YOUR RENAISSANCE YEARS

YOUR RENAISSANCE YEARS

*Making Retirement
the Best Years of
Your Life*

Robert L. Veninga

Thorndike Press • Thorndike, Maine

Library of Congress Cataloging in Publication Data:

Veninga, Robert L.
   Your renaissance years : making retirement the best
years of your life / Robert L. Veninga.
      p.   cm.
   ISBN 1-56054-309-4 (alk. paper : lg. print)
   ISBN 1-56054-939-4 (alk. paper : lg. print : pbk.)
   1. Retirement—United States. 2. Retirement—United
States—Planning. 3. Large type books. I. Title.
[HQ1063.2.U6V46   1991b]   91-33288
646.7'9—dc20   CIP

The author is grateful for permission to include the
following previously copyrighted material:
   Letter from the Dear Abby column by Abigail Van
Buren. Copyright 1989 Universal Press Syndicate.
Reprinted with permission. All rights reserved.
   Letter from the Ann Landers column by Ann Landers.
Reprinted with the permission of Ann Landers and
Creators Syndicate.

Thorndike Press Large Print edition published in 1992
by arrangement with Little, Brown and Company, Inc.

Cover design by Ralph Lizotte.

The tree indicium is a trademark of Thorndike Press.

This book is printed on acid-free, high opacity paper.

This book is affectionately dedicated to

Otila Veninga
Frank Veninga
Katherine Smit
Pieter Smit

Contents

Acknowledgments

I am indebted to a number of organizations and people who contributed to this project. I want to express appreciation to 135 retirees who provided case history material for this book. Not only did they take time to respond to a written questionnaire, but they willingly responded to my inquiries when additional information was needed.

Since much of the information they shared is personal, I have kept their identities confidential. Therefore all case studies have been disguised. In some instances composites have been drawn for illustrative material. But in all examples, the case studies are realistic depictions of the tough issues the respondents addressed in their pursuit of a successful retirement.

I want to acknowledge four retirement organizations that assisted in this project: the United Auto Workers (Local 623 retirees), the Cooperative Older Adults Ministry, Sunrise Seniors, and the Seniors Club of the Hamline United Methodist Church, St. Paul, Minnesota.

Then, too, I am indebted to three professionals in finance who gave timely and pertinent information: Roberta Cole, CFP, stockbroker and financial planner for Paine-Webber; Neil Kittlesen, CLU, chartered financial consultant for Lutheran Brotherhood; and Warren McLaughlin, certified public accountant. While their insights have been helpful, the information provided in Part 1 is my own, based upon my research and interviews with retired adults.

I want to express appreciation to William D. Phillips, Vice President, Little, Brown and Company, for his enthusiasm for this work and for the valuable guidance given through the years. I want to thank my editor, Ellen F. Denison, for her insights and suggestions, which are imprinted on each chapter. And I especially want to express appreciation to Susan Lescher for her encouragement, ideas, and confidence in this project.

Finally, I want to acknowledge four special individuals to whom this book is dedicated. My parents, Otila and Frank Veninga, have taken an interest in this book since its inception. I want to thank my father for his editorial assistance and express appreciation to my mother for her heartfelt encouragement. Then, too, I want to thank my parents-in-law, Katherine and Pieter Smit of White Bear Lake,

Minnesota. They have been supportive at every turn in my family's life, and I will always be grateful that I could be a part of their extended family.

Introduction: A Personal Note from the Author

Dear Reader:

I'll never forget the first time I seriously thought about retirement. I had just turned forty and was attending a workshop on financial planning.

I took a seat in the back of the room, keenly aware of the fact that my wife and I had little to show for fifteen years of hard work. While it was true that we (and the mortgage company) owned a modest home, it was equally true that we had been unable to save for our future.

"No need to feel guilty," said the financial planner I consulted later. "You've been too busy raising your family and establishing your career to think about money."

I was thankful for his understanding, even if it seemed a bit contrived. But then the tone of the conversation changed: "At some point you have to get serious about saving for your son's education," he noted. "Equally important, you need to start saving for retirement."

I found myself resisting his advice. I wasn't ready to think about retirement. More to the point: how could we save money for retirement when the automobile needed to be replaced and the bills from last summer's vacation had yet to be paid?

But with good humor, my wife gently reminded me that I was forty years old, and with my receding hairline it was perhaps time to get serious about our financial future.

In subsequent months I attended numerous seminars on financial planning, and I read everything I could lay my hands on related to retirement. I learned that you are never too young to plan for life without work. But I also discovered that even if you are fifty, sixty, or seventy years of age, it's never too late to realize your dreams.

For the first time in our married life, we took seriously the notion that retirement was in our future, and if we wanted to be financially independent we had to become knowledgeable about employee pension plans, individual retirement accounts, Keogh plans, and 401(k) and 403(b) savings accounts. And we discovered that no matter how small the investment, it would be possible to *double* the value of our savings in nine years — using safe, sound, and predictable investment strategies.

14

While financial planning was the cornerstone of our preparations for retirement, a long-distance telephone call from my father forced me to examine retirement from a broader perspective. "How would you feel if your mother and I retired in Minneapolis?" he asked. "We would like to be near you and your family."

Without hesitation my wife and I encouraged them to retire in the Twin Cities. Four months later they moved into a lovely town house in a Minneapolis suburb.

The following years were full of excitement and challenge for my parents. Although retired, my father couldn't resist getting involved in a local church. "I'm busier now than when I was working," he would say with relish. My mother, a gregarious person, found it easy to make new friends. And seeing her grandson mature into adulthood was a source of great joy.

But not everything went well. On a bitterly cold Minnesota evening, my father telephoned me from his bed. His voice was weak, his speech hesitant. "I'm not feeling well," he confided.

I raced to his home and discovered that he could barely walk twenty-five feet without collapsing from oxygen insufficiency. The next morning he was in the operating room as a cardiac surgeon desperately struggled to save his life. Fortunately the surgery was successful. But I learned that even the best-drawn retirement plans can be altered by an unanticipated illness.

In the years that followed I had an opportunity to visit with many retirees. I learned the importance of developing avocations that challenge the mind and renew the spirit. I learned why it is important to be a good steward of one's money and how to live in a spirit of thankfulness, even when negative events affect our lives.

I learned what can be done to protect health, and strategies for renewing family relationships, especially when there has been estrangement between parents and adult children.

But most of all I learned the importance of developing a mature faith — a faith that sustains us when everything goes well and comforts us when our step is unsettled.

In the pages that follow you will learn how these concepts apply to your life and to your retirement. My hope is that as you read this book you will experience a personal renaissance — a deepened conviction that the next decade of life can be the best one ever. For implicit in every page is the strong belief that no matter your age or physical or fiscal condition, it's *never* too late to dream big dreams and to take charge of your future.

Before I go much farther, I would like to tell you how this book is organized. Chapter 1, "The Secrets of a Successful Retirement," takes aim at one of the myths associated with growing old, and that is that you ought to slow down, bake bread, sleep late, and spend the rest of your life on the golf course. Implicit in this advice is the admonition that your life should become predictable, safe, and comfortable.

Unfortunately it would also be boring. As Garrison Keillor said: "You're supposed to get reckless as you grow older. That way you keep saying yes to life. And perhaps saying yes, not being safe, is the real point of life."[1]

How do you "say yes to life"? The starting point is to take control of your finances, because if you worry about money, you may never be content in your retirement years.

In part 1, *Money Sense: Handling Your Finances,* you will learn that today's financial landscape is pitted with potholes — any one of which could seriously diminish your financial security. Investments that increased your wealth in the 1980s may not be appropriate for the 1990s — especially if you are about to retire.

In this section you will learn about rock-

17

solid investments that provide peace of mind. You will also take several tests that will enable you to assess your financial condition. If you find that you cannot afford to leave your job, do not despair, for there are many ways to augment income and reduce expenses.

But if the test indicates that you are financially prepared for the future, then you may want to examine strategies designed to protect and maximize your investments. It is important, for example, to know how to verify the money in your pension and to become knowledgeable about Social Security benefits. You may need a yardstick by which to evaluate financial planners. And you will want to know how to protect your money from hucksters and financial charlatans who have a special interest in the investments of retirees.

There is, however, a more fundamental lesson that needs to be learned: a successful retirement is not based on how much money you may have accumulated, *but on whether you are at peace with yourself about the money you have.*

If there is one thing about which I am convinced, it is this: a successful retirement is not contingent upon great wealth. But a successful retirement is dependent upon living as if you are wealthy. Chapter 5, "How to Retire on a Modest Income," will demonstrate how this can be done.

Part 2, *House and Home: The Relocation Question,* is packed with housing information. There has been a virtual explosion in the types of housing markets available to older Americans — and not only in the sun belt communities. Today in almost every city there are town houses, condominiums, apartments, and retirement communities that provide *quality* living for individuals fifty-five years of age or older.

Here are a few examples of the many types of living arrangements available to retirees: Gottingham Retirement Community in Cincinnati, Ohio, has a full-time Montessori day care center so that residents can enjoy their grandchildren who live nearby. The twenty-million-dollar Benchmark development in Hoffman Estates, Illinois, offers a concierge, access to limousine service, sauna, greenhouse, and a multitude of amenities. If you have a scholarly bent, you might consider College Harbor, which is a retirement community located on the campus of Eckerd College in St. Petersburg, Florida. If you are a secretary, you might focus on Vista Grande, in Rio Rancho, New Mexico, where half of the 189 retirees in this complex had a secretarial career. And if you are an equestrian, you can retire to Fairbanks Ranch, near San Diego, which offers stables, corrals, and riding trails.[2]

There is, however, a downside to all of these housing options, and it isn't necessarily costs, although they can be formidable. Some retirement communities deliver what they promise. But an alarming number do not keep their commitments. In this section you will learn how to evaluate retirement housing and what legal steps to take in order to protect your investment.

Part 3, *Health Wisdom: Strategies for Long Living*, takes a creative look at how to stay healthy in retirement. The starting point is to take control over worry and depression. But it is also important to understand the role that diet and exercise have on health. And regardless of where you live, you must locate a physician who will provide competent and compassionate medical care.

Chapter 10 takes aim at one of the biggest fears of retirees: *How will I pay for a catastrophic illness?* Such fears are well founded, since a prolonged illness can be a financial disaster. Fortunately there are ways to guard against unexpected health expenses. And there are excellent insurance plans that will provide peace of mind. The key, however, is to obtain insurance protection *before* you need it.

Part 4, *Leisure Pursuits: Enjoying It All*, addresses an intriguing question: "Once retired, what am I going to do with my time?"

The John Hancock Insurance Company estimates that the typical retiree has about 40,000 lifetime leisure hours to fill. That's a lot of time, and there are those who have difficulty finding meaningful ways to use their leisure.

Many people retire *from* something. A demanding job. A punitive boss. Complex work assignments.

But they don't know what they are retiring *to*. Consequently after a few months of leisure they are bored and restless.

If you have wondered what you are going to do with your time, this section is for you. Chapter 11 focuses on the wonderful new world of retirement travel. We will learn how to rent an inexpensive European villa and how to take a magnificent Caribbean cruise at almost half the usual cost. We will even discover how to swap your home for one abroad! If establishing new friendships is your goal, read carefully the paragraphs describing Elderhostel, a program that will introduce you to people with similar interests.

Of course one of the best ways to use leisure time is to help others. In every community there are churches, hospitals, and other philanthropic organizations that desperately need volunteers. I promise you this: if you are bored in retirement, Chapter 12 will give you many ideas as to how to make your life productive and worthwhile.

Without tipping my hand too much, I must tell you that a good share of part 5, *Relationships: Men, Women, and Change,* is designed to help married adults *strengthen* their relationship. The reason? Retirement can be hard on marriages, especially during the first year. The day after retirement starts, two individuals who have lived an active life are thrust together — not for a few hours each evening, but for most of the day and night. It is not uncommon for conflicts to come crashing to the surface as spouses vent frustrations, many of which they had suppressed while raising children and pursuing busy careers.

In this section we will learn the secrets for staying in love throughout life. We will learn how to diagnose and solve problems that threaten marriages. We will note practical strategies for dealing with adult children who meddle too much in our lives, or, conversely, do not meddle enough! But most of all we will discover how to keep our family and friendships together throughout our retirement years.

The book concludes by taking a new look at faith and religious experience. If there is one thing I feel strongly about it is this: *faith matters*. Not only when you are getting married or raising a family or building a career. It matters as you age.

The well-known psychologist Eric Erickson stated that one of the pivotal tasks in later life is to come to grips with the meaning of faith and the impact it has had on our past and will have on our future. He suggested that unless we have a well-founded philosophy of life, we may reach old age in despair rather than with a sense of peace and tranquillity.[3]

In preparing for this book I asked retirees what their faith meant to them as they entered into the sixth, seventh, and even eighth decade of life. Not surprisingly most expressed doubts as to whether they would ever get all of their religious questions answered.

But most acknowledged that as they grew older, their faith became richer and more meaningful, especially when confronting disappointments and the loss of lifelong relationships.

In the closing paragraphs of this book we will take a new look at what faith means — not when things are going well, but when confronted with setbacks and tragedies. We will learn that faith is not a crutch to lean upon when wounded. Nor is it a creed that neatly prescribes moral conduct. Nor is it belonging to a particular type of religious organization.

Rather faith is the knowledge that life has direction, purpose, and meaning. Perhaps, ultimately, that is the foundation for a successful retirement.

Robert L. Veninga, Ph.D.
St. Paul, Minnesota

CHAPTER ONE

The Secrets of a Successful Retirement

The secret is growing up without growing old.
Casey Stengel
(1890–1975)

Jack McLaughlin, a sixty-three-year-old former high school English teacher, can't say enough good things about retirement. "I love every minute of it," he confides. "If I knew that retirement was going to be this good, I would have taken it years ago." What makes Jack's retirement so special?

With a twinkle in his eye he notes: "I'm still in love with my wife. I have three wonderful grandchildren. And I have enough projects to keep me busy for the next thirty years."

Not everyone is as fortunate. I think of Marsha Honnicker, fifty-seven, a former assistant vice president for nursing services at a metropolitan hospital. Owing to budget constraints, Marsha's position was eliminated.

"I had no choice but to retire," she confides. "I tried to find employment, but hit dead ends. I thought volunteer work might be the answer, but the challenge wasn't there. I joined a retirement club, but the topics of conversation didn't interest me. I just can't get my life untracked."

Marsha paused and added poignantly, "Retirement is supposed to be the best time of life. But for me, it has been one discouraging day after another."

Now the question is, Why is it that some people find retirement to be the best period of life, while for others it is a time of melancholy and apathy? Why is it that some people are able to stake out a claim to their future, while others simply drift into retirement, without any sense of what they will do or how they will use their time? And why is it that some people are able to engage life at its deepest level right up until the moment they die, while others become overwhelmed with perplexing problems and nagging worries?

To answer these and other questions about retirement, I interviewed 135 people who represented many walks of life.[1] Included in this group were former executives, teachers, nurses, clergymen, physicians, and individuals who had spent their careers working on the assembly line. I also received information from women who had never worked out of the home and whose views on retirement were different from those who worked for pay.

These respondents pulled no punches in answering my questions. They shared their hopes and dreams. But they also shared their disappointments and regrets. As they talked, I listened — not only with my head, but with my heart. Here is what I learned.

Retirement Blues

When I asked retirees to evaluate their lives, most responded optimistically: "I'm having more fun than ever." "It's good to be out of the rat race." "I'm busier now than when I was working!"

Such responses are not surprising, since most surveys paint a fairly upbeat portrait of retired Americans. In one national study, 50 percent of the respondents stated that retirement was as satisfying as they had expected it would be, while a full 24 percent of the sample indicated that it was *better* than anticipated. In general, as people age, most express a deeper sense of appreciation for their friendships, finances, and marriages than they did in their younger years.[2]

Nevertheless, some questions troubled respondents: "Was your retirement good from the outset? Were there frustrations in adapting to a new life?"

Suddenly the expressions changed as smiles gave way to a hint of worry. Jack Sutherland, sixty-seven, a retired engineer, put it this way:

> Everything went well during the first few months of my retirement. We vacationed in San Diego. I built a deck on the house. I took my grandchildren fishing.
>
> Then one morning I woke up and realized that I had nothing to do. I began to ask disturbing questions:
>
> . . . "Why am I bored, when I have time to do anything I want? Why do I miss work, when I could hardly wait to get out of the company?" I really felt confused, and the worst thing was that I didn't feel comfortable telling my feelings to anyone. It all seemed a little crazy, especially when my buddies kept telling me how lucky I was to be out of the rat race.

After hearing comments such as these, I began to realize that while some adults move into retirement without missing a beat in their busy lives, many do not. In fact, most of the respondents told me that it took them from one to three years to fully come to grips with what it meant to be retired.

28

What did they find troubling? In this survey retirees frequently targeted "money worries" as their number one concern. Some expressed regret over their inability to build a significant retirement nest egg during their working years. Some were mystified by the vast changes made in American financial services, and others were puzzled about how to locate sound financial advice. Many fretted over the volatility of the stock market. "My pension is directly tied to how the stock market performs," said Aaron Blake, a sixty-year-old retired executive. "When you see twenty percent of your portfolio wiped out in one day of trading, as happened in 1987, it makes you nervous." He added plaintively, "I always thought that I had ample money for my retirement years. Now I am not so sure . . ."

Those living on a fixed income often have the greatest difficulty making financial ends meet. Said Jack Rotwoski, seventy-three, a retired engineer:

My wife and I had no difficulty paying our bills during the first six years of retirement. But now it is difficult to meet our financial obligations. The problem is that my pension is not adjusted for inflation. But everything we buy goes up in price. Frankly, if we live another fifteen or twenty years, like we hope, it's going to be almost impossible to meet expenses.

Some of the gravest financial worries were expressed by older women who had never been in a pension plan. Compounding their financial problems is the fact that women tend to outlive their husbands by eight to thirteen years. When their husbands die, Social Security payments may drop by 50 percent. The financial prospects for divorced women can be even bleaker: if the marriage lasted ten years or less, a woman will not receive *any* Social Security benefits based on her ex-husband's earnings.

A second issue contributing to retirement blues was even more personal and, for some, more difficult to verbalize. Nevertheless, a number of respondents confided that the quality of their marriage had suffered because of the retirement of one or both spouses.

"Retirement is hard on marriages," said one fifty-seven-year-old woman. "You get on one another's nerves. Roles have to be defined. Conflicts which you thought were resolved come crashing to the surface. And if your spouse is down in the dumps, it can't help but affect you."

Janet Harrington is an energetic woman who

awakens at 6:00 A.M. and is out of the house by 7:00 A.M. Her mornings are filled doing volunteer work for the American Heart Association. At noon she has lunch with her friends, and if the weather is good, her afternoon is spent playing nine holes of golf. At least two evenings a week Janet works in a community theater, helping to design costumes for the acting company.

Janet enjoys life, but her husband's forthcoming retirement has her worried:

> I love my husband. But I wonder how *his* retirement is going to affect the quality of *my* life.
>
> His view of retirement is that we should do everything together. He expects me to be available twenty-four hours a day to do things he wants to do. What he doesn't understand is that *he* is retiring, not me. I want to go on living my life just as I always have. It's not that I don't love him, but the truth of the matter is that I don't want to be around home twenty-four hours a day.

As she shared her dilemmas I thought of an old vaudeville line in which the heroine quips: "I married him for better or for worse — but not for lunch!"

Fortunately, there is a flip side to all this, and that is that retirement can make marriages more meaningful, more fulfilling. Says Ethyl Kranston:

My husband and I are closer than ever. When our four kids were growing up we were so busy that we kind of neglected each other. And then his career took him away from home for long periods of time.

Now we spend a lot of time together, and we love every minute of it. We have learned to be more tender to one another and more considerate of each other's needs. We have developed new hobbies and made new friends. Retirement is turning out to be the very best time of our lives.

A third concern of retirees boils down to a very simple question: *What am I going to do with the rest of my life?* Dick Listiano, a sixty-five-year-old shipping clerk, said:

Most of my work life has been spent responding to orders: "Do this. Go there." Now I have to figure out how to spend my days. That probably isn't a big deal for most people. But it means learning how to plan for the rest of my life, and I want to tell you that is a *very big deal.*

When respondents told me that they couldn't find enough things to do to fill up their calendar, I admitted to some skepticism. For after all, weren't there concerts to attend, ball games to see, and books to read?

But then I realized that some people develop a fairly predictable pattern for life. The alarm clock rings at the same time each morning. Work assignments seldom change. Vacation customs may not vary. In general, there is a rhythm in life that most find reassuring.

But when retirement begins, routines are dramatically changed. And many become anxious when confronted with an empty calendar.

If you are about to retire, remember this: it may take a while to adjust to your leisure years. And this is true even if you have taken the time to plan for your future. Leland Bradford, former director of the Training Laboratories in Arlington, Virginia, thought he had prepared himself for retirement. But he later noted:

The organization moved on without me. No one called for advice. I found that golf did not fill a day. Life felt empty. I became uncertain of my identity. I knew who I had been, but I was not certain who I was.[3]

Once you leave your place of employment for the last time, be prepared for a letdown. It doesn't happen all at once. But it does take place, often after the new town house has been built and the fiftieth round of golf has been played. Then, in a vulnerable moment, perplexing questions surface: "What's next?" "How do I redefine myself so that life has excitement, purpose, and direction?"

Now the question is: how do you avoid retirement blues, and what can be done to enhance the quality of your retirement years? The starting point is to understand that if your retirement is to be successful, a new mission in life must be discovered.

Success After Fifty-Five: Factors That Make or Break a Retirement

Retirees who report high life satisfaction share one important trait: *they live active lives.* They are not slowing down. They are not disengaged. They are not drifting aimlessly, nor are they bored. Rather their energy is focused on achieving important goals.

When I think of someone who has his goals sharply focused, Ray Karhu comes to mind.

Ray had a terrific career as a high school teacher. Because of his personality and training, Ray was assigned some of the toughest kids in school to advise — the truants, low achievers, and those addicted to alcohol and drugs. He saw the good in each of these adolescents, and from all reports was able to establish meaningful relationships with them.

But several years before his retirement I could detect expressions of concern:

> Two years from now I will be retiring. I need to find a new dream. I have to have something in place the day I retire which will excite me. I want to walk into something that is fun — not simply walk out of a good career.

In the months that followed, Ray identified a new mission for his life. He had always wanted to build a rustic home in the north woods. After a long search, he located a beautiful wooded lot near a beautiful seventy-seven-acre wilderness lake. With pride he showed me the land, indicating with careful precision where the foundation was to be laid and where the path leading to the home would be carved into the woods.

If you were to visit Ray and Gladys Karhu in their northwest Wisconsin home, you would see what ten years of planning and joyous hard work have accomplished. Nestled in the woods is a gorgeous home resembling a Swiss chalet. It's not quite finished, but it is a home filled with love. "I know every nail in this house," says Ray proudly. "And I have all types of plans for a guest cabin in the woods. There has to be a special place up here for our friends."

Why is Ray's retirement filled with meaning? Because he was able to direct his energy toward achieving an important goal.

Without a doubt, *the happiest people in retirement are engaged in meaningful activities.* They are going to concerts, traveling abroad, establishing new friendships, and serving as volunteers in philanthropic organizations. But many individuals who could be retired are engaged in full-time employment.

Why would older adults continue to work when they could be enjoying life on the golf course or at the beach? Some need the money. Others fear that if they retire they would lose their friendships with colleagues and customers.

But most continue to be employed simply because they love what they do. As attorney Melvin Belli, seventy-nine, recently said: "I'd like to go for fifty more [years]. I love what I do, and there's no reason to stop as long as the Lord lets me continue."[4]

Of course many people *do* retire. But not for a lifetime. Fifty percent of all executives, for example, return to work within two years of their retirement, and of this number 87 percent will be back in the executive suite within six months.[5]

The late Mary Martin took a twelve-year retirement from acting and then signed a contract to co-star with Carol Channing in *Legends,* a musical comedy. "I'd been having a lovely time just relaxing," she recalled. "Then I thought: 'enough of that. Why was I given a talent to use if not to use it as long as I can?' "[6]

When asked why she was working instead of relaxing, she replied: "Because acting is my life. If you decline to be what you can be, that's when you start losing yourself and going from the world."

Carol Channing, at sixty-two, agreed: "I'm not going to sit and stagnate. If I'm not working, I'm not living. Every night I am revalidated by the audience response."[7]

While some are renewed by returning to their careers, others find that their retirement is revitalized by helping others. Today 43.5 percent of all people between the ages of fifty and seventy-four are engaged in some type of formal volunteer activity.[8]

In Florida, for example, retired engineers are teaching students new technology, while other retirees provide eyewitness accounts of significant historical events. Elsewhere retired executives are helping young executives start new companies. And many older Americans are serving in the Peace Corps. "It was the most wonderful time of my entire life," said Pat Lockwood, reflecting on her assignment, at age fifty-three, in Malaysia.[9]

Why is volunteer work so rewarding? Listen to Marie Dennison, sixty-one, who retired after a thirty-six-year secretarial career: "One day I woke up and had nothing to do. I knew that if I was to stay happy, I had to find some productive place to use my skills."

At the suggestion of a friend, Marie volunteered to help in a children's hospital. She donates twenty hours a week helping children and their families cope with surgery.

Marie's day begins by meeting with parents of the children. She explains what will happen to their child during hospitalization. After a child returns from surgery, Marie is waiting with the parents. If the news is good, she helps celebrate the joy of the occasion. But if it is bad, she is there to give support.

"The best part of retirement is the volunteer hours I spend at Children's Hospital," said Marie. "Every day is different, with its own drama and its own rewards. When a child leaves the hospital and says 'Thank you,' it's the best gift you could ever receive."

To repeat, if a retirement is to be successful, there must be a goal that you want to realize. It might be starting a new business, discovering a new friendship, or taking part in philanthropic work. But the goal you define must be significant. And ideally, *it should contain a measure of risk.*

Now some might object: "Become a risk taker? Aren't you supposed to grow conservative with age?"

There is a natural desire to play it safe, especially as we approach our retirement years. Some of this reflects a desire for security. Some of it reflects a fear of failure. But part of the reason for avoiding risk is that we listen to admonitions of younger people who suggest that we ought to slow down, scale back, and take it easy as we enter our retirement years.

Such advice may be well intentioned. But it often leads to mental atrophy and physical illness. Said one physician:

Most of my patients owe their physical problems to emotional and psychological ones. They've been told by their bosses, their younger co-workers, their neighbors, and their children that the game of life is over. They feel worthless, shoved aside, and they get the big hint society has been giving them: go home and die. The ones who buy the old idea that retirement means dropping out often do that — they succumb to ailments and disease.[10]

If there is one thing you don't want to do in retirement it is to drop out of life. Nor do you want to play it too safe, especially if you never had opportunity to fully explore your talents and abilities.

It is a fact that when older people review their lives, they often indicate that they were too cautious. If they had to do it over again, they would set higher goals, worry less about things which they could not control, and experience more of life. They would commit themselves to causes more passionately and see beyond self-limiting points of view. And perhaps most important — they would take more risks.

When Franklin Thomas, president of the Ford Foundation, was on the verge of making a major career decision, he was offered some advice by his friends: "They told me that life isn't about security, about holding on to the trunk of the tree. If you want to enjoy the fruits of life, they said, you've got to be willing to go out on a limb because that's where all the fruit is — not on the trunk."[11]

To put it another way: Life is not some destination that you hope to someday reach. It's the process itself. Life isn't an effort to make everything secure, predictable, and safe, although it can be all of those things and more. Rather, life is discovering new ideas — ideas that make the whole journey worthwhile.[12]

Tom Duck knows all about taking risks and starting a new journey. He had a successful thirty-five-year career as an insurance and investment agent. But at age seventy-three he founded the Ugly Duckling Rent-A-Car system. Today the Ugly Duckling Rent-A-Car system is an $84.5 million enterprise and has the fifth largest number of locations of any auto rental firm in the United States.

When he started the company, the odds were heavily stacked against him. "Everyone told me that I couldn't get insurance coverage, wouldn't find a sufficient supply of good used cars, and that no customers would be interested in any case," he said. "But I knew in my guts that I was right, so I went ahead anyway."[13]

Duck took a big risk. But it produced huge rewards. Does he regret his late start on a new career? Not at all. "Everything I did in earlier years prepared me for my success today."

41

Now the last thing you may want to do in retirement is start a new business. But that misses the point. The point is that no matter the state of your health or your wealth, your retirement will be revitalized by taking some calculated gambles.

I think, for example, of Charles Nation, who stumbled on an unusual advertisement in the Casper, Wyoming newspaper.

WANTED: Year-round valentine. Happy disposition. Fun loving. Good cook. Widowed lady would like to find friend 55 or over. No swingers (but like to dance) need apply.

Charles could have shrugged off the ad. But instead, he sent a letter of inquiry. What he did not know, however, was that the ad was a prank, pulled on Elaine Thompson by two of her best friends.

When the fifty-seven-year-old "widowed lady" heard about their prank, she roared with approval. "I was in hysterics," Elaine recalled. "Then I began to fret. What if someone answered the ad? I decided I would apologize and explain the whole thing to him. By Sunday, though, I thought, 'Gee, what if *no one* answers?' "[14]

Elaine received eleven letters, but responded to Charles Nation's letter. She can't explain why she responded to his letter. Perhaps it was because they both had two sons and a daughter. Or it may have been the straightforward tone of Charles's letter as he wrote about his first wife's battle with bone and breast cancer.

Whatever the reason, they decided to meet. The rest is like a happy ending to a romance novel. Soon they were driving three hundred miles each weekend to be together. Four months later they were married.

Today Charles is president of the local Audubon Society and promotes solar energy around the state. Elaine is a member of the town's economic development committee and is involved in establishing a food bank for the needy. But most of all, they are thankful they put their fears aside, took a risk, and met one another. As Charles said: "You see the opportunities and do the best you can."

In ancient China two calendars differentiated the life of every citizen. One calendar began at birth and recorded events through age sixty. A second calendar was presented on the sixty-first birthday. This calendar was called *Kanreki,* which means "the second childhood."

What did it mean to enter a second childhood? It meant that as you grew older you were free to make new discoveries, form new relationships, and take a few risks. Perhaps most important — if you failed, there would be no disgrace.[15]

Now let me pause for a moment and share with you one of the central discoveries that emerge from my conversations with retired adults.

When I started this project my major goal was to suggest strategies that would help readers feel more secure in their retirement. But what I have learned is that the happiest people are not those searching for security. The happiest people are those who are pushing against the current and moving into uncharted waters.

Hilda Crooks understands this fact. Ms. Crooks climbed the highest mountain in the contiguous United States when she was sixty-six years old. By the time she was eighty-five she climbed it for the twentieth time. Why does she climb mountains when she could be resting in a rocking chair?

I once lived next door to an older single man, and every morning I'd go out into the garden in the backyard where there was just a fence between us. He'd be out there and I'd say: "Good morning, neighbor. How are you today?"

He'd always say: "I'm just waiting for

the Grim Reaper." That was his reply, every morning. "I'm just waiting for the Grim Reaper."

At the same time I knew another man who I often met on the street. He was a hundred and one years old. I'd see him on the street going to the library to read. He died before he was a hundred and two, but he never stopped trying to increase his knowledge, to improve himself.

No matter where you are, keep moving. There are always higher areas. When I can't walk anymore, then I'll crawl. It's the way we started and not a bad way to finish. I'd rather die on a mountain than in a nursing home.[16]

And now we come to perhaps the most important ingredient in a successful retirement: *you must reclaim your freedom.*

Freedom — it's a word bantered about in so many contexts that it often loses its meaning. But when I use this word in this book, it suggests that you have the capacity to write the next chapter in your life. A chapter brimming with stories of love, joy, and hope.

To be certain, there are those who have difficulty projecting a joyous retirement. Some have health problems. Some worry about their children, while others have economic concerns.

I do not want to minimize these problems, nor will I overlook them in the pages ahead. But implicit in this book will be a consistent theme: *You are free to choose your response to each day you live.* And you are free to make your retirement years the very best ones of your life.

What are you free to do?

You are free to enjoy life. Agatha Christie, the mystery writer, discovered a "second blooming" that came to her after age fifty. A whole new life opened up before her as she went to picture exhibitions, concerts, and the opera. "It's as if a fresh sap of ideas and thoughts were rising in you."[17]

You are free to be yourself. Pianist Arthur Rubinstein felt liberated from having to hit every note correctly as he grew older. Consequently he became a more daring performer, willing to take risks with his music.[18]

You are free to work for the common good. Lillian Carter was sixty-six years old when she decided to join the Peace Corps. She survived a rigorous training program and learned to type so that she would be qualified to serve abroad. She went to India because it was like her native Georgia, "A dark country with a warm climate." There she brought a sense of optimism and a spirit of hope to a destitute people.[19]

Finally, *you are free to discover your abilities.*

To do this, says Caroline Bird, author of *The Good Years: Your Future in the 21st Century,* you have to go back to a forgotten or undeveloped part of yourself. "It may be a challenge you dared not take, a truth you could not face, a talent you never were able to use, an opportunity you could not or would not take the first time you discovered it."[20] But it is a risk worth taking if you are to discover that you are a unique person, different from any individual on the face of the earth.

How do you discover a challenge that will put a renewed spark of optimism in your retirement years? How do you nurture a talent you never had time to develop? How do you rediscover the joy of working for the common good?

In the six sections of this book we will examine *practical* strategies through which we can discover new meanings in our lives. But for now remember this: the happiest people in retirement are those who stay active. They find new challenges and they take a few risks. And they plan for their future. In so doing, they come to understand a poignant observation made by the American philosopher George Santayana: "Never have I enjoyed youth so thoroughly as I have in old age. . . . Nothing is inherently and invincibly young, except spirit."[21]

CHAPTER TWO

Early Retirement: Is It For You?

I always looked forward to the day I could retire. But the closer it came, the more apprehensive I became. I wasn't so sure about leaving my job, and I was unsure whether I had saved enough money. I don't think there is a magical formula that tells you when to retire. It's kind of a gamble.
Sixty-three-year-old salesman

In chapter 1 we learned that one of the keys to happiness is to have the freedom to do the things you truly enjoy. For many that means taking an early retirement.

Today the typical employee retires at age sixty-one.[1] Some leave their company because they want time for their hobbies and avocations. But others terminate employment because they are the recipients of early-retirement programs that are too good to turn down. Since 1986, over 100,000 workers have been offered these programs from such companies as IBM, CBS, and Metropolitan Life.

Initially most employees are elated when they think about life without work. But then a number of disquieting issues surface: Do I have enough money for retirement? What happens if I don't accept the company's offer? And perhaps most important: Am I actually ready to bring my career to a close?

The purpose of this chapter is to provide *practical* information that will enable you to assess early-retirement programs. More important the next few pages will provide a clearer understanding of whether you are *psychologically* and *financially* ready for retirement. Before we get too far along, however, let's take a close look at the phenomenon called "early retirement" and learn why so many employees are forsaking their nine-to-five routine.

Getting Off the Workaday Treadmill: Why We Do It

Until recently only a few people had the option to retire before age sixty-five. But in the past ten years early-retirement programs have given millions of workers new options as well as new concerns.

Why the interest in early retirement? Economists point to an important fact: for the first time in our nation's history a significant number of people can actually afford to retire before age sixty-five. This does not imply that everyone over fifty is wealthy. But it does suggest that many middle- to older-age adults can live comfortably by combining Social Security benefits with their pension and investments. As David Carboni, co-owner of Retirement Counseling in Westport, Connecticut, states: "More people can afford to retire early. With the advent of older two-career families, Social Security Benefits at sixty-two, and more 401(k) plans, it's increasingly viable for people to retire early."[2]

Today many companies offer attractive retirement programs employees can't pass up. When Dupont presented a one-shot early-retirement plan to 121,000 domestic employees, the company's projection was that no more than 6,500 of them would sign up. To their surprise, 11,500 checked out.

Ken Aerstin, of Johnson and Johnson, is a case in point. When first offered an early-retirement package, he refused. "I rejected the offer outright," he stated. "I felt really reluctant to leave behind all the challenges and opportunities at J & J. I thought, 'Retirement isn't for *me,* it's for *older folks.*' "

But the offer was too good to turn down. Not only could he retire five years ahead of schedule, but he would receive half his current

51

salary until he was eligible for Social Security. In addition, he would be given comprehensive medical coverage for life. "My wife and I realized that we could live just as comfortably as before. As soon as we understood the plan, we decided that we should go for it."[3]

Of course not everyone is employed by companies that provide generous early-retirement programs. In fact during the past decade, millions of American workers have been forced out of the workplace with few benefits as companies streamlined their work force in order to become more competitive.

Fortunately, many who were the victims of a layoff found new jobs, while others simply decided that it was time to do something radically different with their lives.

Ken and Shelly Cassie, both in their early fifties, were professionally secure. Yet they quit their high school teaching jobs so that Ken could spend more time making pottery at their Brielle, New Jersey, home. Said Ken: "It's given us a chance to start again while we're young. Yes, we're aiming to make a certain amount of money, but the biggest thing is that this is fun. We do what we want when we want. I see this as a luxury we've earned."[4]

Whatever the motivation, one thing is clear: most retirees are enjoying life to the fullest.

In one study 90 percent of those surveyed said early retirement was as good as or better than they had expected. Perhaps more significant, the fears that workers project about retirement are frequently exaggerated. For example:

* Sixty-six percent of nonretirees believe that they will be faced with financial difficulties once they leave their jobs. In reality, fewer than 25 percent of all retirees have money problems.
* Thirty-two percent of nonretirees believe that "cutting back on extras" will bother them. Only 14 percent of all retirees agree.
* Thirty-seven percent of workers believe that retirement means boredom. In reality fewer than 18 percent of all retirees expressed boredom. In fact many say they are "busier now than ever before."
* Thirty-one percent of nonretirees believe they will be lonely in retirement, yet only 21 percent of those who are retired indicated that they are lonely.[5]

In reviewing the above data, Alice Goldberg, director of research for D'Arcy, Masius,

Benton, and Bowles, the New York-based advertising and communications firm that undertook this study, concluded: "In reality, older people are much more satisfied with their lives and more positive in their attitudes than ever before."[6]

Will the trend to early retirement continue? Many indicators suggest that it will. If you are considering retirement — whether it be an early, phased-in, or full retirement — here are the issues to consider: First, are you ready to leave your career? Second, can you afford to be retired? And third, how will you spend the additional three thousand hours of leisure you will have each year?

Retirement: Early, Normal, Late, or Never? What Factors Should Influence Your Decision?

Issue One: Do you really want to leave your job? Most retirees have few regrets as they leave the office or the assembly line for the last time. In fact within a few months after retirement, most indicate that if they were to make the decision all over again, they would retire earlier, not later.

However, there are those who *do* regret retirement. Robert Brandon, fifty-three, is a case in point:

The day I sold my dental practice was the happiest day of my life. No longer would I have to worry about personnel problems, insurance rates, and overhead costs.

But during the first few months of retirement I found myself thinking about the office. I missed my colleagues and the friendships I had with patients. But what I missed most was being recognized for who I was and what I could contribute.

But now all those things which were so meaningful have stopped. Frankly, I am not sure I will ever get used to it.

As journalist Bob Greene once observed: "Work is a powerful thing in our lives, not easy to leave behind. Many of us claim to hate it, but it takes a grip on us so fierce that it captures loyalties we never knew were there."[7]

What is it about work that captures our loyalties? The answer goes beyond the receipt of a regular paycheck. Marilyn Kramer, sixty-one, a former nurse, put it this way:

I'll never forget the first day of my retirement. I set the alarm for five-thirty A.M. just like I had done for the past thirty-seven years. Then it dawned on me — there was no reason to get up so early.

In fact, I didn't have one thing planned.

In the weeks that followed I felt restless, so I joined a health club and signed up for aerobics. I went shopping. I ate out. I bought tickets to Orchestra Hall.

I had fun doing these things, but there was a sense of sadness in my life that I had never before experienced. What bothered me most was that I didn't have anything of *substance* to do. In effect, I didn't have any reason to get up in the morning.

A strange paradox emerged in my interviews as I began to assess the meaning of work in respondents' lives: there were those who couldn't wait for the day in which they could leave the office or the factory for the last time. But once it arrived, conflicting emotions surfaced.

On the one hand there was relief at not having to balance budgets, write reports, attend meetings, or listen to the admonitions of a foreman or an insensitive boss. But conversely, most said they had lost some very important things in retirement: a steady salary, meaningful friendships, and "a reason to get up in the morning."

Frankly, the worst thing which you can do if things aren't going too well at work is to make an arbitrary decision to retire. Nor should you decide about your future when you are emotionally exhausted. Far better to take a vacation and get a new perspective on life. Then take a hard look at your career, assess its benefits as well as its psychological costs, and determine whether retirement is for you. Here is how to do it.

In Table 1, you will find a test consisting of ten questions that will help you decide when retirement will be right for you. Under each question, circle the number that represents your feelings, then summarize your score.

If your total score was between 35 and 50, you may want to delay your retirement: your answers suggest that work provides you with considerable happiness and fulfillment. While there may be frustrations, the rewards outweigh the deficits by a significant margin. Consider putting retirement plans on hold *unless you have a firm plan as to how you want to spend the next five years of your life.*

If you scored between 20 and 34, you should assertively plan for your future. While your job provides important benefits, there is a current of unrest that makes retirement — particularly an *early* retirement — appealing. A good goal to establish is that twelve months from now you will be retired, or if you can't afford retirement, you will have located a new employer or type of employment.

If you scored between 10 and 19, it is time to move on with your life. Do not act rashly by submitting a letter of resignation. But if you can swing it financially, set a firm day by which to begin a new era in your life. A good goal for you is to expect that in six months you will either be retired or have located a job that better fits your talents and abilities.

You may find after taking this test that work plays a more important role in your life than you thought. But you may also discover that it is time to find a new challenge. If retirement sounds appealing, however, the next step for you is to make an objective assessment of your finances.

Issue Two: Can You Afford to Retire? The number one concern of employees as they think about retirement is whether they have enough money to pull it off. Paul Brickson, a certified public accountant, said:

> My biggest concern is whether I will out-live my savings. The fear of becoming dependent upon my children keeps me working. How do you know when you have enough money for retirement? And how do you determine whether your savings will last a lifetime? I can't find any satisfactory answers.

TABLE 1
Should You Retire?

(Circle the appropriate score.)

1. Do you look forward to going
   to work each day?   *Score*

Never		*Sometimes*		*Always*	
1	2	3	4	5	_____

2. If you retired, would you miss
   your work associates?

Not at All		*Some*		*Yes*	
1	2	3	4	5	_____

3. Do you find your work enjoyable?

Not at All		*Some*		*Yes*	
1	2	3	4	5	_____

4. Does your work interfere with
   your personal life?

Always interferes		*Sometimes*		*Never interferes*	
1	2	3	4	5	_____

5. Are you able to take at least
   two weeks of vacation each year?

Never		*Sometimes*		*Aways*	
1	2	3	4	5	_____

TABLE 1 (*Continued*)

6. Do you find yourself daydreaming about walking away from your job?

Yes		*Sometimes*		*Never*	
1	2	3	4	5	_____

7. Do your relatives think you should retire and get away from the pressure?

Yes		*Some*		*No*	
1	2	3	4	5	_____

8. Do you feel challenged by the nature of your work?

No		*Sometimes*		*Yes*	
1	2	3	4	5	_____

9. Do you like the idea of earning additional money before you retire?

No		*Somewhat*		*Yes*	
1	2	3	4	5	_____

10. Do you feel physically and mentally fit?

No		*Somewhat*		*Yes*	
1	2	3	4	5	_____

TOTAL SCORE: _____

These *are* tough questions to answer primarily because everyone's financial needs and resources differ. Nevertheless, there are certain guidelines that can give you an accurate portrait as to whether retirement is financially feasible.

The first task is to know *exactly* what your employer would offer in the event you decide to retire. It is important to remember that retirement packages come in many sizes, shapes, and descriptions. Some offer king-size inducements to retire before age sixty-five. Others look attractive on the surface, but when you dig behind the figures, it becomes apparent that the company is the primary beneficiary of your resignation.

Here are the issues on which to focus: How much will your employer pay per month until you are eligible for Social Security? Will an early retirement influence your future Social Security payments? Can you obtain medical insurance through your employer? If so, what will it cost? Will your company pay for life insurance? If not, can you continue the coverage without taking a medical examination?

While there is no one plan by which to measure the strength of your company's offer, the following represents a fairly typical package, particularly if you are in management.

Early Retirement Plan
XYZ CORPORATION

If you are over 50 with 10 or more years of service, you will accrue the following benefits:

Time added to age for
pension computations ..... 5 years

Cash-separation payment .. 4 weeks
per each
year
employed

Extra annual payment
Social Security begins ... 20% of
base salary

Health insurance ..... Continues to
age 65[8]

In evaluating your retirement plan, it is particularly important to determine how an early retirement might affect your *future* pension. In general, payments are trimmed by 1 percent to 2 percent for each year that precedes the normal retirement point. If, for example, you leave at sixty, your monthly pension check may be as much as 10 percent smaller than if you retire at sixty-five.[9]

However — and this is an important point

— sometimes staying with your employer past age sixty will not necessarily improve your pension. David Wise, a Harvard professor of political economics who has studied hundreds of retirement plans, states that pension formulas typically increase your annual benefit more slowly once you have reached age sixty.[10] Consequently, the only financial benefit you might receive from working an extra year or two would be your salary for that year or years.

The long and short of all this is that it is imperative to ask your company benefits department what your pension will be *if you leave at various ages.* You might be in for a surprise: early retirement might have only a negligible impact on your final pension payout. But remember, the way your pension plan is written may affect whether or not you would want to retire. Some plans base their benefits on the employee's average salary throughout his or her career. Others base benefits on the last three or five years of service, and still others on the three or five best-paid years. If you think a significant raise is in your future, staying employed for another year might dramatically increase your retirement income.[11]

The first task in evaluating your finances is to assess your company's pension program. The second task is to make a hard-nosed calculation as to how much money you will need to maintain your current lifestyle. The work sheets in Tables 2 and 3 provide an easy, accurate way to assess your financial resources. But before you get out your calculator, a few explanations are in order.

Most retirement experts are agreed that you will need between 70 and 80 percent of your preretirement income to maintain a similar lifestyle. If, for example, you earn $60,000 before retirement, you will need between $42,000 and $48,000 to meet expenses and maintain the lifestyle you now enjoy.

TABLE 2
Financing Your Future Retirement

Many people fall short at retirement not because they made poor investments but because they didn't save enough, early enough. This work sheet, created with assistance from the accounting firm of Coopers & Lybrand, will assist you in determining how much money you need to maintain your current lifestyle throughout retirement. It will also indicate whether your savings and investments plans will permit you to reach that goal.

1. Current annual salary: $_____
2. Retirement-income target
   (multiply line 1 by 0.8)   _____

TABLE 2 *(Continued)*

3. *Estimated annual benefit from pension plan, not including IRA's, 401(k)'s, or profit-sharing plans _____

4. Estimated annual Social Security benefits (see Table 3) _____

5. Total retirement benefits (add lines 3 & 4) _____

6. Income gap (subtract line 5 from line 2) _____

7. Adjust gap to reflect inflation (multiply line 6 by factor A, below) _____

8. Capital needed to generate additional income and close gap (multiply line 7 by 16.3) _____

9. Extra capital needed to offset inflation's impact on pension (multiply line 3 by factor B, below) _____

10. Total capital needed (add lines 8 and 9) _____

11. Total current retirement savings (includes balances in IRA's, 401(k)'s, profit-sharing plans, mutual funds, CD's) _____

12. Value of savings at retirement (multiply line 11 by factor C) _____

TABLE 2 (*Continued*)

13. Net capital gap (subtract line 12 from line 10)   _____

14. Annual amount in current dollars to start saving now to cover the gap (divide line 13 by factor D, below)   _____

15. Percentage of salary to be saved each year (divide line 14 by line 1)   _____

Accounting for Inflation, Savings and Capital

Years to Retirement	Factor A	Factor B	Factor C	Factor D
10	1.5	7.0	2.2	17.5
15	1.8	8.5	3.2	35.3
20	2.2	10.3	4.7	63.3
25	2.7	12.6	6.9	107.0
30	3.2	15.3	10.1	174.0

Lines 3 and 4: Employers can provide annual estimates of your projected retirement pay; estimates of Social Security benefits are available from the Social Security Administration at 800-234-5772. Table 3 lists typical benefits. Both figures are stated in current dollars, not the high amounts that you will receive if your wages keep

TABLE 2 (*Continued*)

up with inflation. The work sheet takes this into consideration.

Line 6: Even if a large pension lets you avoid an income gap, proceed to line 9 to determine the assets you may still need to make up for the effect that inflation will have on a fixed pension payment.

Line 8: This calculation includes a determination of how much you will need to keep up with inflation after retirement and assumes that you will deplete your capital over a twenty-five-year period.

Line 14: This amount includes investments earmarked for retirement and payments by employee and employer to defined contribution retirement plans, such as 401(k)'s. The formula assumes that you will increase your annual savings at the same rate as inflation.

Line 15: Assuming earnings rise with inflation, you can save a percentage of gross pay each year, and the amount to be saved will increase annually.

Note: Inflation is assumed to average 4 percent a year, and the annual return on investments and savings is assumed to be 8 percent.

Source: U.S. News and World Report, copyright July 30, 1990, p. 79.

However, in assessing whether your resources are adequate, it is important to consider how inflation may affect your savings. Average life expectancy at age fifty-five is twenty-nine years; at fifty it is thirty-three years; and at age forty-five, thirty-eight years. If you project that you will need $35,000 for the first year of retirement, you'll need more than $90,000 in the twentieth year in order to enjoy the same standard of living, assuming that inflation will rise at 5 percent per year. If you believe that inflation will run at a 7 percent clip, plan on more than $135,000.

If after completing the work sheets in Tables 2 and 3 you discover a financial shortfall, Table 4 will show you how much you can accumulate by putting away $100 per month.

Now we come to the third issue in determining whether to retire: *Do you have a plan for retirement that brings a smile to your face and a focus to your life?*

In one sense this is perhaps the most critical issue in determining when to retire. For if you can satisfactorily define how you will use your time, the probability is high that your retirement will be a success.

There are, of course, many activities that can fill up a day. You can travel, swim, or sail a boat. You can visit friends, dig in your garden, or play golf. You can even cut the grass!

What you do, however, is not the critical issue. The crucial issue is whether your activities provide purpose and structure to life.

Most people tell me that their greatest desire in retirement is to have a life filled with meaning. Yet, as Joseph Campbell has voiced in his book *The Power of Myth,* "meaning" is perhaps not what should be pursued: "People say that what we're all seeking is a meaning for life. I don't think that's what we're really seeking. I think that what we are seeking is an experience of being alive, so that our life experiences on the purely physical plane will have resonances within our innermost being and reality, so that we actually feel the rapture of being alive. That's what it's finally all about . . ."[12]

I do not think that Campbell is rejecting the idea of meaning as much as he is nudging us to identify those things that provide a purpose to life. What are those things? Listen to some of the responses of those whom I interviewed:

My greatest joys are my grandchildren. When my own children were growing up, I was preoccupied with my career. But in retirement I have an opportunity to watch my grandchildren grow and develop. I feel very fortunate, for I have

TABLE 3

What You Can Expect from the Government

Social Security retirement benefits are based on how much you earn during your working years. The projected benefits below assume that you will be working steadily over the years and that your real wages will increase at the rate of 1 percent annually. The amount saved is in current dollars and does not reflect future increases to offset inflation.

Estimated Monthly Social Security Benefits at Retirement:

Worker's Earnings in 1989

Worker's Current Age:	$25,000	$30,000	$35,000	$40,000	$48,000
35 Worker	1,098	1,199	1,289	1,357	1,484
Worker and spouse	1,647	1,798	1,933	2,035	2,226
45 Worker	1,006	1,101	1,168	1,234	1,332

Worker and spouse	1,509	1,651	1,752	1,851	1,998
55 Worker	906	986	1,027	1,071	1,126
Worker and spouse	1,359	1,479	1,540	1,606	1,689
65 Worker	832	896	925	946	975
Worker and spouse	1,248	1,344	1,387	1,419	1,463

Note: Worker and spouse are assumed to be the same age. A working spouse may qualify for a higher retirement benefit based on his or her earnings record.
Source: U.S. News and World Report, copyright July 30, 1990, p. 62, and the Social Security Administration.

TABLE 4
How to Build Your Nest Egg

The following table shows you how much you will have at the end of the period indicated if you save or invest $100 a month, assuming various annual returns. Results for amounts other than $100 can be calculated as fractions or multiples of $100.

How $100 will grow!

Years:	5 1/2%	7%	8%	9%	10%
5	$6,920	$7,201	$7,397	$7,599	$7,808
10	16,024	17,409	18,417	19,467	20,655
15	28,002	31,881	34,835	38,124	41,792
20	43,762	52,397	59,295	67,290	76,570

Source: Reprinted by permission from *Changing Times*, the Kiplinger magazine, November 1988, p. 32.

been given a second chance with my family, and I am enjoying every minute of it.

The best thing about retirement is being able to spend time with my husband. After raising four children and owning our own business for forty-two years, we finally have time to be with one another. What we have discovered is that we are still the best of friends.

The best thing about retirement is serving as a volunteer at Methodist hospital. I bring magazines and books to patients. I love doing it and have made some wonderful friendships. It's also provided me with a lot of happy memories.

Retirement has given me an opportunity to start a new career. In the back of my mind I always wanted to be a real estate salesman. Now I am getting my chance. Starting next week I am enrolling in a course of study that will qualify me for a real estate license. I am so excited about it I can hardly get to sleep at night.

As I listened to these people speak, I could hear the excitement in their voices as they talked about the things that gave them joy. One gentleman with a marvelous sense of humor put it this way: "For most of my life I have been a frustrated writer. But now I have a goal: to get published. Therefore, each winter I devote my time to writing, and I have had some publishing success. Then in the spring I go to my lake home and get physically fit. In other words, in the winter I will take care of my brain, and in the summer, my body." He added, with a twinkle in his eye: "My friends tell me my body is ahead."

Now let me pause a moment and return to the subject of money. As you are reading these words you might be thinking: "Well, I know that I could identify a lot of things that would be fun to do, but unfortunately, I don't have the money to do them."

Money. The subject came up again and again in my interviews. It became quite apparent that for many, the chief stumbling block to having a good retirement was their lack of money.

Now if this is your situation, I have a suggestion: think about ways to increase your standard of living or to reduce your expenses. Because if you are absorbed with financial concerns, your entire vision of retirement can become clouded.

How can you increase your standard of living? Perhaps an early retirement is not in your best interest. Maybe an additional year or two of salaried employment might make the difference between a satisfying retirement and one that leaves you financially strapped.

Or you might consider part-time employment. If so, you may be amazed at the number of jobs available in your community. According to a recent survey 32 percent of 456 companies were actively recruiting older workers. Not only will you augment your income, but you will meet new friends and perhaps discover skills you never had an opportunity to develop.

Now you may be thinking, "If I worked in retirement, all I would earn is minimum wage."

That may be true, but if you work twenty hours a week you could easily accumulate $5,000 over the course of a year. This is the equivalent of what could be earned in interest from a $70,000 bank deposit. Rather than lament the fact that you don't have a $70,000 investment, affirm the following: with a little work you may have the resources to do the things you always wanted to enjoy.

Colonel Sanders had many financial worries when he retired. His first Social Security check amounted to a grand total of $99! He stared at the check and knew that he could never live on that paltry amount.

Therefore his first order of business was to determine how to augment his income. Unfortunately he had little to offer an employer. He didn't have a formal education. He had few financial resources. And he certainly didn't have his youth.

But what Colonel Sanders *did* have was one asset: a marvelous chicken recipe! He decided that the best way to escape poverty was to market the recipe to restaurants in his community.

Full of enthusiasm, Colonel Sanders hit the streets, going from one restaurant to another with basically the same message: "I've got the best recipe in the world, and I'll give it to you right now for absolutely nothing. All I want is a percentage of the increased profits you make from your chicken sales from now on."

The restaurant managers were unimpressed with the sales presentation. In fact, it probably is a safe bet to say that most restaurant owners looked at the gray-bearded man as a crazed senior citizen. "I've already got a good chicken recipe," said one owner. "Why would I give up a part of my profits for another one? Thanks, but no thanks."

Now if the colonel were like most people, he probably would have thrown in the towel.

He might have said: "Selling things is for younger people. I'm too old." Or, "Maybe my recipe isn't very good after all. Maybe I'm just kidding myself."

But the colonel brushed aside his doubts. He spent the next two years of his life traveling from one end of the United States to another, sleeping in the back of his car, going from one restaurant owner to another and planting the seeds for Kentucky Fried Chicken.

Time after time he met with rejection. But he drove to the next restaurant, planning his next sales presentation.

The colonel was turned down by ten restaurants, then twenty, then two hundred. But he simply would not give up.

Imagine — here was an elderly gentleman, chasing around the country for *two years*, living out of the back seat of his car, only to be faced with one rejection after another. Why did he do it? And what kept him going?

The answer, as chronicled in the *Financial Freedom Report*, was that he had the courage to fulfill his dream.

Colonel Sanders and his chicken recipe were turned down by 1,009 different restaurants before he finally achieved success. Why was success inevitable? "Because if the positive response hadn't come on the 1,010th try, the Colonel would have kept driving and talking through another one hundred or one thousand rejections until he got the answer he wanted."[13]

When an individual has that type of persistence — the courage to keep a dream alive in the face of overwhelming opposition — success in retirement becomes inevitable.

Now you may be thinking: "I could never make it that big." Perhaps not. But that misses the point. The point is that if you are going to have a truly great retirement, you must believe in yourself, your ideas, and your ability to make every day count.

How do you do it? First look at the dreams that you had ten, twenty, or even thirty years ago that you never had a chance to realize. Now might be the time to act on them. That's what Ken Aerstin did. The week after he retired, Aerstin enrolled in broadcasting courses at a local community college. Why? He wanted to pursue his lifelong dream of becoming a disc jockey.

"Since my youth, I've sustained an affection for and unbounded interest in great American music — Gershwin, Richard Rodgers," he said. "I've always kept alive the hope that when I retired, I would become a part-time disc jockey, playing all this great music for people my age."

In evaluating his retirement, Ken said: "I

don't *feel* retired yet. And until I do, I want to sit at a console with my headset on, a stack of records on one side and my program plan on the other, playing all my old favorites: Cole Porter . . . Benny Goodman . . . Harry James . . . Ah, that'll be the Holy Grail for me."[14]

Of course the "Holy Grail" differs from one person to another. Ken Aerstin's lifelong ambition was to be a disc jockey. Your lifelong ambition might be to volunteer in a local hospital, serve on a board of a church, start a new business, or simply hoe in your garden.

But what if all of your dreams have been realized? What if you have been a successful executive and your whole life revolved around work? Then how do you discover a new mission for your retirement?

My suggestion is to head to the nearest retirement organization in your community. You shouldn't have trouble locating one, since almost all cities have retirement centers devoted to the members' hobbies, investments, and/or travel aspirations. But if you have difficulty, contact the local affiliate of the American Association of Retired Persons, and they will assist you in finding a retirement organization that is right for you.

Peter Coners was a vice president for a major company, and he will tell you that his company's retirement club was the catalyst for getting him out of the doldrums.

When Peter was sixty-one years old, his employment was terminated when his company was acquired by a conglomerate. For fifteen months he struggled with his feelings about "being put out to pasture." Then one day he was invited to attend a meeting of his company's retirement club. He was hesitant about attending because he wasn't ready to retire. Nor did he want to be associated with people who were spending their time on the beach.

But with a little coaxing from his wife, he accepted the invitation. Later he reflected on what he had experienced:

It was quite a night, and frankly, it changed my attitudes about retirement. There were several former executives whom I hadn't seen in years. They seemed in the peak of health. Most of them were more relaxed, tanned, and seemed to be enjoying life.

There was one executive with whom I used to work. I asked him how retirement was going for him, and he told me that he wished he had done it five years ago.

I asked him whether he missed his job, his title, and all the perks that went with it. He smiled and told me that he was the chairman of the board of a local hospital. He said he had received more recognition out of that volunteer work and a deeper sense of accomplishment than anything he had ever done at the company. Just talking to him made me feel more optimistic about the future.

I went home and told my wife what had happened. As we talked I realized how much I had changed since I was terminated. I had always been an optimistic person, but I had become withdrawn.

I was determined not to let that happen. I still don't know what I will do with the rest of my life — but I know one thing: I am going to work very hard at keeping a healthy, positive attitude. The future of my life might depend on it.

The future of *your* life might depend on your attitude as well. Never forget that within you are countless ideas waiting to hatch. And a future that may be far different — and better — than you might have imagined. Here is how Ruth Bousman assessed her retirement:

I wish someone had told me how enjoyable and wonderful retirement can be. Just before our retirement we heard sto-

81

ries of retirees dying soon after retiring, of other retirees being bored, and of some going back to work just to fill the hours.

But now we have time for our hobbies, time to enjoy meals and not have to dash somewhere, time to bike, swim, fish, and garden. We have time to be a little lazy — to sit down and look around, to watch a bird building a nest.

We didn't know that after forty years of hard work we could adapt so easily to a whole new life — and find it such a blessing. So I am telling you the way it is. Don't be afraid. Jump in and enjoy.[15]

Here, then, is what to do in determining whether to retire early. First, take out a sheet of paper and write down on the left side of the page the benefits of your job (money, friendships, a challenge, etc.). Then on the right-hand side record what your job might be costing you in terms of your happiness and/or your health. If the costs outweigh the benefits, retirement might be in your future sooner than you thought.

Then make a hard-nosed assessment of your finances using the work sheets that follow this chapter. If there is a financial shortfall attached to early retirement, think of ways to reduce expenses or augment income.

Finally, take a one-week vacation at home and pretend that you are retired. If you get up in the morning with a smile on your face and an agenda for the day dancing in your head, see your personnel officer and apply for the benefits you richly deserve.

PART I
MONEY SENSE

Handling Your Finances

The brokerage firm Merrill Lynch recently undertook a study to identify the major concerns of individuals preparing for retirement. Here is what they were:

Top Worries Among Pre-Retirees

* Inflation
* Health of spouse, family
* Ability to afford medical bills
* Physical health
* Ability to afford daily living expenses
* Ability to live near family
* Ability to care for aging parents[1]

You will note that three of the concerns relate directly to financial considerations, and the remainder have indirect although important economic implications. Studies repeatedly demonstrate that the *principal* concern of pre-retirees is economic: "Will I have enough money to enjoy my retirement years?"

The purpose of this section is to help you achieve lifelong financial security. To achieve that goal you will want to avoid mistakes that can cripple your financial security (chapter 3). You will want to protect your nest egg from the ravages of inflation (chapter 4). And if short of cash, you will want to discover creative ways to increase income and reduce expenses (chapter 5).

Implicit in this section is that we all share a fundamental belief: No matter how many years of work you have before you, it is not a moment too soon to think about life after your paycheck stops. And if you are already retired, it is important to manage your money aggressively so that you are maximizing every retirement dollar you own.

Before we examine the essentials of managing your retirement dollars, one important caveat is in order: The suggestions in this section should be carefully analyzed in terms of your needs and financial resources. You and you alone should be the final arbiter of how you invest your funds and plan for the future.

Nevertheless, I believe that a careful reading of this section will provide you with creative ways not only to manage your retirement savings, but to make your retirement dreams come true.

CHAPTER THREE

A Short Course in Financial Planning

The first rule of survival is not to depend on the kindness of strangers.
Don Underwood
Vice president, Merrill Lynch

If you are about to retire, you may have financial concerns. You might wonder whether you have accumulated enough money to achieve your retirement goals. You may be puzzled about where to invest a large lump sum distribution. And you may be contending with the nightmare of all retirees: no matter how much they have saved, inflation could significantly erode their retirement dollars.

The purpose of this chapter is to examine the *fundamentals* of managing your retirement money.[1] We will learn the importance of keeping accurate financial records. We will discover ways to meet health care expenses, which are rocketing out of sight. And we will learn how to avoid financial mistakes that can seriously undermine your financial future.

The starting point, however, is to make a careful examination of your attitudes about money. For no matter how much or how little you may have accumulated, your attitudes toward money may be the most important factor in making your retirement dollars last.

Develop a Positive Financial Attitude

Many people feel downright guilty about their inability to save for retirement. Says one fifty-two-year-old executive:

> I know that I should be putting away money for retirement. But after I pay the mortgage and the tuition payments, there isn't much left over. Maybe when my kids graduate, I will be able to salt away a few bucks. Of course, by then it might be too late.

Feeling guilty about not saving money for retirement seems to grow with age and reaches its apex when employees make their first serious analysis of their company's retirement plan. Often they discover that their pension represents but a fraction of their annual salary. James Brandt, an English teacher at a small midwestern college, is a case in point.

By his own admission, James paid little attention to his pension fund. "I thought I would teach until I die, so I never planned for retirement."

But at age sixty-one James had a mild heart attack, forcing him to reconsider his future. With some reluctance he went to the college's personnel office and inquired how much he would receive if he retired at age sixty-two. He was in for a nasty surprise: he would receive $742 per month, which was less than 25 percent of his monthly salary.

At the suggestion of a colleague, James made an appointment with a financial planner, who made a thorough analysis of his financial resources. Then she asked a penetrating question: "What's your biggest concern about retirement?" James's anxiety came tumbling out: "How in the world am I going to live on $742 per month? I won't be able to afford a new car. I won't be able to travel. I won't be able to do anything that's fun!"

The financial planner agreed that it would be difficult to live on $742 per month. "But," she noted, "there are many ways to augment your income."

In the weeks that followed, James took a crash course in financial planning, and the results were rather amazing.

The first thing he learned was that rather

than taking a retirement annuity offered through his employer, he would be better off to transfer his pension into an individual retirement account. Because of the higher interest being paid on an IRA, he would be able to boost his retirement income from $742 per month to $813.

He discovered that if he sold his house he would be able to invest the proceeds, which would bring in an additional $852 per month. And if he delayed retirement until age sixty-five, Social Security benefits would amount to $822 per month. Suddenly Jim's financial world looked a lot brighter.

Today Professor Brandt is fully retired, in the peak of health, and renting a beautiful apartment overlooking one of the Twin Cities' most picturesque lakes. To make matters better, every winter he takes a trip to San Diego to visit his daughter. What did he learn from his experience?

Don't panic. That's the most important thing I discovered. There are a lot of financial options, even if your savings are small. The key is getting good financial advice. If you do, you will probably be able to make your money last.

If you are growing pessimistic because you

don't know how to make financial ends meet, chapter 5, "Retiring on a Modest Income" is for you. In the meantime, remember one important rule of financial management: It's not how much money you may have accumulated for retirement that ultimately counts. *It's how it is managed.* As we will see, even the smallest amount of money can be creatively invested to increase monthly income.

Organize! Organize! Organize!

The first rule in planning for your financial future is not to panic over the size of your nest egg. The second is even more important: *get organized.* This means making a pre-retirement budget so that you have a clear understanding of how your money is being spent.

No matter your age, you need to have a budget. I am not talking about an elaborate record-keeping system. Nor am I referring to penny-pinching schemes that keep you from enjoying life. But what I am suggesting is a simple ongoing system by which you can monitor your pre-retirement finances.

Why is a budget so important in retirement planning? The primary reason is that you need to know how much your present lifestyle is costing. Once that has been established, you will be able to get a good fix on how to save money for retirement.

The form in Table 5 will enable you to summarize your monthly expenses. Every evening jot down what you have spent during the day. At the end of the month summarize your total expenditures and ask yourself: "How much of this money would I have expended if I were retired?"

Most people are surprised to learn that at least *20 to 30 percent* of their expenditures will be reduced in retirement. Your transportation costs, for example, will probably decrease, since you no longer commute to work. You will no longer have to pay for work-related lunches, nor will you have to pay dues to a union or to professional organizations. And perhaps most significant, you will no longer pay Social Security tax, which siphons as much as $4,085.10 from your salary and $8,172.20 from self-employment income.[2]

Of course, everyone's situation is different. Some might find that their expenditures will actually *increase,* particularly if they have plans to remodel their home or travel abroad.

Nevertheless most retirees are in for a pleasant surprise: their income needs in retirement are not as great as they imagined. Jack Carlson, of Portland, Oregon, says:

TABLE 5
Assessing Your Financial Expenditures

	Month:_____	Retirement Projection
INCOME:		
Take-home pay	$_____	$_____
Other income	$_____	$_____
Total	$_____	$_____
FIXED EXPENDITURES:		
Mortgage or rent	$_____	$_____
Property taxes	$_____	$_____
Income and	$_____	$_____
Social Security taxes not withheld by employer		
Alimony, child support	$_____	$_____
Installment and credit card payments	$_____	$_____
Insurance		
Auto	$_____	$_____
Homeowners	$_____	$_____
Life	$_____	$_____
Health and other	$_____	$_____
Savings and Investments		
Emergency Fund	$_____	$_____
Investment Fund	$_____	$_____

TABLE 5 (*Continued*)

	Month:_____	Retirement Projection
Vacation Fund	$_____	$_____
Other	$_____	$_____

VARIABLE EXPENDITURES:

Food	$_____	$_____

Utilities

Gas or oil	$_____	$_____
Electricity	$_____	$_____
Telephone	$_____	$_____
Water and Sewer	$_____	$_____
Home Maintenance, furnishings and improvements	$_____	$_____

Automobile

Gas and oil	$_____	$_____
Repairs	$_____	$_____
Public Transportation	$_____	$_____

Pocket Money

Wife	$_____	$_____
Husband	$_____	$_____

Clothing (including dry cleaning)

Wife	$_____	$_____
Husband	$_____	$_____
Personal care	$_____	$_____

(haircuts, gym membership, hobbies, etc.)

TABLE 5 (*Continued*)

	Month:_____	Retirement Projection
Medical and dental bills not covered by insurance	$_____	$_____
Educational expenses	$_____	$_____
Entertainment, recreation, and gifts	$_____	$_____
Charitable contributions	$_____	$_____
Miscellaneous		
_____	$_____	$_____
_____	$_____	$_____
_____	$_____	$_____
_____	$_____	$_____
Total amount spent during the month		$_____
Amount that could be saved in retirement		$_____

Note: As a general rule, most retirees will spend approximately 20 to 30 percent *less* in their retirement years.

Source: Adapted from *Success With Your Money,* by permission of *Changing Times,* 1987, by the Kiplinger Washington Editors, Inc., page 13.

I have learned that I can get by on a lot less [money] in retirement. My cars don't wear out as fast. No longer do I have to "dress for success." We are living a bit more simply — but we sure aren't suffering.

I don't want to mislead you: it takes money to enjoy a successful retirement. But you can probably save more than what you might project. To see what you can save, record every expenditure for a one-month period of time. Then ask yourself this question: "If a financial catastrophe occurred and I needed to save serious money, where would I cut?" You might be amazed at your ability to roll back expenditures — *without compromising your values or the opportunity to do the things you enjoy most in life.*

As you approach retirement, it is also important to keep accurate records, whether of the results of an examination conducted by your physician or of yearly statements sent from your pension fund. Not only might such records be a lifesaver in the event of a health emergency, they might save you considerable money if you are audited by the Internal Revenue Service. Here is how to do it.

First, assess your present record-keeping system. If you have an up-to-date, readable file that lists your important papers, investments, and health records, you need not read further. But if your records are in disarray, now is the time to put them in order.

Items targeted for a safe-deposit box include: deeds, contracts, household inventories, genealogical charts, and photos or videotapes of every room in your house (which can be used to support insurance claims in case of theft or fire).

Your will should *not* be kept in a safe-deposit box. The reason for this is that your heirs might have difficulty retrieving the document. Other items that should be kept at home are bank/thrift passbooks, records of stock purchases, loan payments, income tax records, and life insurance policies.

In addition you should have a file labeled "Important Papers." Included in the file should be the following information:

People to Contact in an Emergency
* Physician
* Pastor/priest/rabbi
* Attorney
* Accountant
* Relatives

Savings and Investments
* Checking accounts
* Bank/thrift savings accounts

99

* Money market funds
* Pension accounts
* Individual retirement accounts
* Keogh plan
* Brokerage accounts
* Stocks/bonds (purchase date, price, certificate or serial numbers, dividend payments received, selling prices — all needed for tax purposes)
* Real estate
* Mutual funds

Life Insurance

* Insurance policies, including life, health, automobile, and home
* Insurance annuities

Mortgages and Loans

* Home mortgage
* Outstanding consumer loans
* Other indebtedness

Additional Information

* Location of birth certificates
* Location of will and/or trusts
* Location of income tax records
* Social Security number/tax identification number
* Credit card accounts
* Business associates to be contacted in the event of an emergency
* Other pertinent information

You should review your records every year to ensure that they are current. And you should keep all tax-related materials for six years and your actual tax returns forever.

Determine How You Will Meet Health Care Expenses

After organizing your financial records, you should take aim at a critical issue: How will you finance the cost of your health care in retirement? And, if you are married, how will your spouse's health expenses be financed?

Most people are not wiped out by making poor investment decisions. Rather they are caught off guard by unexpected medical and hospital expenses. According to Edward R. Roybal, chairman of the House Select Committee on Aging, older Americans are paying a whopping *18.1 percent* of their income for health care — up substantially from 12.7 percent in 1980.[3]

The Employee Benefit Research Institute in Washington reports that since 1960 health expenditures have risen 800 percent, which is eight times faster than the rate of inflation.[4] In middle-size cities like Seattle, Washington, health care costs have roughly doubled in ten years.

In 1979, a simple chest X ray would have

cost $27.50. Today it is $59. A set of dentures cost $350 a decade ago, but in 1991 you would be lucky to get out of the dental chair with a bill of $600. And if your physician prescribes coronary bypass surgery, be prepared to mortgage the house if you aren't covered by Medicare or insurance. In 1979 bypass surgery came to $18,000. Today the tab comes to over $38,000.

Because of the escalating costs of medical care, what you are about to read represents one of the most important messages of this chapter: *Before you retire make certain you and your dependents have adequate health care insurance.* Because if you aren't adequately insured, the results could be disastrous.

Consider George Linford, who worked in the airline business for thirty-two years. When given a chance to take early retirement, George jumped at the opportunity. The offer included a $2,000 bonus, 100 percent medical coverage, and a pension that amounted to eighty-five percent of his current salary.

But there was a downside to the equation: George's fifty-six-year-old wife, Sara, would receive medical/hospital insurance coverage for only eighteen months. And to make matters worse, because of a preexisting medical condition, it was doubtful that Sara could obtain affordable health insurance.

George and Sara gambled that her medical condition would not deteriorate. Everything went well during the first two years of retirement. Then the bottom fell out when Sara was diagnosed as having ovarian cancer. In the next fourteen months the Linfords' entire savings were devoured by thousands of dollars in medical bills.

Today George and Sara have to count every penny in order to get by. "It's not the kind of retirement we dreamed of," laments George.

Before you terminate employment, it is important to determine how you are going to meet the health insurance needs of you, and, if married, your spouse. Here are some important principles to factor into your decision.

First, you need to know exactly who is going to pay for your health care costs once you are retired. Unless you have the wealth of an Arab sheik, you need to protect yourself from catastrophic health care costs. For even wealthy people can see their financial resources erode after a lengthy illness.

Second, remember that Medicare was never meant to be an all-inclusive health insurance program. It was originally designed to offer *partial* relief from the costs of hospitalization, surgery, and skilled nursing care. But it was not intended, nor does it today, cover all of your medical expenses. And while improvements are being made in Medicare coverage, only *49* percent of the average senior's health care costs are covered by the federal government.[5]

Medicare will not reimburse you for private duty nursing, nor will it pay all the costs of your medications. Most important, if you end up in a nursing home for an extended period, you have little chance to be reimbursed for expenses that typically run $2,000 to $3,000 per month.

So what should you do? *Shortly before retiring, enroll in a health care program that will provide relief from major medical expenditures.* Here is how to do it.

Your first line of defense in locating appropriate health insurance is with your employer. Before submitting a letter of resignation, visit the personnel office and ask what health insurance options they offer to retirees. If your employer has at least twenty workers, you and your dependents will be able to continue health insurance coverage for at least eighteen months, as mandated by the Consolidated Omnibus Budget Reconciliation Act of 1985 (COBRA). If you are disabled and eligible for Social Security disability benefits when you terminate employment, you can obtain an additional eleven months of coverage, for a total of twenty-nine months.

What happens if you work for an employer with fewer than twenty workers? If your state requires "continuation of benefits," you may be able to stay with your employer's group policy for as little as three months in some states or as long as eighteen months in others.[6]

Insurance protection under COBRA legislation does not come cheap. COBRA requires that you pay 102 percent of your group insurance premium. If your employer has been paying a portion of your insurance expenses, you may have to assume that cost in addition to what you were previously paying plus an extra 2 percent for administrative costs. Disabled individuals who take COBRA coverage may pay as much as 150 percent of the premium for the extra months.

Another option is to piggyback on your spouse's insurance program, providing, of course, that your marriage partner is employed outside the home. This option should be evaluated carefully, however, because your spouse's policy may not be as good as the one you formerly owned. Ask for a copy of the plan and note the deductible, which should not be more than $500. Also inquire about the lifetime cap on benefits, which is usually around $1,000,000.

A third possibility is to join a Health Maintenance Organization (HMO). An HMO is designed to hold down health expenditures by paying hospitals and doctors a set yearly fee. HMO's can save you money — up to 28 percent compared with traditional health insurance policies. While the monthly premium is approximately the same as what you would have to pay for private insurance, the difference is that HMO's cover virtually *all costs* after payment of the premium. Furthermore, private insurance almost always has deductibles and requires you to pay a percentage of your medical expenses, usually 20 percent.

There are pitfalls to enrolling in an HMO — primarily the fact that you may lose the freedom to select your own physician and hospital. But if you are looking for an economical way to finance your health expenses, an HMO might be your best choice.[7]

A final option is to purchase a health care policy through a private insurer such as Blue Cross/Blue Shield. Here are the key issues to explore before making a decision on a particular carrier:

1. Are there age requirements that would keep you from owning the policy? (Entrance ages vary depending upon the insurer. Some policies can be purchased at any age.)

2. Does the policy cover preexisting health conditions? Many do not. If not, what will it exclude in your case, and for what period of time?
3. Is the policy guaranteed renewable?
4. What is the deductible?
5. What is the maximum benefit? A maximum benefit can be expressed as an *interval of time* (full coverage in a semiprivate hospital room for sixty days) or a *maximum dollar* ($350 for outpatient surgery).
6. What is the cost of the policy, and how does it compare with other health insurance programs? What have been the premium increases for each of the past five years?[8]

One concluding thought about health insurance: Regardless of the plan you select, determine where you will be hospitalized and the number of physicians sponsored by the plan. The reputation of the hospital as well as your plan's willingness to reimburse a wide variety of medical specialists will give you a clue as to the quality of the plan.

Avoid Serious Financial Mistakes

Finding an appropriate health plan might save you from financial ruin, but it won't guarantee a financially secure retirement. To be financially secure you must invest your retirement monies prudently.

In the next chapter we will examine various strategies that will preserve and enhance your capital. But for now, let's consider some of the most common mistakes that retirees make as they plan for their financial future.[9]

The first is what *Fortune* magazine calls *playing pigeon*. The closer you get to retirement the more you resemble a plump target to brokers, insurance salesmen, and even con artists who will beguile you with magic words like "guaranteed return," "liquid," "100 percent safe," "risk-free income." These people know that you have a chunk of money to invest and will pounce on you like a hungry cat seeking its prey.

Virginia Kent, sixty-eight, is a retired widow living in Mystic, Connecticut. Three years ago, on the questionable advice of a stockbroker, she invested $200,000 of her $427,000 savings in thirty-year tax-exempt bonds. She was also advised to purchase a $75,000 single-premium life insurance policy.

The advice was not helpful. While bonds can be an appropriate investment for retirement, Ms. Kent bought when interest rates were low. In addition, the insurance company had a poor track record in building up cash values. The cost for this advice: more than $8,000 in commissions.[10]

An entire financial industry has sprouted up during the past decade, designed to help you invest your retirement dollars. Most financial planners will give you credible advice. But others see you ripe for the picking.

How should you respond to those who offer financial advice? Be wary. Talk to more than one financial planner. And above everything else, trust your instincts. If the advice sounds too good to be true, it probably is.

The second mistake is a *failure to diversify*. Pete Stocker, fifty-two, was only three years from retirement as a credit manager from Weyerhauser, the giant forest-products company in Tacoma, Washington. The bulk of his assets were invested in Weyerhauser stock through a 401(k) plan. Unfortunately for him and his wife Barbara, doomsday struck in the October 1987 stock market crash. Weyerhauser shares fell precipitously from a precash high of $52 to $30. The value of Pete's retirement fund dropped 42 percent for a loss of $15,000. "I realized I was in deep trouble the moment I heard that the stock market had hit bottom."[11]

Many retirees load up on one type of investment. Some buy only bonds or utility stocks because they want predictable income. Others purchase gold or gold stocks because they are terrified of inflation.

The best approach, however, is to have an investment program that balances relatively safe investments, such as bonds, with more risky investments, such as stocks. Table 6 illustrates a recommended risk according to age.

The third mistake is to *ignore growth investments*. In general, investments come in two broad categories: *income* and *growth*. The most commonly used income investments include savings accounts, money market funds, certificates of deposits, treasury bills, and bond funds. Growth stocks are investments which, although more risky than income investments, will generally give you a larger financial return.

Some retirees, particularly people in their seventies and eighties or nineties, need only income. Consequently they are best advised to keep their retirement dollars in safe and predictable instruments, such as savings accounts, certificates of deposit, and treasury bills.

TABLE 6

Investing Your Retirement Dollars According to Your Age

Age	Recommended Asset Mix	Total Return 20 Years*	Average Annual Rate of Return
35-50	75% stocks 25% bonds	420%	8.6%
50-65	50% stocks 50% bonds	301%	7.2%
65+	25% stocks 75% bonds	208%	5.8%

*Assumes annual return of 10% for stocks and 4.4% for bonds.

Source: Copyright *Fortune,* 1989, the Time Inc. Magazine Company. All rights reserved.

But most people need investments that will grow in value. Charles DeRose, a New York investment advisor, states: "People who retired to Florida with only certificates of deposit or long-term bonds are desperately budgeting today to offset the rising cost of living."[12]

It is important to remember that bonds will provide a steady stream of income, but the purchasing power of that income tends to shrink as inflation rises. Furthermore, if interest rates rise, the market value of bonds falls. Far better to have a balanced portfolio that will give you both income and growth. How do you do it?

Financial specialists suggest that your financial investments should be adjusted according to your age. At forty-five to fifty, your retirement strategy should tend toward growth. Thus you should hold approximately 50 percent to 60 percent of your assets in stocks. You can place another 30 percent of your holdings into bonds and the rest in certificates of deposit or a money market fund.

As you approach age fifty-five you should consider reducing stocks to 30 percent of your portfolio and boost bonds to 40 percent and cash to 30 percent. In so doing you are reducing your risk to market gyrations.

Once retired, your portfolio should be conservatively managed with approximately 50 percent in bonds and 30 percent in money market accounts. However — and this is a key point — *20 percent of your savings should continue to be in growth stocks.* And if you retire early, say at age fifty-five, you are best advised to keep 20 percent to 30 percent of your assets in stocks.[13]

Which stocks should you select? You might

want to concentrate on blue-chip stocks. In a recession they tend to hold their value better than other securities, such as stocks in small companies. In addition, most pay predictable dividends. "Not only does the increased payout give you a higher income each year — which is more than you can say for bonds — it also helps boost the price of the stock," says Geraldine Weiss, editor of *Investment Quality Trends Newsletter*.[14] Examples of stocks which have raised their dividends each year for at least the past fifteen include American Business Products, American National Insurance, H&R Block, Delux, Emerson Electric, Minnesota Mining and Manufacturing, National Gas and Oil, and Pfizer.[15]

There is one additional way to diversify your retirement nest egg, and that is to purchase annuities from an insurance company. When you purchase an insurance annuity, you give the company a lump sum deposit. The company, in turn, provides monthly income at a rate that can be guaranteed. The amount you receive each month will depend on how much you wish to draw as well as the number of years the contract will be in force. Before purchasing insurance annuities, visit your local library and obtain an independent analysis of various insurance companies made by A. M. Best Company, Standard and Poor's, or other independent raters.

In summary, the portfolio that will protect you from inflation as well as market crashes will have a mixture of stocks for growth, some taxable government or tax-exempt municipal bonds for income, and money market funds, short-term certificates of deposit, or Treasury bills for liquidity and safety. The conservative investor may also wish to take advantage of annuities that guarantee income for life.

Will such a mixture of investments really protect you in the event of a market crash? Not entirely. Whenever you invest in stocks you take a risk. But a well-diversified portfolio can mitigate the losses and, in the long term, protect the value of your retirement investments.

A fourth mistake made by pre-retirees is *not considering the tax implications of their savings.* One San Francisco executive took a three-month trip shortly after receiving a $600,000 profit-sharing settlement. The executive intended to roll over the money into an Individual Retirement Account, which would have delayed the onset of a tax bill. But the Internal Revenue's deadline for such a rollover is strictly enforced at sixty days. It was an expensive trip: the tax due on his settlement totaled about $250,000.[16]

The most important financial decision you

make, suggests Leon Nad, a tax expert from the accounting firm Price Waterhouse, is to figure your taxes *before* you retire. The reason is simple: a lot of money is often at stake.

At retirement you will typically receive more money than at any other point in your life, especially if you have been investing in a company savings plan. Most of your assets will be in tax-*deferred* retirement plans. These funds are subject to complex tax laws, and the penalties for mistakes are high. And the decisions you make are almost always irreversible.[17]

How do you avoid such errors? The starting point is to have an accountant and/or tax attorney review your finances. But it is equally important for you to learn everything you can to protect your savings and nurture their growth. How can you educate yourself about money, particularly if you are not financially inclined?

In most communities there are banks, brokerage houses, and community colleges that sponsor programs aimed at helping you plan for retirement. In addition, there is a wealth of reading material at your fingertips. *Changing Times* and *Money* magazines provide astute advice in helping invest your hard-earned dollars. *Business Week, Forbes,* and *Fortune* magazines can assist in spotting economic trends.

And retirement newsletters such as *United Retirement Bulletin* (617-267-8885), and *The Retirement Letter* (301-424-2700) provide valuable financial information as well as pertinent advice on retirement housing, health care, and travel.

Finally, don't forget the local library. "Many libraries," according to Kenneth Fisher, a money manager in Woodside, California, "now have better research material than a typical stock brokerage office."[18]

Obtain Competent Financial Advice

Let's pause a moment. If you are like most pre-retirees, you probably have a savings account, a pension, a few shares of stock, and equity in your house.

It may not be a big pot of money. But to you it represents not only a lifetime of work, but your financial future. Now the issues are: How can you protect your retirement money from the relentless pressure of inflation? And how do you diminish the big bite that Uncle Sam will take out of your tax-deferred savings?

To answer these questions, you may want to turn to a financial adviser. Today 13 percent of American households are utilizing financial advisers.[19] Why? Because the average person can't keep up with the complexity of federal and state tax laws as well as new investment opportunities.

You should consider obtaining financial help under the following circumstances:

* You have had little experience in managing money.
* You are considering an early retirement and need to know whether your income can support your lifestyle.
* You have financial responsibility for an aged parent or a dependent child and need to assess whether your retirement savings can care for them as well as yourself.
* You are five to ten years away from retirement and have not been able to accumulate savings for retirement.
* You are ten to fifteen years away from retirement, but your investments have not produced positive results.
* You have been an aggressive investor in the stock market but have little knowledge of income-producing investments.
* You have successfully invested in

income-producing instruments such as savings accounts and certificates of deposit but have little knowledge of growth investments.

* You have a financial plan for your retirement but want it analyzed for accuracy by a professional accountant, lawyer, planner, etc.[20]

If you turn to a financial planner for help, you will probably be pleased with the outcome. In one survey 71 percent described themselves as "very satisfied" with the results, while 21 percent were "somewhat satisfied." Only 1 percent indicated that they were "not at all satisfied."[21]

One word of caution is in order. There are unscrupulous individuals in the financial planning field just as there are in other disciplines. Gustave Hoehn, seventy-two, and thirty-five other investors lost $4,500,000 when their funds, which were to have been deposited in bank-issued certificates of deposit, were siphoned off by a promoter who bought four houses, a thirty-three-foot yacht, antiques, furs, and a Rolls-Royce. Hoehn, a physician, figures he lost $438,000. Says he: "I'd be retired right now if this hadn't happened."[22]

How can you find a competent financial adviser? Here are five points to remember.[23]

1. *Reputation.* Your best recommendation will probably come from neighbors, friends, family, and associates at work. Another source is your accountant, who knows your finances, or a banker who has had experience in working with financial planners in your community.

In addition, you may ask one or more of the organizations that accredit financial planners for lists of planners in your area. One of these is the International Association of Financial Planners in Atlanta, Georgia (404-395-1605). Upon your request the association will provide a free booklet, *Consumer's Guide to Financial Independence.* Another financial planning organization is the Institute of Certified Financial Planners, which is located in Denver, Colorado (800-282-PLAN). This group will provide the names of five certified planners in your area and provide biographical information. They also offer a free booklet, *First Steps to Financial Security: A Guide for Selecting a Certified Financial Planner.*

2. *Competence.* How do you assess competence? Here are the key questions to ask:

1. What is your professional training?
2. How long have you been a financial planner?
3. How long have you been in the community?

4. May I have a list of references?
5. How often do you keep in touch with clients after you have made your recommendations?
6. Will you be doing the work on my financial plan or will you be delegating it to others?
7. How long does it usually take for you to draw up a financial plan?
8. How do you charge for your work?
9. What companies, if any, do you represent?
10. What percentage of your clients are planning for retirement?

3. *Legal compliance.* Always insist on proof of registration or certification in the event that your financial planner is selling you a product. Firms that offer securities advice must register with the Securities and Exchange Commission and the National Association of Securities Dealers. This means that your financial adviser is required by law to give a written description of his or her fees, types of clients, investment specialties and strategies, education and background, and industry connections.[24]

4. *Financial Costs.* According to the columnist Jane Bryant Quinn, there are basically

four ways in which planners are reimbursed. (1) Commission only: these planners make their living by selling a financial product, such as a mutual fund or insurance policy. The amount you will pay will be dependent on the product purchased. (2) Fee and commission: these planners will draw up a financial plan that typically will cost between $250 and $1,500. Most of their money, however, will come from commissions. (3) Fee offset: planners who use this method of compensation will give you a fixed fee for their advice. You will be billed by the hour, the job, or a percentage of the assets under their management. If they earn commissions from your business, these are offset against their fee. (4) Fee only: financial planners who are "fee only" charge only for advice and will not take any commissions.

Many people are turned off by fee-only planners because their price appears to be high. It is important, however, to remember that the "low-priced" service might actually be more expensive once you compute the commission charges you are paying (see Table 7).

In working with a financial adviser, be honest about your retirement goals, your experiences in investing money, and your tolerance for risk. Be prepared in addition to make full disclosure of your financial resources as well

TABLE 7
Comparison of Costs Associated with Financial Planners

Financial planning promotional pitches can be deceiving. Planner B asks for a low fee for constructing a plan but takes a large sales commission. He ends up costing more than planner A, who charges only for the plan and the consulting fees. The moral? Before entering into any agreement with a financial planner, be sure to obtain in writing a complete description of costs associated with the services offered by your financial planner.

Product	Planner A Amount	Planner B Amount
Financial plan	$6,000	$1,500
Life insurance premium: $1,500	750*	975
Disability insurance premium: $2,000	750*	1,300
Mutual funds: $150,000	1,500**	9,000
Limited partnership: $20,000	200	1,600
TOTAL COST:	$9,200	$14,375

*$150 an hour
**1% a year
Source: Hopewell Rembert Advisors, in Jane Bryant Quinn, "Who Calls The Tune?" Newsweek, July 31, 1989.

as financial obligations. Never give your planner power of attorney in which he or she has sole authority over your money, and be wary of turning over any assets for the planner to manage. The primary role of a financial planner is to give advice, not to manage your money.[25]

A competent financial planner will help you avoid a maze of financial problems. But if in doubt about the value of the advice, show your financial plan to an accountant or lawyer who, by virtue of his or her training, can assist you in identifying a questionable recommendation or claim.

Determine How Your Estate Will Be Distributed

Now we come to one of the most important fundamentals of money management, and that is estate planning. A good estate plan has two objectives. First, it will ensure that your financial resources will be distributed to your heirs in a manner consistent with your wishes. Second, it will protect your estate from excess taxation.[26]

Estate planning begins with the creation of a *will*. This will is designed to instruct your survivors about how to distribute your property. It designates someone who will serve as the estate's executor. The executor is responsible for taking inventory of all property, paying creditors and taxes, and dividing assets among heirs.

If you have never drawn up a will, see an attorney. If you do not have a will and if you are not married, the court at the time of your death will appoint an administrator for your estate. While most courts prefer to name a relative as an administrator of your estate, there is no guarantee that they will do it. Sometimes they will turn over your assets to a professional administrator, who will charge 3 percent to 5 percent of your estate in fees per year — an arrangement which provides little incentive to settle your estate quickly.

You may want to enclose in your will a *letter of intent*. While not legally binding in all states, such a letter will make clear your personal wishes. It permits you to make specific bequests of your personal property, including your heirlooms and antiques, and allows you to explain some of the provisions in the will.

While a will is considered the most basic of all estate planning tools, you may also need a *trust*. A trust represents a legal device that holds assets for your beneficiaries. In a revocable trust you serve as a trustee, manage the assets yourself, and can alter the terms at any time. After your death, a successor trustee, usually a family member or a trusted friend, will distribute the assets to your beneficiaries according to instructions you state in the trust document.[27]

Now if all of this sounds like a legal document for the rich, think again. There are some very important reasons for a trust, even for individuals of modest means.

First, if you have minor children or a disabled adult child, a trust can be an effective mechanism for caring for them in the event of your death. Consider, for example, a fifty-five-year-old single parent who has a net worth of $150,000. The parent has one child, a college freshman. The parent, fearful of financial mismanagement, does not want the eighteen-year-old child to be the sudden recipient of a $150,000 windfall. Therefore, he or she establishes a trust that reimburses the college for tuition expenses, pays the child a reasonable monthly stipend, and then distributes the bulk of the estate to the child over a five-, ten-, or even twenty-year period. Not only is the deceased parent caring for the child's educational needs, but the estate is being professionally managed and, in all probability, growing in value.

Another advantage of implementing a trust is that it protects your privacy. Neighbors, work associates, and distant relatives cannot ascertain how the assets have been distributed.

In fact, the terms of the trust may become public only if someone objects to the provisions or lack of provisions designated for him or her. This tends not to happen, however, for it is more difficult to contest a living trust than a will.

The most important reason for establishing a trust, though, is to protect your family in the event that you are incapacitated. Upon notification that you are no longer able to take care of your financial affairs, a successor would manage your investments consistent with instructions you had previously given. This process is particularly useful if a spouse and/or next-of-kin have little experience in managing money.

One word of caution is in order: a trust is not for everyone. The initial costs for setting one up through an attorney can be substantial, and you should be prepared to spend considerable time reviewing your finances and determining how they should be allocated in the event of your death. In addition, there are many types of trusts and it is important to find the one that is best for you. Nevertheless a trust might be the most appropriate mechanism for you to use in making sure that the estate you have accumulated over a lifetime will be distributed fairly and promptly to your heirs.

What, then, are the priorities in determining

a sound financial plan for retirement? Budget your income. Organize your files. Obtain adequate health insurance protection. Diversify your assets. Establish a will and possibly a trust. If you do these things you will not only have mastered the fundamentals in financial planning, but you will leave an important legacy for the people you love.

CHAPTER FOUR

New Rules: Protecting Your Retirement Money and Making It Grow

Resolve not to be poor. Whatever you have, spend less.
Samuel Johnson
(1709–1784)

Retiring used to be easy. After working for the same company for twenty or thirty years, employees would collect their pension starting at age sixty-five.

Today, however, employees have worked for three, four, or more employers. They have invested in individual retirement accounts (IRA's), 401(k)'s, Keoghs, or company-sponsored savings plans. And, thanks to inflation, the biggest equity many retirees have is in their home.

Now the question is, How do you bring your pension, Social Security payments, and investments into a coherent retirement package? And how do you make sure you take full advantage of the many investment opportunities that exist, regardless of the size of your nest egg? Here are the new rules for managing your retirement monies.

Rule One: Minimize Your Debt

It used to be that debt was essentially a problem of the young. Not so anymore. Says John Laskey, senior vice president of Insured Credit Services, in Chicago: "The young borrowers [who defaulted on loans] often had short-term jobs, recently bought new houses with a minimum down payment, and were already carrying considerable debt when they applied for yet another loan. But now the average defaulter is forty years old, holds a steady job, and has lived in his home for five years."[1]

Why is debt a problem, even to people who are in their fifties or early sixties?

For one thing, many parents have heavy financial obligations to their adult children. Today 53 percent of all eighteen- to twenty-four-year-olds live with their parents or are dependent upon them financially while attending college, compared with forty-three percent in 1960. Even as children approach middle age, they often need shelter: 11 percent of all twenty-five- to thirty-four-year-olds live at home, up from 9 percent in 1960. And countless other children live away from home but rely on Mom and Dad for financial support. Consequently, parents who could be saving for retirement are putting their money where their hearts are — their children.

Increased housing costs also contribute to the debt load of many older adults. When the kids finally leave home, parents may pursue more suitable housing. Many, however, don't trade down. They trade up, which is well and good in terms of lifestyle and comfort. But the mortgage payments are increased, which means that fewer dollars can be put away for retirement.

Then, too, there are the more mundane things that keep people from enlarging their retirement nest egg, including credit card payments, automobile loans, and increased insurance expenses.

Regardless of the reasons for accumulating debt, one thing is certain: *You can't enjoy retirement if you are loaded with financial obligations.* Nor can you make sound plans for the future if you can't see beyond the Mastercard statement, the car payments, and the consumer loan that floated last summer's vacation. If you are serious about retirement, you have to become equally serious about reducing your financial obligations.

But how do you do it? Suppose you are in

your fifties or early sixties, and find it almost impossible to pay off the bills? First, determine whether your debt load is too high. In Table 8 you will find a brief exercise that will let you know whether you are overextended. As a rule of thumb, your consumer installment debt should not exceed 20 percent of your income. If you are planning on retiring within the next five years, be even more conservative and use *only* net income from work. This means excluding interest dividends and other nonemployment income.[2]

Should you use your savings to pay off debt? Most financial planners say yes.[3] As Kathryn Maxell, a partner in Ascent Cash Flow Systems, in San Francisco, states: "The fastest way to make eighteen percent is to pay off your credit card."[4]

Not only should you take aim at reducing debt associated with credit card bills and consumer loans, but you should also accelerate your mortgage payments. True, you will lose the tax advantage when paying off a mortgage. Most people, however, are ahead by taking clear title to their home. The reason? Mortgage expenses are usually higher than what most people can earn on conservative investments. Therefore it is usually prudent to pay off the mortgage rather than invest the same money elsewhere.

TABLE 8
Are You Carrying Too Much Debt?

As a rule of thumb, your consumer installment debt should not exceed 20 percent of your "take-home" income from work. As you reach the retirement planning stages be even more conservative and use only net income from work. Don't include interest, dividends and other non-employment income. Hold back this non-work income as a protective cushion that you can put into savings/investments.

If you are retired, assess what you consider to be your "take-home" income — which might include Social Security, annuities, pension plan, Individual Retirement Accounts, or similar. Do not include the interest, dividends from longer-term investments — say those maturing in five, ten years.

A. Your total net income from
   work: _____

B. The 20% installment-payment
   debt maximum safety level
   (20% of line A): _____

C. Your present total annual
   consumer installment debt
   payments, including:* _____
   Autos . . . . _____
   Other vehicles . . . . _____
   Furniture . . . . _____
   Appliances . . . . _____

TABLE 8 (*Continued*)

Home entertainment
   equipment . . . . _____
Sports equipment . . . . _____
Vacation trip . . . . _____
Other:

_____   _____

_____   _____

_____   _____

                                     Total: _____

D. Amount of total annual
consumer installment-debt
you can afford — in
addition to present amount
(B minus C) . . . .   _____
This amount (D) is your
present margin of safety.
If your present amount (C)
exceeds the 20% level (B),
you are in trouble already.

E. To figure your current debt
ratio, divide your present
total debt (C) by your
annual net income (A) . . . .   _____

*Other than mortgage, education and business loans

Source: Sylvia Porter, *Sylvia Porter's Your Finances in the 1990s.* Copyright © 1990 Prentice Hall Press, a division of Simon & Schuster, New York, p. 54.

In addition, once the note is paid off, most people experience great relief. Never again do they have to worry about a monthly mortgage payment. And if by chance they lose their job or their investments fall on hard times, they can take comfort in knowing that they are beholden to no one when it comes to owning their home.

If you are serious, then, about wanting a worry-free retirement, dig yourself out of debt. This does not imply that you have to be a miser in your fifties in order to enjoy life in your sixties, but it does suggest that the key to financial freedom is keeping expenses under control.

Rule Two: Accelerate Your Retirement Savings

Many people in their forties and fifties have the vague hope that "someday" they will be financially secure. Yet the facts indicate that fewer than 5 percent of all Americans are financially independent at age sixty-five and more than 20 percent must work after retirement in order to maintain their lifestyle.[5]

If you are five, ten, or fifteen years away from retirement, now is the time to invest aggressively for the future. Why? Because there still is time to make your money grow in value.

Equally important, you want to save now so that you are not totally dependent upon your company's pension later.

Many people are lulled into a false sense of security because they are enrolled in a pension plan. But Social Security and a pension *combined* usually account for only 40 to 60 percent of what you need in retirement.[6] Therefore it is important to accelerate your savings, so that you have control over your financial future. What strategies will maximize your savings?

Your best bet is to participate in tax-sheltered, corporate-sponsored savings plans, which have grown at a phenomenal rate during the past decade. Today more than 82 percent of large and medium-size employers offer 401(k) plans, compared to only 2 percent in 1983.

Under 401(k) legislation, you are entitled to stash up to $7,979 annually (1990) in tax-deferred accounts, although most companies have specific plan-eligibility requirements. This means that if you are in the 28 percent tax bracket, you spend only $72 to save $100. And if your employer adds fifty cents to your account for each dollar you contribute (a typical formula), you have an immediate 50 percent return on your savings.[7]

You will have to make several investment

decisions when enrolling in a 401(k) plan (or, for public employees, a 403(b) plan). If you are ten or more years away from retirement, you probably want to invest in a growth mutual fund or in your company's stock plan. If retirement is around the corner, government securities with fixed income returns are usually the safest bet.

However, it is important to think of your tax-sheltered savings in conjunction with other assets. If the bulk of your savings is in low interest-bearing bank accounts, you probably should make monthly investments in a growth-oriented mutual fund. The reason for this is that monies stashed in savings accounts rarely keep up with inflation.

What if your company does not offer a 401(k) plan? If neither you nor your spouse is covered by a corporate pension plan, take out an IRA offered through banks, mutual funds, brokerage houses, and insurance companies. Or if self-employed, enroll in a Keogh plan by December 31 to take advantage of tax savings for that calendar year. A Keogh plan will produce more dramatic investment results than an IRA, since you can make tax-deductible contributions to it of up to 20 percent of your net income, to a maximum of $30,000.

Then, too, you might wish to consider purchasing annuities from an insurance company, particularly if you are getting a late start on retirement planning. One of the most attractive offerings is a single-premium deferred annuity (SPDA) in which you invest a lump sum such as $5,000. The total return on your investment can be guaranteed and your taxes are deferred until the day you actually receive the money. Additional information on annuities is presented later in this chapter.

The amount of money you can accumulate in tax-sheltered plans can be dramatic. The chart in Table 9 shows how $100 invested biweekly grows over five, ten, and fifteen years.[8]

A word of caution is in order, however. There is a downside to most tax-sheltered plans due to the fact that your invested money is usually locked up until you are fifty-nine and a half. If you need this cash before then, the Internal Revenue Service will hit you with a 10 percent penalty tax. If you own an annuity, you will be forced to pay not only the penalty tax but sometimes a surrender fee charged by the insurance company.

In spite of these restrictions, *the fastest way for most people to accumulate wealth is through tax-sheltered investing.* If you are ten or more years away from retirement, you should strive to save through tax-sheltered savings plans — provided, of course, that you have an emer-

TABLE 9
How Savings Grow

The following illustration demonstrates the dramatic savings that can occur through tax-deferred savings plans. The example shows how an employee contribution of $100 from a biweekly paycheck would grow after 5, 10, and 15 years in one of four different investments. The money is assumed to increase at 9% a year compounded, except in the tax-free bond fund, where the rate is 7.3%. Taxes are assessed at 28%. The best savings plan is the 401(k) tax-deferred plan with a 50% matching contribution from the employer. The 401(k) with no employer contribution comes in second.

$100 invested biweekly in a taxable bond fund yielding 9%

Net worth after five years	$11,038
Net worth after ten years	$26,293
Net worth after fifteen years	$47,378

$100 invested biweekly in a tax-free bond fund yielding 7.3%

Net worth after five years	$11,277
Net worth after ten years	$27,514
Net worth after fifteen years	$50,892

$100 invested biweekly in an investment contract (GIC) at 9% in a tax-deferred 401(k) plan

Net worth after five years	$11,795
Net worth after ten years	$30,280
Net worth after fifteen years	$59,247

TABLE 9 (*Continued*)

$100 invested biweekly in an investment contract (GIC) at 9% in a tax-deferred 401(k) plan with 50% employer matching contribution

Net worth after five years	$17,693
Net worth after ten years	$45,420
Net worth after fifteen years	$88,871

Source: Reprinted from *Money: Family Wealth*, Spring 1988, by special permission; copyright 1988 The Time Inc. Magazine Company.

gency fund that equals from three to six months of your annual salary.

If it is difficult to save, consider investing a small amount — say, $25 or $50 a month. You will be surprised at how fast that money will accumulate. And once you discover the "eighth wonder of the world" — the miracle of compounding — you will probably find ways to enlarge your retirement nest egg.

Rule Three: Yes – You Can Count on Social Security

Now we come to one of the most troublesome worries of pre-retirees: *Will Social Security be there when I need it?*

Many people have reservations about the future of Social Security. In a recent study 69 percent of the respondents indicated that they were not confident about the stability of the system.[9] And others doubted they would ever receive as much from the government as they paid in.

Is such apprehension warranted? Will Social Security be there when *you* need it?

The answer is a qualified yes.[10] But medical entitlement programs might be altered as health costs soar. In addition, some caps may be placed on automatic cost-of-living increases.

Nevertheless, the Social Security Act, signed into law on August 14, 1935, is President Franklin D. Roosevelt's most important domestic achievement and lasting legacy — "the greatest democratic revolution in our history," states noted historian Henry Steele Commager, professor emeritus at Amherst College in Massachusetts.[11] And it's not likely to be fundamentally changed for the following reasons.

First, contrary to popular myth, the Social Security system is not going bankrupt. In fact, one indicator of its financial health is that it is starting to amass sizable reserves that will swell to twelve trillion dollars by the year 2020, when the first wave of baby boomers is well into the system.

Second, it is not contributing to the federal deficit. Over the first fifty years, Social Security operated at a more than $50 billion *surplus*. During the period 1987–1992 it will produce a $330 billion reserve, with a multi-trillion-dollar surplus appearing in the early decades of the next century.

Third, Social Security continues to be an immensely popular program with the American electorate. As authors Merton and Joan Bernstein note in *Social Security: The System That Works:* "Most Americans support Social Security because it preserves a modicum of human dignity and independence for our parents, the disabled, 3.2 million children with disabled, retired, or deceased parents, and sooner or later, ourselves. The trustees of the Social Security funds say the program can meet its obligations over the next 75 years. Everyone can rely on it. For how many things in this world can that be said?"[12]

Nevertheless many people are uncertain as to what they are entitled to under Social Security legislation. And many are confused about whether they can earn additional monies after age sixty-two without sacrificing benefits. Here are straightforward answers to some of the most frequently asked questions about Social Security.[13]

Once retired, how much money will I receive

from Social Security? There is an easy way to determine your future Social Security benefits: Call 1-800-234-5772 and ask to have form SSA-7004 sent to you. This form will request information about your current earnings and the age at which you plan to retire. Mail the form to the Social Security Administration, and four to six weeks later you will receive a "Personal Earnings and Benefit Estimate Statement." This statement will show what benefits you can expect to receive under three conditions: 80 percent benefit if you retire at sixty-two, full benefit at age sixty-five to sixty-seven (depending on your year of birth) and the 33 percent larger benefit if you delay receiving Social Security entitlements until age seventy. The statement will also provide information about disability benefits and how much your children and surviving spouse will receive in the event of your death. In the meantime, Table 10 will provide a good estimate of what you are likely to receive provided you made the maximum contribution during your career.

Can I collect Social Security even if I continue to work beyond age sixty-two or even age sixty-five? Yes, but your benefits may be reduced. In 1991 individuals between the ages of sixty-two and sixty-four are able to earn $7,080 before there is a reduction of benefits, while individuals between ages sixty-five and sixty-nine could earn up to $9,720. Once you reach age seventy you can work to your heart's content, without ever again worrying whether your Social Security payments will be reduced.

How much money will you lose if you earn more than the Social Security Administration prescribes? As a rule of thumb, expect to lose one dollar in benefits for every three dollars earned above the maximum for your age group. But remember: these earnings limits cover only salary and wages and not income from dividends, investments, pensions, insurance, and so forth. For further information on how earnings influence Social Security payments, contact your local Social Security office.

Can a divorced spouse collect a deceased husband's Social Security benefits? A divorced spouse is permitted to receive the same benefits as one who was still married at the time of the spouse's death provided the marriage lasted at least ten years and you didn't remarry before age sixty. You can still receive benefits if you did remarry before age sixty and that marriage ended in death or divorce. You're eligible for full benefits when you turn sixty-five and partial benefits as early as age sixty.[14]

I will be sixty-five soon, but my husband is only sixty-two and will not retire until he is at least sixty-five. I have never been employed. Do I have to wait until my husband retires to get Medicare? No. You are eligible for Medicare at sixty-five, even though your husband is younger than you and is still working, provided he is entitled to Social Security benefits once he retires. Don't make the mistake, however, of waiting until your birthday to apply for benefits. You should file your application for hospital insurance at least three months before you reach age sixty-five.[15]

I am a fifty-two-year-old married woman and have never been in Social Security. Is it important for me to find a job in order to be eligible? Probably, particularly if your personal savings are limited. Once eligible, you will not have to wait for your husband to retire before you receive benefits. If disabled, you would be protected, as would your dependents.[16]

I retired several years ago and received the maximum Social Security paid. But now I don't. Why not? Some people are disappointed when they learn a neighbor or friend is receiving a larger Social Security payment than they. The reason for this is that your Social Security benefits are computed from your average yearly covered earnings over a period of years up to your retirement. The maximum amounts covered by Social Security before you retired some years ago were much lower than the higher limits of recent years. Those years of lower limits were taken into account in calculating your average covered yearly earnings, and this average determined the amount of your check.

As a consolation, remember this: although your benefit may be less than that of a similar worker age sixty-five who is retiring today, your Social Security deductions were less and you probably have been collecting and using your benefits for a long time.[17]

How should I apply for Social Security benefits? Visit a Social Security office in your community and bring the following information: (1) Social Security card; (2) proof of age, such as a birth certificate or baptismal certificate; (3) evidence of the relation of other eligible family members, such as a marriage certificate in the case of your spouse; (4) your W-2 forms, if any, for the past two years; (5) if self-employed, your tax returns for the past two years plus proof of filing, such as canceled checks. It is also helpful to have proof of citizenship if you are a naturalized U.S. citizen.

Can I have my Social Security checks deposited directly to my bank? Yes. To do so, complete Form SF-1199, which can be obtained from your local Social Security office, or call 800-234-5772.

One of the best booklets describing the benefits to which you are entitled is *Your Social Security Benefits,* published by Retirement Living Publishing Company, Inc., 28 West 23rd Street, New York, NY 10010.

Rule Four: Maximize Your Pension

Now we come to one of the most important new rules in making your retirement financially secure, and that is to manage your pension *assertively.* Why? Because old-fashioned company paternalism is all but dead.

In the past, employees had few options concerning their retirement assets. But today employees are often required to determine whether their assets should be placed in stocks, bonds, or fixed-income accounts. And at the time of retirement, a bewildering set of possibilities may be presented as to the distribution of benefits.

Frankly, managing a lifetime of retirement savings can be an awesome task. In fact, one of the most gut-wrenching decisions you may confront is how to take your benefits. At stake may be the core of your wealth. A miscalculation could cost thousands of dollars in taxes. And perhaps most frightening, the choices are often irrevocable. "Of all the decisions people face at retirement," observes

TABLE 10

What You Can Expect from the Government

The following table shows benefits payable to the worker and spouse. To use the table, find the age which is closest to your age and the earnings closest to your earnings in 1989. These figures will give you an estimate of the amount of your retirement benefits at various ages.

Approximate Monthly Retirement Benefits if the Worker Retires at Normal Retirement Age and Had Steady Lifetime Earnings

Worker's Age in 1990	Worker's Family	Retired Worker's Earnings in 1989								
		$10,000	$15,000	$20,000	$25,000	$30,000	$35,000	$40,000	$45,000	$48,000 or more[1]
25	Retired worker only	$648	$830	$1,013	$1,196	$1,296	$1,381	$1,467	$1,553	$1,604
	Worker and spouse[2]	972	1,245	1,519	1,794	1,944	2,071	2,200	2,329	2,406

Age		1	2	3	4	5	6	7	8	9
	Final year earnings[3]	13,700	20,550	27,400	34,250	41,100	47,950	54,800	61,650	65,760
	Replacement rate[4]	57%	48%	44%	42%	38%	35%	32%	30%	29%
35	Retired worker only	599	767	935	1,098	1,199	1,289	1,357	1,436	1,484
	Worker and spouse[2]	898	1,150	1,402	1,647	1,798	1,933	2,035	2,154	2,226
	Final year earnings[3]	12,700	19,050	25,400	31,750	38,100	44,450	50,800	57,150	60,960
	Replacement rate[4]	57%	48%	44%	41%	38%	35%	32%	30%	29%
45	Retired worker only	547	700	852	1,006	1,101	1,168	1,234	1,296	1,332
	Worker and spouse[2]	820	1,050	1,278	1,509	1,651	1,752	1,851	1,944	1,998
	Final year earnings[3]	11,700	17,550	23,400	29,250	35,100	40,950	46,800	52,650	56,160
	Replacement rate[4]	56%	48%	44%	41%	38%	34%	32%	30%	28%
55	Retired worker only	496	632	771	906	986	1,027	1,071	1,107	1,126
	Worker and spouse[2]	744	948	1,156	1,359	1,479	1,540	1,606	1,661	1,689
	Final year earnings[3]	10,700	16,050	21,400	26,750	32,100	37,450	42,800	48,150	51,360

TABLE 10 (Continued)

Worker's Age in 1990	Worker's Family	$10,000	$15,000	$20,000	$25,000	$30,000	$35,000	$40,000	$45,000	$48,000 or more[1]
	Replacement rate[4]	56%	47%	43%	41%	37%	33%	30%	28%	26%
65	Retired worker only	456	582	708	832	896	925	946	965	975
	Worker and spouse[2]	684	873	1,062	1,248	1,344	1,387	1,419	1,447	1,463
	Final year earnings[3]	10,000	15,000	20,000	25,000	30,000	35,000	40,000	45,000	48,000
	Replacement rate[4]	55%	47%	42%	40%	36%	32%	28%	26%	24%

[1]Earnings equal the Social Security wage base from age 22 through 1989.   [2]Spouse is assumed to be the same age as the worker. Spouse may qualify for a higher retirement benefit based on his or her own work record.   [3]Worker's earnings in the year before retirement.   [4]Replacement rates are shown for retired worker only.

Note: The accuracy of these estimates depends on the pattern of the worker's actual past earnings, and on his or her earnings in the future. It is assumed that there are no future benefit increases after January 1990 and no average wage increases after 1988. Estimated benefits are adjusted upwards by 1 percent for each year that the year of initial eligibility exceeds 1990, to reflect expected real wage gains.   *Source:* United States Department of Health and Human Services, Social Security Administration (Baltimore, Maryland: SSA Publication 05-10035), January, 1990.

Paul Westbrook of Watchung, New Jersey, a retirement specialist, "this one causes the most panic."[18]

Nevertheless, there are practical things you can do to maximize your pension and give you peace of mind. First, make an appointment with your company's *plan administrator*. This should be done at least once every five years so that you are knowledgeable about any changes made in your company's pension plan.

Under law you are entitled to three types of pension information. The *Summary Plan Description* is a booklet that describes how your retirement plan operates, the date at which you are eligible to receive benefits, and a description of the method through which to calculate benefits. The *Summary Annual Report* contains information on the financial activities of your pension plan and must be provided annually. The *Survivor Benefit Statement* will inform you as to how your spouse and/or dependent children might be covered.

You should also request an *Individual Benefit Statement,* which will provide the dollar amount of benefits earned.[19] Your employer may voluntarily provide this information, but if not, request it in writing from the plan's administrator.

Approximately six months prior to retirement determine the options through which you can tap your retirement funds. Here are the possibilities:

1. You may take the money as a monthly annuity.
2. You may take the money in a lump sum.
3. You may be able to roll the money over into an individual retirement account.

Which method should you select if given the choice? Here are some important things to consider.

ANNUITY PAYMENTS

Monthly annuity income is the most popular method through which companies make pension payouts. Often it is the only option available.

The popularity of annuities is due to the fact that retirees receive monthly income that's guaranteed to last as long as they live. *You can never outlive a lifetime annuity, which is perhaps the biggest benefit of this type of pension settlement.* If you are married, your spouse will also receive income for life, unless you specifically decline the "survivor-option."

The disadvantages of an annuity are significant, particularly if there isn't any cost-of-living escalator built into the retirement plan. A 5 percent annual inflation rate will *halve* the real value of your checks after only fourteen years. In addition, if you die before your spouse, his or her monthly pension from your plan may be approximately 50 percent of what the two of you received. That's a significant reduction that could adversely affect your spouse.

There is, however, a creative way to get around this limitation. Consider John Remington, who plans on retiring at age sixty-five. His company, Arrow Manufacturing, will provide a single-life annuity of $1,000 per month. If he elects a joint-and-survivor annuity based on his spouse's age (sixty-two), the benefit will be reduced by 27 percent to $730.

In order to obtain the maximum monthly income, John takes the single-life option, purchases a life insurance policy, and names his wife as beneficiary. The selection of the single-life annuity gives them an additional $270 per month, and the life insurance policy provides income for John's wife in the event of his death.

There are a few drawbacks to this plan. You need to be in good health in order to be eligible for a life insurance policy. Then, too, by the time you are in your late fifties or early sixties, life insurance costs might be prohibitive.

Nevertheless, the advantages may outweigh the disadvantages, assuming your insurability. Your spouse's need for financial security is met through life insurance. You receive more monthly income if you do not elect the joint-and-survivor option. And you may, depending upon the size of the insurance policy, provide for a *higher* standard of living for your spouse in the event of your death. If your spouse is three or more years younger than you and/or is in poor health, this option has considerable appeal in maximizing financial resources. For further information, consult a life insurance agent or read "Testing Life Insurance as a Substitute for Survivor's Pension Benefits" in the March 1988 issue of the *Journal of the American Society of CLU and Ch FC.*

LUMP SUM PAYOUTS

Some individuals wish to receive their retirement savings in one lump sum. The primary motivation is a belief that income taxes will be raised in the future. Therefore it is best, they reason, to withdraw their money, pay the income and capital gains taxes, and live off the proceeds.

If you believe that tax rates have nowhere to go but up, a lump sum payout should be considered. But you should also consider a lump sum payout if you are in poor health and if you don't believe you can beat the actuarial odds on which annuities are based.

Before receiving a lump sum distribution, however, see your tax accountant, because there are a myriad of tax laws that will affect the amount of money you will ultimately receive. Ask your accountant about five- or ten-year forward averaging, which could significantly reduce the tax bite. "Forward averaging" means that you will be taxed as if you had received ordinary income evenly over a five- or ten-year period. Five-year averaging tends to benefit investors with distributions *in excess of $473,700* while those with distributions of *less than $473,700* generally save money by utilizing the ten-year method. To be eligible for ten-year averaging you must have turned fifty before January 1, 1986 (those born before 1936).[20]

Of course one of the big disadvantages of taking out a lump sum distribution is that the burden to invest it rests squarely on your shoulders. If you have not managed large sums of money, you may want to stick with an annuity offered through your company's retirement plan. Or you may want to contact a certified financial planner and tax accountant who can advise how the money can best be invested.

ROLL YOUR PENSION MONIES INTO AN INDIVIDUAL RETIREMENT ACCOUNT

If a lump sum payout is appealing to you but you don't want to pay the tax, consider rolling your pension into an IRA. Placing your distribution into an IRA within sixty days protects the money from taxation until it is withdrawn, a process that *must* begin no later than April 1 of the year following the year in which you become seventy and a half. If you do not choose the rollover within the sixty-day waiting period, you will be taxed on the amount withdrawn. If you are younger than age fifty-nine and a half, you must pay an *additional* 10 percent nondeductible excise penalty tax on the entire lump sum. The exception to this occurs when companies offer a special retirement option for employees at age fifty-five.[21]

Once you roll the monies into an IRA, the distribution rules apply: any withdrawals made before age fifty-nine and a half incur the 10 percent excise tax in addition to the regular income tax. There is one exception: if you make substantially equal withdrawals geared to your life expectancy or to the joint life expectancy of you and your spouse, you may be able to avoid the 10 percent penalty tax.[22]

Now the question is, Which of the above three methods is best for you, assuming that your employer provides these choices? Many things should be factored into your decision, not the least of which is your comfort at managing relatively large sums of money. But if you want a hard-nosed assessment of the financial implications of each method, consider Table 11. As you will see, the best option generally is to use an IRA rollover and let your money grow untouched for five years.

One word of caution is in order, however. Don't make any major decisions when under pressure. If uncertain as to what you should do with a large distribution, follow pension rules and park your money in a safe place, such as a money market account, bank certificates of deposit, or short-term U.S. Treasury bills. Then, with adequate time, you will be able to construct a thoughtful investment plan that will keep pace with inflation and provide for growth.

Rule Five: Minimize Financial Risk

Now we come to an old rule for managing your retirement monies, but one that has gained considerable credibility since the stock market crash of 1987. Unless you have money to burn, *never gamble* with your retirement savings.

TABLE 11

Choosing Between a Lump Sum and an Annuity

You and your spouse are both 65 and set to retire on January 1. You can take a $2,000 check monthly for life or a $250,000 lump sum. What's a couple to do? As the following table shows, the safe annuity course would shrink your annual income of $24,000 ($17,280 after taxes) to $10,608 in 1988 dollars by the time you reach 75 if inflation were to run at a modest 5% a year.

By taking a lump sum instead, you would have four options, under which you would invest the $250,000 either in a tax-free bond fund paying 7.3% a year or in a taxable bond fund yielding 9%. In each case, you could withdraw $17,280 after taxes the first year and increase that 5% a year to keep up with inflation. If you needed income, you could pay income tax on the $250,000 right away using 10-year forward averaging. Then you could put the remaining money in the tax-free fund, and it would last until you were 79. The next two options — using less favorable five-year averaging or rolling the money into an IRA with immediate withdrawals — would provide income until you were 78 and 80, respectively. The last course is best: roll the money over into an IRA and let it grow for five years untouched. Then the sum, invested in the taxable fund, would last until age 93.

Option	Initial Tax	Net Sum Invested	Income Age 65*	Income Age 75*	Balance Age 75	Age When Income Ends
Pension (annuity)	$0	$0	$17,280	$10,608	$0	Death

TABLE 11 (*Continued*)

Option	Initial Tax	Net Sum Invested	Income Age 65*	Income Age 75*	Balance Age 75	Age When Income Ends
Lump sum with 10-year averaging	50,770	199,230	17,280	17,280	87,552	79
Lump sum with 5-year averaging	60,110	189,890	17,280	17,280	70,053	78
IRA rollover with immediate withdrawals	0	250,000	17,280	17,280	148,759	80
IRA rollover with no withdrawals for five years	0	250,000	0	17,280	389,638	93

*In after-tax 1988 dollars, assuming inflation of 5% a year

Source: Reprinted from *Money* magazine by special permission; copyright 1988 The Time Inc. Magazine Company.

The 1980s represented a time of unprecedented economic growth for the United States. Yet on Monday, October 17, 1987, the stock market dropped 508 points, erasing more than a year's gains in a single day. And it took only five days for the New York Stock Exchange to lose 6 percent of its value when Iraq invaded Kuwait in August of 1990.

In researching this book, I heard heartbreaking stories of people who were just about set for a financially secure retirement, when suddenly their portfolio was reduced by twenty to twenty-five percent by the stock market debacle. Some had to delay their retirement, while others were forced to accept lower-than-expected annuities. And some had to restrict their lifestyle, simply because there wasn't enough money to fund their retirement dreams.

Economies stall. Even in relatively good economic times there are periods in which the market retreats — sometimes at breakneck speed. You don't want to get caught in a financial downdraft in retirement. Therefore it is important to invest your retirement savings in conservative instruments. Here are some of the best.

LOW-RISK INVESTMENTS

Certificates of deposit. If you want safety,

take your money to a bank and invest in a government-insured "certificate of deposit" (CD). When you take out a CD you agree to leave your money with the bank for a pre-determined period of time. Generally, the longer you leave the money with the bank, the higher will be your rate of return. Some banks will accept as little as $250 for time deposits and offer maturities as short as one month.

When making a deposit, keep in mind that you will be penalized if you want to make an early withdrawal. Federal law requires that banks withhold at least one month's interest on early withdrawals of CD's with maturities between thirty-one days and a year. On longer CD's, the minimum penalty is three months' interest. Some banks, however, will impose even tougher restrictions.

Treasury bills. Guaranteed by the government, Treasury bills are considered the ultimate risk-free investment.[23] Treasury bills come in three-month, six-month, and one-year maturities and can be purchased from banks and stockbrokers for modest sales fees. Or you can purchase them commission-free directly from the nation's twelve Federal Reserve banks. (For purchasing instructions call 202-287-4113.) Treasury bills can be sold if you need cash before they mature. A shortcoming is that you must invest at least $10,000. Nevertheless, if you are looking for safety and a relatively high rate of return (6.25 on a one-year Treasury bill, March 7, 1991), Treasury bills represent an appropriate way to invest your retirement dollars.

Money market funds. Money market funds invest in short-term government securities, bank certificates of deposit, and other low-risk securities. Such funds pay money market rates of interest (6.19%, March 7, 1991), and withdrawals can be made from them at any time at a predictable per share value.

Money market funds are typically purchased through a mutual fund family, such as Fidelity, Vanguard, or Twentieth Century Investors, or through a brokerage firm, such as PaineWebber, Merrill Lynch, or Shearson Lehman Hutton. Although they are generally not insured, there has been only one time where a fund lost any of its investors' principal.[24] Each Thursday the *Wall Street Journal* lists yields for hundreds of money market funds, which will vary depending upon the fund's expenses and investment objectives.

United States savings bonds. Investors with a small amount of money might wish to consider Series EE savings bonds, which can be purchased through banks or payroll deduction plans offered by employers. Available in denominations as low as $50, savings bonds do not pay current interest. Rather you buy them at a discount, and when you redeem them at face value, the sum you receive includes accrued interest on which you pay only federal tax. If you hold a savings bond five years or longer, you are guaranteed a minimum yield of 6 percent.[25]

How long will it take to double your money in any of the above investment vehicles? It's easy to compute, using the "rule of seventy-two." Divide seventy-two by the rate of interest you can expect to earn on your money. The resulting figure will be the number of years it will take to double your investment. For example, suppose you earn 9 percent on an investment. Seventy-two divided by nine means that it will take eight years to double your money.

MODERATE-RISK INVESTMENTS

Some people are willing to take a higher risk with their money in order to obtain higher income. If this be your case, here are some moderate-risk investment opportunities particularly suitable for your retirement account.

Treasury bonds. If you believe that interest rates are tending downward, you may want to consider Treasury bonds. You can purchase Treasury bonds from the government commission free. You can make a minimum purchase of $1,000 for all denominations except two- and three-year notes, whose minimums are $5,000. With Treasury notes (two to ten years) and bonds (more than ten years) you don't risk default.

As interest rates fall, the price of Treasury bonds rises. The longer the maturity of the bond, the greater the price increase. For example, suppose you purchase a thirty-year Treasury yielding 9 percent. Five years from now yields plunge to 7 percent. If you sell, your total compounded return will be approximately 13 percent a year. Of course, your greatest risk is if interest rates rise, which would cause the price of your bonds to drop.[26]

One advantage of Treasury bonds is that there is a secondary market for Treasuries, so you are unlikely to have trouble selling bonds or notes at a profit if interest rates tumble.

Corporate bonds. Corporate bonds generally carry interest rates higher than Treasuries of comparable maturity. Most financial planners recommend that if you are counting on this money for retirement, you should stick with high-grade utilities and major corporations such as Exxon, IBM, Citicorp, General Motors Acceptance Corporation, AT&T, and any of the Bell operating companies.

Brokerage firms can recommend corporate

bonds and will assist you in purchasing them. But you can also buy shares through a mutual fund. Among the best are: Boston Company Managed Income (800-225-5267) and Vanguard's Fixed Income Securities Fund — Investment Grade (800-662-7447). A star performer sold through stockbrokers has been American Capital Corporate Bond, which during a recent twelve-month period yielded 9.8 percent (800-231-3638).[27]

Tax-free bonds. Issued by state and local governments to finance the building of highways, bridges, and sewage plants, municipal bonds typically generate tax-free interest, which makes them suitable for investors in higher tax brackets. Municipals are particularly attractive if you live in a high-tax area such as New York City, California, or Massachusetts, where the interest earned may be free of state and local taxes.

Top mutual funds investing in high-quality bonds include Financial Tax Free Income (800-525-8085) and Safeco 23 Municipal Bond (800-426-6730). If you wish information on a diversified municipal portfolio that may provide higher yields, consider Vanguard Municipal High Yield (800-644-7447). But be careful: higher yields always imply you are taking a greater risk in the pursuit of a higher rate of return.

INVESTING FOR GROWTH

The above investments will provide income, but they will not necessarily protect you from the ravages of inflation. To do that you need growth investments.

Stocks. What is a "growth-oriented" investment? Essentially it is an investment made in a stock, or a group of stocks, that holds promise for a return exceeding inflation.

Now, you may regard stocks as about as safe as driving a Corvette at 160 miles an hour on an ice-covered road, but it could be a major mistake to shun stocks entirely. "Equities deserve a major role in virtually all portfolios," states Anthony Sulvetta, managing director of Ferris Investment Advisory of Washington, D.C. The reason is that stocks provide you with capital expansion — growth that will give you an important inflation hedge.[28]

In spite of the volatility of the stock market, most people should have a portion of their savings in stocks. It is important, however, to understand the risks as well as the rewards of stocks so that you do not panic at the wrong time.

For example, after the stock market crash of 1987, thousands of investors frantically sold their holdings and put them into government certificates of deposit paying approximately 8 percent. Over the next two years, 8 percent barely covered inflation and income taxes. If the same investors had left their money in the stock market, they would have earned three times as much money.

Should you really own stocks, given the market's volatility? Here is the historical record, calculated by Stephen Janachowski of the San Francisco money-management firm Brouwer and Janachowski. Five thousand dollars invested in 1969 in the Standard and Poor's index of 500 stocks was worth $512,000 twenty years later, assuming that dividends were reinvested. But the same amount invested in Treasury bonds would have paid approximately $335,000, and Treasury bills, only $263,000. As you can see, stocks were far and away the best investment, even though that twenty-year period included two bear markets (1973–1974 and 1981–1982) and the 1987 crash.[29]

How do you pick a portfolio of stocks that will let you sleep at night? Professional investors use a "beta analysis," which permits them to measure a stock's volatility — the extent to which it mirrors the ups and downs of the stock market. A stock that mirrors the stock market perfectly would have what's called a beta of 1.0. But if it tends to fall 25 percent less than the Standard and Poor's 500, it would have a beta of 0.75.

To find a stock's beta, consult *Value Line Investment Survey,* which is available in most community libraries. Or turn to a stockbroker who can advise you on blue-chip and/or high-dividend stocks with low betas.

Mutual funds. If you like the idea of investing in a group of stocks, consider mutual funds. A mutual fund is managed by an investment company that raises money from shareholders and invests it in stocks, bonds, and other types of securities. Most mutual funds are open-ended, which means that fund managers continuously sell new shares to investors and are prepared to buy back shares at their net asset value.

The 1980s were a period of explosive growth in the mutual fund industry, both in the number of funds offered to the public and the amount of money they managed. Today there are more mutual funds available — over three thousand — than there are stocks on the New York Stock Exchange. These funds hold a whopping *one trillion* dollars in value.

What is the appeal of mutual funds? Why should you consider funds a central part of your investment portfolio? Here are the advantages as compared with other types of securities.

First, mutual funds *spread the risk* of owning

securities by diversifying the portfolio. Declines in one or more stocks are generally offset or reduced by gains in other issues of the portfolio.

Second, mutual funds benefit from *professional management*. Many of us do not have the financial inclination to attend to economic and political events that affect our investments. But professional money managers monitor a wealth of data, carefully adjusting your fund's holdings to reflect economic uncertainties.

Third, you can *redeem your funds* with a minimum of hassle. Mutual funds buy back shares, so investors may liquidate their holdings for cash whenever they wish. Usually this can be accomplished with a toll-free telephone call to the mutual fund company.[30]

Perhaps one of the best advantages of mutual funds is that you can *choose the level of risk* at which to invest. Here are the categories:

High risk:	Aggressive growth funds
Moderate to high risk:	Growth funds
Moderate risk:	Growth and income funds
Moderate to low risk:	Balanced funds
Low risk:	Bond funds with short maturities

TABLE 12
Outstanding Mutual Funds 1987–1990

	*Average Annual Return**	*1 Year*
Aggressive Growth Stock Funds		
Kaufman 800-237-0132	29.8%	-3.1%
AIM Constellation		
800-347-1919	15.5%	-0.4%
Oppenheimer Target		
800-525-7048	15.3%	2.8%
Growth Stock Funds		
Gabelli Growth		
800-422-3554	24.1%	2.0%
Pasadena Growth		
800-822-2855	21.3%	2.5%
Fidelity Growth Co.		
800-544-8888	19.4%	11.0%
Growth and Income Stock Funds		
Vista G&I 800-348-4782	30.1%	1.2%
Composite Northwest 50		
800-543-8072	18.8%	4.4%
Cigna Value	17.4%	5.0%
Equity Income Stock Funds		
Financial Industrial Income		
800-525-8085	15.4%	3.6%
Helmsman Equity Income		
800-338-4345	13.6%	0.8%

TABLE 12 (*Continued*)

	Average Annual Return*	1 Year
United Income 800-366-5465	13.0%	-1.7%

*Performance is net of annual expenses and brokerage costs but excludes sales loads. Three-year return through 12/31/90; one-year through 1/18/91.

Source: Fortune, Copyright 1991 The Time Inc. Magazine Company. All rights reserved.

Which funds should you consider for your portfolio? One of the most important criteria in selecting a mutual fund is its track record. Table 12 lists funds that performed admirably between 1987 and 1990.

There are, of course, many investments not covered in this section that are appropriate for retirement portfolios, including convertible bonds, zero-coupon bonds, international bonds, and utility stocks. The advantage of these investments is that most provide a predictable stream of income. For further information on these and other investments consult a stockbroker and/or credentialed financial planner. Or telephone the American Association of Retired Persons (AARP) and request a no-cost brochure entitled "Investing for Monthly Income" (800-253-2277).

No matter your age, now is the time to re-evaluate your retirement savings and the monies that have accumulated in your pension plan. Here are some practical things to do to prepare yourself for a financially secure retirement:

* Reduce debt
* Accelerate savings
* Calculate Social Security benefits
* Maximize pension assets
* Minimize financial risk

CHAPTER FIVE

Retiring on a Modest Income

All we have is our home and a small pension. But we have never been as happy as we are right now.
                Annette Olson, sixty-six

Most people retire with little more than Social Security, a modest pension, and the equity in their homes. If this fits your circumstances, you may wonder how you are going to make it financially.

I do not minimize the difficulties that arise when you are short of cash. But I want to affirm a lesson I repeatedly learned from my research: A great retirement is not contingent upon wealth. It *is* contingent upon managing money wisely and taking full advantage of the numerous ways to stretch your retirement dollars.

How do you expand your retirement dollars? And how can you augment income so that you are not always running short of cash?

The starting point is to take full advantage of the many cost-reduction programs marketed to senior citizens.

The Financial Joys of Being a Senior Citizen

If reducing expenses seems like an impossible task, consider Bill McDonald, who retired after a twenty-nine-year career driving buses in Chicago, Illinois:

The first six months of my retirement were a financial nightmare. I obviously had misjudged how much money it would take to enjoy my retirement.

But my best buddy was having a financially successful retirement, and he didn't have a great big pension. How did he do it? He was a "coupon-clipper." He knew every place in town which gave him 10 percent to 50 percent price reduction because he was over fifty-five.

One week I went shopping with him and I counted up all the money he was saving. He saved money on an oil change for his car because of a coupon he found in the paper. He went to a theater that saved him 50 percent on a ticket because he was over sixty-five. He shopped in a grocery store where he could take advantage of day-old bakery goods.

It was really something to see him aggressively save money. Perhaps the biggest eye opener was when he went to a travel agency giving huge discounts on Caribbean cruises if you are over sixty years old. He booked a January cruise that saved him hundreds of dollars.

Right then I decided that I would become assertive about my money. Since that time I have saved hundreds of dollars by taking advantage of all the specials for senior citizens. My wife tells me that if I would have clipped coupons all my life, I would be a millionaire!

You might not become a millionaire by shopping smart, but there are many ways to reduce expenses in retirement. Here are some of the best:

Grocery Bills

Clip coupons. The average store coupon shaves *20 percent* off the regular price of an item. A 20 percent reduction on a monthly grocery bill of $250 will save $600 per year.[1]

Dine at home. The average cost of a hamburger, French fries, and a medium drink at a fast-food restaurant is $2.10. The same food can be bought for 90 cents at home. If you and your spouse take one less meal per week at a fast-food restaurant, you will save $128.80 per year.

Appliance and Clothing Expenses

Shop discount stores. You will generally save between 20 percent and 30 percent by shopping at a discount store. And if you shop at outlet stores, where the manufacturers sell direct to the public, the savings are usually between 30 and 50 percent. If you spend $1,161 for clothes, as does the typical family earning $25,000, you will reduce your clothing bill by 30 percent. Savings to you per year: $348.30.[2]

Prescriptions

Use mail-order pharmacies. You can save a bundle of money by using mail-order prescription services, such as the one offered through American Association of Retired Persons (AARP Pharmacy Service, 1 Prince Street, P.O. Box 13671, Richmond, VA 12231, 800-950-8777). Your prescriptions will be filled with high-quality brand-name or generic drugs at low prices. Your order is shipped directly to your door via UPS or first-class mail. Write or call for additional information prior to sending in prescriptions. Depending upon your medication needs, *this service could save you hundreds of dollars per year.*[3]

Vision Care

Purchase eyewear at optical companies catering to senior citizens. For example, the Vision One optical program at Sears, Roebuck and Company will save you up to *50 percent* on high-quality eyewear products. Call 800-334-7591 for more information.

Transportation and Automobile Expenses

Mass transit. Most metropolitan areas offer senior citizens dramatic price reductions for trips on buses and local trains. For example, Chicago's Transit Authority will issue a special discount card to people sixty-five and older providing 50 percent savings on bus and train fares throughout some 38 Chicago suburbs.

Know what your new car will cost you. Senior citizens can receive a computerized printout package that shows you the dealer's invoice cost and markups for most models of new cars, including options. Call 800-753-6000 and request information about "Car/Puter."

Purchase a used car at rock-bottom prices. As a subscriber to *Mature Outlook* magazine/service, you are eligible for a $300 discount off the regular retail price of any late-model used car you purchased from any corporately owned Hertz Used Car Sales. Included in this special price is Hertz's 12-month/unlimited mileage, limited power train warranty covering labor and parts on your engine, transmission, drive-shaft, and differential for one year, no matter how or where you drive in the continental United States. In addition, you can join the Allstate Motor Club at 10 percent off the regular fee, a discount that applies to club renewals as well. (Mature Outlook, P.O. Box 1205, Glenview, IL 60025.)

Homeowners Insurance

Reduce insurance costs. You can save between 10 percent and 15 percent on your home insurance bills by enrolling in the AARP Homeowners Insurance Program. For further information write to: AARP Homeowners Insurance Program, The Hartford, P.O. Box 2807, C, Hartford, CT 06101-9937.[4]

Credit Cards, Bill Collection, and Banking Services

Keep an eye on your banking expenses. Many banks will provide *free* checking for senior citizens. On average, financial institutions charge a flat rate of $7 per month for checking privileges. Savings to you: $84 per year.

Reduce dependence on credit cards. Avoid charging bills on a credit card, unless you can pay off the balance every month. If you have numerous credit card bills you can't pay off, consider a consolidation loan from a bank. Your credit card company might be charging you interest between 16 percent and 24 percent. You probably can obtain a consolidation loan at a much lower rate. Better yet: once you obtain the loan, cancel the card. Your savings per year: $25 or more on the annual fee.

Delay paying your bills. If you have an interest-bearing checking account, pay your bills as close to the due date as possible to collect every bit of interest on your balance. If, for example, you have $500 worth of bills to pay every month, and you let the money sit in an interest-bearing checking account at 5 percent for an extra month before paying creditors, you would collect $25.00 in interest every year.

Vacation Expenses
Obtain a federal pass to our nation's parks. Any U.S. citizen aged sixty-two or older can get a Golden Age passport good for *free*

admission to all parks, historic sights, monuments, recreation areas, and wildlife refuges administered by the federal government. Passholders are also entitled to 50 percent off boat launching, camping, and parking fees. You can usually obtain a pass at parks, but for information on how to obtain one before starting your travels, write to the Consumer Information Center, Dept. 594-N, Pueblo, CO 81009.

Stay in hotels that honor senior citizen discounts. Here is a partial listing of hotels/motels offering lodging for senior citizens at a significant discount:

* Best Western   800-528-1234
* Budgetel Inns   800-428-3438
* Days Inns   800-325-2525
* Econo Lodges   800-446-6900
* Exel Inns   800-356-8013
* Imperial Inns   800-368-4400
* Knights Inns   800-722-7000
* Motel 6   800-386-3004
* Red Carpet Inns   800-251-1962
* Super 8 Motels   800-843-1991

In addition, Mature Outlook members are eligible for savings of up to 20 percent on rooms at participating Holiday Inn Hotels worldwide. Even if you are not a guest at the hotel, you can take 10 percent off the cost of a meal in the restaurant. For further information call 800-HOLIDAY.

Obtain a special senior pass when traveling in Europe. You can reduce the costs of travel in Europe by 50 percent when you obtain a senior pass offered by the national railways of Austria, Denmark, Great Britain, Norway, Portugal, and Sweden. In Britain everyone sixty and older is entitled to travel first class at 10 percent to 15 percent off the regular rate. For further information write to each country's tourist office in New York City or ask your travel agent.

Legal Assistance

Obtain affordable legal help. If you cannot afford an attorney, write to the National Senior Citizens Law Center, 1709 W. Eighth Street, Los Angeles, CA 90017 or National Paralegal Institute, 200 P Street NW, Washington, DC 20036. They will put you in contact with agencies near your community that will assist you at no or low cost. In addition, consult with your United Way, who may be able to put you in touch with low-cost legal assistance.

If you are short of cash, don't forget to take full advantage of government programs. *Half of all elderly poor who are eligible for financial and medical assistance are not receiving it —* apparently because they're either not aware of programs providing assistance or are unaware of their own eligibility. For example, Supplemental Security Income (SSI) was designated to assist low-income, blind, and disabled individuals. SSI provides a maximum of $368 per month for an eligible individual and $553 per month for an eligible couple. Yet in one study 48.5 percent of those who were eligible did not receive benefits. In most instances they either had never heard about the program or had incorrect information about the program's eligibility requirements.[5]

How to Retire on the Equity in Your Home

Many older Americans who are hard-pressed for income are discovering flexible ways to cash in on the biggest blue chip they own: their homes. Today 75 percent of Americans over sixty-five own their own homes, with an average of more than $50,000 in equity waiting to be tapped.[6]

Real estate experts suggest three ways to tap the equity in your house. First, *trade down to a smaller home,* possibly a condominium or town house. Second, sell your house, claim the $125,000 capital gains tax exclusion and *rent an apartment* — preferably one that provides a 10 percent or more price break for senior citizens. Third, if you don't want to move out of your home, determine if you are eligible for a *reverse mortgage.*

OPTION ONE: TRADE DOWN

The federal government has given older Americans a tremendous incentive to purchase a smaller home by dramatically diminishing the capital gains tax on any profit you make when selling your house. Today you can declare $125,000 of the appreciated gain tax-free. In addition, if your gain is more than $125,000 it is possible to tax-defer the excess by plowing some of the profits into a new home. In effect, you are receiving two tax breaks for the price of one.

Here is how the world of real estate swapping works. Suppose you purchased your home for $40,000 and could sell it today for $253,000, netting a $213,000 gain. You are able to deduct the $10,000 spent on improving your home over the years and the $3,000 you spent on fix-up expenses before the sale. In addition you can exclude $125,000 from tax. That leaves $75,000 eligible for taxation by the Internal Revenue Service. But if you replace your house with one worth $75,000 or more, your remaining taxable profit is deferred.[7]

By avoiding all taxes, you are left with a sum of money to invest for income. If the home owner in the above example had no mortgage on either property, he or she would have freed up approximately $160,000. If that money was invested in Treasuries paying 9 percent, the income would be $14,400 per year.

Remember, however, that you have only *one* chance at the $125,000 tax break. Once it has been used, it is gone forever. "Therefore," says tax expert Mark Bloom, "don't take the exclusion if your gain is less than $125,000."[8] The exception to this would be if you have made a decision to sell the house, invest the equity, and become a permanent renter. Otherwise, it is generally best to wait for your house to appreciate prior to using the one-time $125,000 tax exclusion.

Of course there are nonfinancial reasons for purchasing a smaller home. Perhaps you are tired of spending your weekends raking leaves or painting the fence. Perhaps you would like to live closer to your children. Or maybe you just want a change of scenery.

Whatever the reason, you need to make a careful examination of how a trade-down would affect your overall finances.[9] Specifically you should:

Estimate your profit in advance. Before putting your home on the market, know how much a suitable replacement will cost, especially if you intend to move to another section of the country. If your potential profit is relatively small, trading down might not free up the equity for income purposes.

Nevertheless, you might be amazed at the amount of money you will save on lower mortgage payments, insurance costs, and taxes if you move into a smaller home. "Lower costs might make it worthwhile to move even if your profit from the trade-down is only $50,000," states Laura Adams, a certified financial planner in Princeton, New Jersey.[10]

Time your sale to take advantage of tax benefits. Remember — you must be fifty-five or older before you are able to exclude from taxes up to $125,000 of the capital gain on the sale of your home. If you have lived in your home for less than three of the five years preceding the sale, you will not be eligible for the exclusion.

Consider lending the buyer part of the purchase price. One excellent method of receiving income through the sale of a house is to extend a loan to your buyer, called "owner financing." Insist on a down payment of at least 20 percent, which will protect your principal if the buyer defaults. Consult with an attorney in drawing up a contract with your buyer.

Pay cash for your new home. While it may be possible to take out a mortgage on a smaller home and invest the money in a diversified portfolio, this may not be the best course of action for someone short of cash. The reason is that most conservative investments will not generate enough money to cover the loan payments.

The better option is to sell a large home, buy a small one with cash, and invest the money you have left in conservative investment vehicles, such as Treasury bills, certificates of deposit, or money market funds.

Avoid variable-rate mortgages. If you have no option but to take out a mortgage on a smaller home, strive for a fixed-rate mortgage so that you will *never* have to worry about sharply rising payments. This is particularly true if the variable rate can jump more than five percentage points over the life of the loan.

OPTION TWO: RENT RATHER THAN BUY

Many older Americans are discovering that it makes financial sense to rent rather than purchase another home. Consider Jimmy and Jacki Whitney, who have used their seven-room traditional brick house in Dallas, Texas, as the financial foundation for their retirement.

The Whitneys sold their house in 1987 for $148,000. They paid off the $76,000 mortgage, put down $5,000 on a new Lincoln Town Car, and moved to Oklahoma City in order that Jacki, fifty-seven, could be with her eighty-three-year-old mother. Unwilling to purchase a home that might be difficult to sell, Jimmy and Jacki rented a seven-room ranch-style house for $650 a month.

Jimmy invested the $67,000 remaining from the sale of the house in a balanced portfolio of mutual funds he estimates will earn a tidy 8 percent to 10 percent per year. He projects that the mutual fund income, plus his $23,000 pension and income from other investments will be more than ample to meet his monthly income needs. "Paying off the old mortgage freed up $1,165 a month," states Jimmy. "On that money we can go to Europe twice a year."[11]

OPTION THREE: IF YOU'RE ELIGIBLE, CONSIDER A REVERSE MORTGAGE

Most older people, when they first hear about reverse mortgages, think it is too good to be true. How, they ask, is it possible to borrow money and not pay it back for ten years, or sell a house and still live in it?

The answer is a concept that first became available to San Francisco Bay area seniors in 1980, when reverse mortgages became available. Here is how it works and how it is affecting the life of Raymond DuBois, a retired insurance agent living in Tenafly, New Jersey.

Dubois, seventy-nine, owns a three-bedroom English Tudor house, which was appraised at $125,000 in 1983 and has appreciated to $200,000. Using a reverse equity mortgage, DuBois receives $350 a month from the American Homestead Mortgage Corporation. He will continue to receive that amount every month until he dies or sells the house. "It's very good for me," says DuBois. "I get a check every month, just like a pension."[12]

A reverse mortgage is essentially an upside-down nonconventional mortgage. Instead of the home owner making monthly payments to pay off a large mortgage, the lender makes a monthly payment to the home owner for a period of years. When the home is sold at the completion of an agreed-upon fixed term, or when the borrower dies or opts for different living arrangements, the borrower or his estate pays the principal and interest in a lump sum. The lender may also receive part of the house's appreciation.[13]

When Mr. DuBois's home is finally sold, American Homestead will receive a lump sum for the principal paid out plus accrued interest. The mortgage company will also receive 60 percent of any appreciation from the time the mortgage was taken out.

For many people a reverse mortgage is an ideal way to utilize the capital in their home. However, you should only consider a reverse mortgage if you intend to live in your home for five years. In addition, reverse mortgages are rarely helpful if you have a relatively small amount of equity in your home, say, less than $10,000.

One word of caution is in order, however. Most reverse mortgages are relatively new, and you may have difficulty qualifying. In addition, each has its unique rules and regulations. To obtain more information on the concept and eligibility requirements write for AARP's free booklet *Home Made Money* (AARP-HEIC), 1909 K Street NW, Washington, DC 20049) or the National Center for Home Equity Conversion's *A Financial Guide to Reverse Mortgages* (1210 E. College St., Suite 300, Marshall, MN 56258).

How do you know whether it is best to trade down to a smaller house, take out a reverse mortgage, or continue to live in your present home? Table 13 analyzes the possibilities. In

TABLE 13
Three Options for Tapping Equity in Your Home

The following tables show three options available to a 65-year-old couple with a mortgage-free house worth $250,000.

I. Trade-down: The couple will get the biggest payoff if they sell the house and buy a smaller one for $100,000. Then they can invest their $150,000 gain in a diversified portfolio of investments, in this case yielding 9%. The income will more than cover their housing costs.

Year	Additional Income	Annual Housing Costs	Home Equity and Principal
1	$13,500	$3,200	$254,000
5	13,500	3,744	271,665
10	13,500	4,555	298,024
15	13,500	5,541	330,094
20	13,500	6,742	369,112
25	13,500	8,203	416,584

II. Reverse mortgage: The couple can take out an Individual Reverse Mortgage Account, which provides fixed payments of $5,676 a year for life. If they live for at least 15 years, their estate will owe the lender an amount equal to the home's value.

Year	Additional Income	Annual Housing Costs	Home Equity
1	$5,676	$ 8,000	$233,312

TABLE 13 (*Continued*)

Year	Additional Income	Annual Housing Costs	Home Equity
5	5,676	9,359	185,293
10	5,676	11,386	106,979
15	5,676	13,853	0
20	5,676	16,855	0
25	5,676	20,506	0

III. Do nothing. If they stay put and leave their equity intact, the couple will retain the full value of their property, which increases by 4% a year in our example. But they will need income from other sources to meet rising costs, including maintenance, insurance and property taxes.

Year	Additional Income	Annual Housing Costs	Home Equity
1	0	$ 8,000	$260,000
5	0	9,359	304,164
10	0	11,386	370,061
15	0	13,853	450,236
20	0	16,855	547,781
25	0	20,506	666,459

Source: Reprinted from *Money: Family Wealth,* Spring 1988, by special permission; copyright 1988 The Time Inc. Magazine Company.

general, the best option is to trade down and invest your equity in income-producing investments.

Is Unretirement in Your Future?

Your first strategy in retiring on a modest income is to reduce unnecessary expenditures. The second strategy is to take full advantage of any equity you have in your home.

But what if you have clipped every coupon in sight and/or don't own a home? Then what do you do to make financial ends meet?

There may be only one practical option: find a challenging job that will pay you for your knowledge and skills. If you decide to go back to work, you will be in good company, for nearly 25 percent of all retirees hold jobs, and half of them work simply because they need the money.[14]

Now you may be thinking: "Wait a darn moment! I didn't retire to go back to work. I retired so that I could get away from the daily hassles of my job. Are you really suggesting that I should spend my leisure days working for a living?"

Well, you may not have a choice. If every month your budget is dripping red ink, the time might be ripe for a part-time job. Marilyn Mathison, sixty-eight, a former social worker who was barely making it on her $433 a month pension, recalls:

After I paid monthly bills, I found myself depressed. There never was any money left over for fun. One day my best friend asked me to a concert. The ticket would cost seventeen dollars. I confessed to her that I didn't have a dime.

That night I did some hard thinking about my finances. I thought to myself: "Is the rest of my life going to be like this? Am I always going to be depressed about money?"

The answer was self-evident. Unless I went back to work, I would always have money worries.

The next morning I looked at the classified ads. It took me fifteen interviews, but I finally found a job as a receptionist for a law firm in my community.

I make seven dollars an hour and I work twenty hours a week. That gives me an extra five hundred sixty dollars a month. But the best thing is that I no longer feel poor. My entire attitude has changed for the better.

If you are short of cash, perhaps it is time to consider part-time employment. If so, you may be amazed at the warm reception you will receive from companies in your community who are eager to take advantage of your knowledge.

Why the interest in older workers? Primarily because there is not a large enough pool of young workers to meet the needs of employers. Between now and the year 2000, American business will create thirteen million new jobs. But there are 44 percent fewer individuals in the twenty-five to forty-four age bracket available for employment in 1990 compared to 1980. And each succeeding year the prognosis is worse: there simply aren't enough young workers to supply the labor needs of many American companies. As former Secretary of Labor William Brock says: "We are simply going to run out of people with the skills to hold the jobs that are being created."[15]

Of course, a labor pool shortage is but one reason why companies are searching out older workers. A more significant reason is that older workers bring an ethic to their job that companies find appealing. A study conducted by the American Association of Retired Persons revealed the following:

* Productivity does not decline with age; older employees are as produc-

tive as younger ones in most organizations.

* Workers over forty-five have an attendance record that is as good as most other age groups. In fact, the American Council of Life Insurance found that older workers take only 3.1 sick days per year.
* Workers over age fifty-five account for only 9.7 percent of all work place injuries, despite the fact that they make up 13.6 percent of the work force.
* Older workers have a strong commitment to their jobs. Employees between the ages of fifty and sixty have been with their employers an average of fifteen years.[16]

But perhaps the most important reason companies are hiring older workers is that mature workers have a stoic work ethic. States Donna Montgomery of Superior Senior Services, a firm in Minneapolis that recruits older workers for companies:

[The attitude of older workers] is cheerful and upbeat, and they're dedicated and dependable simply because they love to be working. They're on time, they take pride in what they do. They don't hang on the phone, shoplift from the company, or slack off in any way. Besides a different work ethic, older people generally have a whole different moral code.[17]

Employers like such an attitude. Consequently, many companies have designed programs specifically for retired workers. For example:

The *Travelers Retiree Job Bank* draws on the services of more than 600 retired workers to fill vacancies. To encourage "unretirement" the company has altered its pension plan, allowing retirees to work nearly half-time without losing benefits.

The *Minnesota Title Financial Corporation* hires former postal workers and metropolitan bus drivers to serve as their couriers.

Bankers Life and Casualty Company has created a temporary workers pool made up of retirees. The company estimates that the program has saved the company $10,000 during its first year of operation.

Control Data encourages retirees to be a part of the company's special "business advisors" division. In that capacity retired workers are hired as independent consultants to firms who need their services.

General Electric has found it is cheaper to retrain veteran engineers at its aerospace electronic systems department in Utica, New York, than to hire young engineers. "The cost would have been three times greater if we had hired new people and instituted layoffs," said a General Electric spokesman.

Georgia Power and *New York State Electric and Gas Corporation* have hired hundreds of retirees to weatherize homes of older adults.

Lockheed, Honeywell, Motorola, Grumman Aircraft, and the *Travelers Companies* have created "retiree pools" so that older individuals can be rehired as work shortages develop.

Now, if you are short of cash or simply need a new challenge, you should consider finding paid employment. But be mindful that while many companies are looking for older workers, some personnel officers have misconceptions about employees older than fifty. Therefore be prepared to answer these questions:

* Have you kept up with your field?
* Can you relate to employees who are the age of your children?
* Can you take criticism?
* Are you willing to learn new technologies?
* If you work part-time, will you have a half-hearted commitment to the company?
* Are you an optimistic person, or have your work experiences made you cynical?

Before seeking employment, take a moment to answer these inquiries. But also devise a coherent plan for finding employment. Here are six strategies that can assist you in locating the perfect job.

STRATEGY ONE: ASSESS YOUR STRENGTHS

Your worst enemy in seeking a job is a negative attitude. Never assume you are "over the hill" and no one wants you. Instead, make a candid assessment of your strengths as well as your limitations.

How do you make such an assessment? Your best bet is to head to a community college that has close ties with local business and industrial organizations. Not only can they put you in contact with prospective employers, but many will give you an "occupational skills inventory," which assesses your career options.

You may be surprised after taking the inventory that your skills are transferable to many occupational settings. A case in point is a man who served as a staff aide to a big-city mayor for over twelve years. The citizens decided that another candidate was better suited for the mayor's position and ousted "hizzoner" as well as the aide.

Fortunately the aide recognized that he had skills transferable to other occupational settings. He noted that during the past twelve years he had planned numerous globe-circling junkets to foreign countries, and that he was familiar with travel schedules and foreign customs. It didn't take him long to find work as a travel agent.[18]

If you feel your skills are dated, consider enrolling in courses that will put you at the head of the class. If you are an accountant, become knowledgeable about recent changes in tax legislation. If you are a secretary, learn the latest word processing programs. And if you are in sales, talk to sales people and learn the latest trends in marketing.

STRATEGY TWO: WRITE A RÉSUMÉ THAT DEMANDS ATTENTION

In writing the résumé use the best-quality bond paper available, and watch out for typos and misspellings. At the top of the résumé put your name, address, and telephone number. Then write a succinct paragraph entitled "Career Objective." Be specific, and tailor it to the position you are seeking.

Next, describe your work experiences. Stress your accomplishments, and build credibility by stating pertinent facts, such as "increased sales 23 percent in one year" or "cut costs 14 percent in six months."[19]

At the end of the résumé list two or three references. State their relationship to you, their address, and telephone numbers. Be sure to check with your references before giving their name to any prospective employer.

Keep your résumé short and to the point. Most recruitment specialists suggest that it not be longer than two pages.

Your résumé should be attached to a cover letter. Indicate why you are applying for a particular position, and briefly summarize your employment history. Indicate that you will be following up with a telephone call on a certain day.

Once again, presentation counts, and may

be the determining factor in whether you receive an interview. If you don't type, spend a few dollars and have your material professionally prepared by a secretarial service. Names and addresses of such services can be found in the yellow pages.

STRATEGY THREE: PERK UP YOUR APPEARANCE

You don't want to look for a job looking destitute! Far better to invest in your future by purchasing a new dress or a business suit. A sharp appearance won't get you the job, but it will leave a positive impression.

STRATEGY FOUR: MAKE A LIST OF POTENTIAL EMPLOYERS

As a general rule, your best option in finding employment is through former employers. There is nothing to be ashamed of in asking for a job, once retired. If you have a good track record and your former employer needs your skills, you will probably be hired immediately. But even if there are no openings, your name will be put in a job bank and you may be contacted in the future.

STRATEGY FIVE: INTERVIEW FRIENDS ABOUT JOB PROSPECTS IN THEIR ORGANIZATIONS

Be frank about your need for employment

and your willingness to work hard and learn new skills. Remember one important fact about finding employment: most jobs are found not through classified ads but through contacts with colleagues and friends.

STRATEGY SIX: CONSIDER TEMPORARY EMPLOYMENT

In most communities there is a tremendous demand for part-time help. The growth rate of the temporary help industry has expanded 17 percent during the past five years, and there is no sign it will abate. Today the temporary help industry has six million workers with an industrial payroll of over nine billion dollars.

Temporary employment offers the best of two worlds to over three million adults over age fifty-five: the chance to make money using their knowledge and skills and the time for whatever else they want to do with their lives.[20]

Of course, many part-time jobs expand into meaningful careers. Caroline Grasso, seventy-seven, works at Papa Gino's fast-food chain in New England. "I was retired, and I was depressed," states Grasso. "And my doctor prescribed part-time work just to get me out of the house."

She started cleaning tables at Papa Gino's for the minimum wage. But today she averages

$8.00 an hour acting as a salad bar expert and hostess for the dining hour. She also organizes birthday parties for children. After she had put on 325 parties for almost 3,200 children, the company president sent her to Florida for a two-week all-expense-paid vacation. "I love my job," states Grasso with a smile. "I'm never going to quit."[21]

When we think of part-time work, blue-collar jobs jump to mind. But some of the best part-time jobs are for retired executives and managers. For example, many retired business leaders are members of the Service Corps of Retired Executives, which helps younger men and women start new businesses (SCORE, 1120 20th Street NW, Washington, DC 20416). If you like the idea of travel, you might wish to apply for a government-sponsored program that sends retired executives around the globe, all expenses paid, to countries needing American know-how in technical, administrative, and educational fields (International Executive Service Corps, 8 Stamford Forum, Box 10005, Stamford, CT 06904).

But regardless of the type of temporary positions you are seeking, begin by contacting employment agencies in your community. Or write to the National Association of Temporary Workers, 119 S. Saint Asaph Street, Alexandria, VA 22324, and request a listing of employment services in your community.

If you hit a lot of dead ends in your search for work, think about unmet needs in your community. If you enjoy being around children, you might want to offer child-care services to working moms and dads. If you like to sew, consider a business in which you repair clothing and make minor alterations. If you are surrounded by professional neighbors, offer to "house-sit" when they are away on business; or if you like to cook, volunteer (for a price!) to assist in the kitchen when they entertain clients. And if you are handy around the house, consider putting a flier in mail boxes announcing a new "handy-man" service. Remember: if you can prune a hedge, paint a door, or tune up a sputtering car, the public will beat a path to your door.[22]

One final comment is in order: finding employment can be a job in itself. In fact, most job placement experts state that you should consider your job search a full-time endeavor.

Therefore approach the search in a professional manner. Evaluate your strengths. Write a neat résumé. Invest in a new wardrobe. Contact previous employers and temporary service agencies. And remember that in many United States cities the American Association of Retired Persons offers valuable educational programs in helping retirees find meaningful work. For further information write AARP, Work Force Education Section, AARP Worker Equity Initiative, 1909 K Street NW, Washington, DC 20049.

As you read the above you may be thinking: "Do I *really* want to go back to work?" Only you can answer that question. But if your life is clouded with financial concerns, this may be the time to target a new job or even a new career. Not only will you be bringing in income, but you will find that employment provides rich psychological dividends. As author Van Arsdale France states in his book *Career Planning:* "Your marriage will be better, you'll meet new people, and you'll have something to talk about. You'll enjoy the discipline of work. Without it most of us are ships without rudders. You'll continue learning, since work forces us to grow. You'll enjoy your leisure; real pleasure in having leisure time is found when it is a well-earned rest from work."[23]

Postscript: What to Do if You Feel Poor

If you have taken the time to read this chapter, you may be worried about money. I hope that some of the strategies I've discussed will assist in helping you augment your income.

But what if none of the strategies is applicable to your situation? What if you have rented living space all your life and have no equity in a home? What if you are in poor health and employment is not a possibility? Then what do you do?

I do not want to minimize the problems associated with being poor. But I come back to an earlier point: *It is possible to live on a modest income and have a good retirement.*

There is, however, an important prerequisite: *Your attitude must be positive.* You dare not compare yourself to neighbors who are traveling to Europe. Nor can you look with envy at those who dine at expensive restaurants and wrap themselves in the latest fashions.

Rather, you must look inward at those things that give you the greatest joy: a walk near your home, a visit with a trusted friend, a trip to the library. And every month, no matter how little your income, you must earmark a few dollars for fun, even if it is only a trip to the theater or a lunch at a favorite restaurant.

When you do these things you are engaged in what one of my dearest friends calls "prosperity thinking." Prosperity thinking is not dreaming of the day that you will strike it rich because you have the winning number in a lottery. It's not going to the mail box, hoping that this will be the lucky day your magazine sweepstakes numbers are drawn. Prosperity thinking means feeling rich in your heart. It means waking up in the morning knowing that there are countless ways of having fun with little expense. It suggests counting your assets, not in a financial sense, but in affirming the meaning of your friendships, your hobbies, your avocations. And it means planning events for your future that are so precious, you can hardly wait for them to happen.

Finally, never forget this important fact: Some of the most contented people in the world are not millionaires. They are ordinary people who have learned to celebrate the joys of life that bear little expense.

PART II
HOUSE AND HOME

The Relocation Question

One of the most exciting aspects of retirement is the possibility of changing your place of residence. This doesn't necessarily imply moving across country, nor does it suggest that you put your car on automatic pilot until it arrives in Sarasota, Florida; Sun City, Arizona; or San Diego, California. After all, only 5 percent of retirees actually relocate to a southern climate.

But when you finally leave your nine to five job, you may wish to consider a move to a new home that better meets your economic and lifestyle priorities.

How do you determine whether you should make a move, once retired? How do you assess whether it is prudent to sell your home and plant your roots in another community?

Chapter 6 focuses on the wonderful new world of retirement housing. You will learn what life is like in a retirement community.

You will discover the advantages of renting an apartment or purchasing a condominium. And you will learn how to avoid six mistakes in housing that can ruin an otherwise successful retirement.

Chapter 7 describes twelve beautiful retirement Edens that are located in various parts of the United States. We will learn the advantages of retiring on the Oregon coast, as well as the particular appeal of living in university communities such as Amherst, Massachusetts, or Chapel Hill, North Carolina. But before examining these locations, we will take a hard-nosed look at how to evaluate a new community and how to determine whether there is a good match between your needs and what the city offers. The chapter concludes by presenting an intriguing option: maybe the best place to retire is not in the United States, but in a foreign country where housing costs are low and where you can live like royalty without spending a fortune.

CHAPTER SIX

Don't Make a Move – Yet

We are thinking about buying a home, with the Lord's help. At these prices, we need all the help we can get.
Mr. and Mrs. Jack Parker
Caldwell, Indiana

When your grandparents were your age, they had few housing options. Most resided in their original homestead. Those who needed extra care moved in with an adult child. And those who were impoverished often had no choice but to enter a county nursing home.

In one short generation, housing possibilities have dramatically changed. Today you can move into a luxury apartment, freeing you from the drudgeries of home ownership. You can join a plush retirement community, providing medical care for life. Or you can purchase an economical garden apartment with golf courses, swimming pools, tennis courts, and private jogging trails.

While today's retirees have an impressive array of housing opportunities, the choices can be difficult. As Janet McLonski, sixty-two, says:

In three years my husband retires and we will be free to move anywhere. I should be excited, but I am worried. Should we sell the house we have lived in for thirty-six years? Would we *really* be happier in Florida or Arizona? Should we move to Baltimore to be close to our children? And what makes the most financial sense? We really don't know how to make this decision — and it looms heavily on our minds.

The purpose of this chapter is to present *practical* information on retirement housing. We will learn whether it is best to reside in a single-family home. We will explore the advantages of retirement communities, and we will discover why purchasing a condominium might be an attractive option. The starting point, however, is to examine several errors in housing that can keep you from enjoying your retirement years.

Retirement Housing: Six Mistakes to Avoid

MISTAKE NUMBER 1: MOVING AWAY FROM FAMILY AND FRIENDS

It's not always a mistake to leave family and friends in pursuit of better living conditions. In fact, tens of thousands of retirees do it every year as they migrate from the northern states to warm climates.

But it is important to understand that such a move might entail emotional costs. Consider Doris Little, who retired to sunny Arizona. Seven years later she returned to her Minnesota home. When she reopened charge accounts at supermarkets and gas stations, the reaction was predictable: "Are you out of your mind?" "Didn't you go in the wrong direction?" or "Why would anyone want to do that?"

She explained that her children and grandchildren lived in Minnesota. "I missed watching them grow," she would comment. No other explanation was needed. There was always the same understanding smile of approval.[1]

Before moving to the sun belt — or anywhere else, for that matter — think about the important relationships in your life. Is your happiness dependent on living near your children? Do their problems give you additional worries? How would *they* feel if you moved to another state?

It is equally important to assess relationships with grandchildren. Do you see them very often? Do you participate in their lives in a meaningful way? If you moved, could you arrange to visit them several times a year?

Of course relationships between parents and adult children sometimes *improve* when separated by hundreds of miles. This is particularly true if there is a history of friction between parent and child. As Gina Savarletti, sixty-seven, noted:

> I moved three hundred miles away from my two children. I love them dearly, but after a disagreement it was apparent that we needed some space between us. Our relationship is now much closer. I don't offer advice and they don't intrude in my affairs. We get together on holidays and on birthdays. This is a good arrangement for everyone.

It is also important to consider how a move might influence your friendships. Some people find it difficult to leave friends and make new ones. Rebecca Norman, fifty-seven, left Mt. Lebanon, Pennsylvania, in order to join a retirement community in Miami, Florida. Seven months later she noted:

> It's been hard. There are some nice people in this retirement community. But I miss having coffee with two women who are my "soulmates." When you move away from people who have been with you through difficult times, the new relationships seem superficial.

If you have a large network of friends, or if you find it hard to make new ones, consider a move very carefully. You can replace a house. But it takes time to replace trusted friends.

MISTAKE NUMBER 2: MOVING TO A NEW LOCATION WITHOUT ADEQUATELY CHECKING IT OUT

According to David Evan Morse, a New York CPA and partner in the law firm of Whitman and Ransom, many people move to a new location because it's cheaper, but they find themselves living where they don't want to be. "Who wants to spend the rest of his life uncomfortable and bored?" asks Morse.[2]

Unfortunately, once you invest in a new home, it might be difficult to recover financially if you suddenly need to move again. This is particularly true if you make a large non-refundable investment in a retirement community.

Therefore, before relocating to a different section of the country, vacation there first. Subscribe to the local newspaper so that you can read about the political and economic developments in the community.[3] And after you retire, rent an apartment for a year or two. This will give you ample time to see what the residents are like, how the medical system meets your needs, and whether the climate is to your liking. In addition, it will give you an opportunity to evaluate shopping centers, churches, libraries, theaters, and the community's transportation system. If there is a chance that you will need to earn money in retirement, be sure to examine job opportunities.

Regardless of where you may move, *define your priorities*. That's what Maurice and Sharon Dralock of Atlanta, Georgia, did, and they haven't regretted their decision to retire close to home.

"First, we wanted to be in an area close to our married son and our two grown daughters," says Sharon. "We also wanted a brand-new condominium that had tennis courts and a swimming pool. It had to have a master bedroom on ground level, because we didn't want to climb stairs all the time. It had to have a second bedroom on that level, because we have elderly relatives who visit often."[4]

They also knew what they *didn't* want. "We didn't want to move to another part of the country or to a retirement community. And we didn't want to be tied to a home in the country, because we like to travel and go to different places."

Even though they had several offers to purchase their home, they waited until they located a condominium community about twenty miles from their house. What has been the net effect? "We don't have the expense of maintaining the landscaping, there is no yard man, and no outside painting. Inside, we find our power bills are lower. This way of living is much to our liking."[5]

The move not only met the Dralocks' psychological needs, it made financial sense. Maurice, fifty-nine, took the one-time capital gains exclusion on the profits made in selling the house and invested a portion of the proceeds. And because they moved to a progressive community, the Dralocks will become eligible for an exemption from county school taxes once they reach age sixty-two.

MISTAKE NUMBER 3: SPENDING MORE ON HOUSING THAN YOU CAN AFFORD

Most people want to diminish their living expenses in retirement. But others want to own an elaborate home, and consequently put themselves at financial risk.

Now more than ever, you want to make a hard-nosed assessment of how much you want to spend for housing. How do you determine an appropriate amount? Here is a formula that will give you an indication of how much housing you can afford:

Step One: Calculate your gross monthly income. Total all sources of income, including Social Security payments, pension and annuity payments, and any dividends/interest from investments.

Step Two: Deduct from the total any monthly payments you make on long-term debts (more than ten months). Included in this would be auto loans, association dues, alimony, and any additional bank loans.

Step Three: Multiply the resulting figure by 36 percent (.36), which will give you your "income-to-debt" ratio. This answer will tell you what you can afford per month. (Note: some mortgage lenders apply more or less strict factors, say 33 percent or 38 percent, especially when your down payment is 5 percent or 20 percent respectively.)

Step Four: Estimate the average annual real estate taxes, plus the annual cost of home owner's insurance. Divide by 12 to obtain a monthly figure.

Step Five: Deduct the monthly taxes and insurance costs from the figures you arrived at in the third step. The result is the maximum monthly payment you can allocate for a mortgage.

What should you do if you can't afford the house of your retirement dreams? One option is to move to a section of the country where housing costs are lower. A two thousand-square-foot, three-bedroom house in an affluent neighborhood of Mobile, Alabama, or Colorado Springs can be purchased for $73,000. The same house sells for $144,000 in Wichita, Kansas, $300,000 in Morristown, New Jersey, and $600,000 in Greenwich, Connecticut.[6]

MISTAKE NUMBER 4: NOT FINDING THE BEST REAL ESTATE AGENT TO SELL YOUR HOUSE

You've worked hard for your money. You probably have spent many years nurturing your investments. Yet upon retirement, some people turn over their largest asset — their house — without giving more than a passing thought to the credentials of their real estate sales agent.

It is important to remember that a good real estate agent can make a difference of *10 percent* in what you will receive for your home.[7] Therefore you want to do everything possible to make certain that you employ the best possible real estate agent. How do you find a competent agent?

First, understand what role a real estate sales person has in selling a home. A competent sales person will (1) help you determine the asking price of your property, (2) suggest ways to fix up your home before it goes on market, (3) aggressively market the house, (4) advise you on the selling techniques they are using to sell the home, and (5) nudge the deal all the way to a successful closing.[8]

In locating the best possible real estate agent, interview at least three real estate sales people. Here are some pertinent questions to ask:

* How will my home be priced? A good agent will make a comparison of houses like yours that have recently sold and will share the selling prices with you.
* How will my home be advertised?
* What has been the average length of time to sell a home in my community?
* May I have at least three references? It is not unreasonable to ask for the names and telephone numbers of the agent's last half-dozen sales. Call these references and determine their level of satisfaction with the agent.
* Does your real estate company have a "guaranteed sales program"? In a guaranteed sale, the real estate company agrees to purchase your home at a predetermined price if it doesn't sell in a reasonable length of time.
* Does the agent give you practical suggestions as to how to improve your house for a quick sale? ("The door is in excellent condition, but the lock needs changing.")[9]

Finally, request three figures in determining a selling price: First, what will my home be worth in a forced sale? Second, if I had all the time in the world to wait for it to sell, what is the highest figure I could reasonably expect? Last, what will my house sell for under normal circumstances?

The agent's responses to these questions will put him or her on notice that you will not accept a low figure simply to get the house sold. The figures may also assist you in doing comparative shopping with other real estate companies.

Above everything else, take your time in selecting an agent to represent your home. If you have a $150,000 house, and if the agent can help you obtain an extra 10 percent, you will have pocketed $15,000 excluding the commission. That $15,000 "bonus" might be the perfect way to begin your retirement years.

MISTAKE NUMBER 5: FAILING TO FOLLOW INTERNAL REVENUE POLICIES CONCERNING THE SALE OF A HOME

Most people are aware that the federal tax law permits home owners to avoid paying taxes on a gain of as much as $125,000 from the sale of a house. But you can take the exclusion only once, and you must be fifty-five years of age or older in order to be eligible. To qualify for the tax break, you must have owned the home and lived in it as your principal residence for *at least three of the five years before the sale.*

If you don't follow the rules and regulations, you could be in for a nasty surprise. Consider a gentleman who had lived in his house for thirteen years before moving to Germany for four years. He kept his old home, returned to the United States, moved into the home for half a year, sold it, then claimed the $125,000 deduction. Although he was fifty-five years of age when the sale was made, the IRS ruled that the profits were taxable because he failed the three-year residency test.

It should be noted, however, that the three years do not need to be taken consecutively. A temporary absence, such as taking a winter vacation in the south, generally counts as time at home even if you rent out your home during your absence.[10]

Because of the complexity of tax laws, *you are advised to consult with a financial planner prior to selling your home.* As you can expect, whenever a break from tax is involved, the fine print gets tricky. In addition, call the Internal Revenue Service at 800-424-3676 and request a copy of Publication 523, "Tax Information on Selling Your Home."[11]

MISTAKE NUMBER 6: IGNORING THE ADVANTAGES OF RENTAL PROPERTY

If you absolutely must own your home, skip this section. But if you have little equity in your present home and/or the expenses of home ownership are crimping your retirement lifestyle, consider renting an apartment, condominium, or even a single-family home. Why rent?

First, equity in your present home can be invested, providing you with a steady stream of income. For example, let's say you own a $100,000 home and have a mortgage of $60,000. If you sell your home and invest $40,000 at 6 percent, you will have an additional $200 per month on which to live.

Second, rental expenses have generally not risen as fast as costs associated with home ownership.[12] In addition, more than one hundred communities have rent controls, providing a safeguard against exorbitant rent increases. With home prices and property taxes rising, rental properties represent an economical way of funding your retirement housing.

Third, renting means you will never again have to shovel the snow, clean the gutter, cut the grass, or paint the house! Nor will you

224

have to replace the roof or mend the fence. If the plumbing needs fixing or the furnace gives out, just call the landlord.

Fourth, you usually have less interior upkeep in rental property because of its smaller size. This is attractive for those who do not want to spend their time cleaning floors and dusting furniture. In addition, one-bedroom studio apartments provide a homey atmosphere. Many retirees welcome a smaller and more cozy living arrangement than is typically found in a large house.[13]

A final advantage is that utilities may be included in the rent — although landlords increasingly require tenants to pay their own utility costs.

Whether you should rent or own a home will ultimately come down to your personal preferences as well as pocketbook considerations. But do consider the benefits of renting. Millions of retirees have adopted a "rent first" philosophy and are happier because of it.

Should You REALLY Sell Your Home?

As we have noted, renting a cozy apartment might be an attractive option. But selling a beloved home has emotional consequences. As Sally McGuinnes, sixty-three, of Chicago, Illinois, states:

My husband wants to sell our home and move into an apartment. It makes financial sense. But every time I think about leaving our home, I shed a few tears. This is where we raised two lovely daughters. We have over thirty years of family history in these walls. I suppose I shouldn't be so attached to brick and mortar, but this home represents my life. It will be very, very tough to leave.

Should you sell your home? According to the American Association of Retired Persons, there are important reasons to stay in your home — and some powerful reasons to sell.

Reasons for Staying

* The expenses of your present home are not a strain on your budget, and you can reasonably expect to pay for them in the future. You do not expect property taxes to increase drastically. Your home does not require extensive maintenance work. You can meet utility expenses.
* You like the climate most of the year where you now live.
* There are an adequate number of

social and cultural events to attend in your community.
* Your home is located near shopping centers, places of worship, recreational activities in which you are interested.
* Your home is located conveniently, and you are able to get to your physician, dentist, attorney, etc., without too much difficulty.
* You like the looks of your neighborhood. It is well maintained. Neighbors take pride in their homes.
* You have friends nearby, and the neighborhood is quiet, pleasant, and friendly.

Reasons for Moving

* Your present housing expenses are excessive and will likely increase in the future.
* Your house is difficult and expensive to maintain. The house is too large and takes too much work to keep clean. It costs too much to heat or cool. The yard requires too much upkeep.
* Your house does not adequately

meet your needs. There are too many stairs to climb. The bathroom/laundry/storage areas are poorly located.

* The weather is often harsh and keeps you indoors too often.
* Your neighborhood is deteriorating.
* There is too much noise.
* You live too far away from shopping centers, your place of worship, recreational facilities.
* You live too far away from your doctor or medical facilities. Emergency help is not readily available.
* Your neighborhood does not provide adequate recreational opportunities.
* Your children and friends have moved and you wish that you were closer to them.[14]

Most retirement specialists suggest that if your pro and con comparisons come out reasonably close, you should consider staying in your present home. Why? Because if the mortgage is paid off, your housing expenses are probably lower than any comparable living arrangement. If you have a significant portion of your income left for nonhousing needs, you are in a truly enviable situation.[15]

Housing Options

What housing possibilities are available if you decide to relocate? Fortunately there are many exciting options. Here are some of the best:

RETIREMENT COMMUNITIES

Shortly before writing this chapter, I telephoned Marjory Kernkamp, a former colleague, who retired in Sun City, Arizona. The excitement in her voice was unmistakable as she shared the joys of living in a retirement community:

> I have met so many new friends. The services are wonderful. The medical system is outstanding. And there are social gatherings every night of the week. I will never regret moving to Sun City.

Many residents would agree. With alluring names like Sun City and Leisure World, retirement villages are self-contained communities that offer older adults tranquillity, security, companionship, and loads of leisure activities.[16]

Today there are over 230,000 people living in over 800 retirement communities. In return for a substantial entrance charge plus a monthly fee, the communities provide an abundance of social activities and, if needed, nursing care.

Retirement communities come in all sizes, shapes, and descriptions. Some are luxury high-rise units with balconies from which to view lakes and mountains. Others are mid-rise apartments that overlook golf courses, while still others are ranchlike configurations with wings of apartments radiating from a common area. In some communities you have the option of purchasing a condominium or a town house.

All retirement communities have communal dining rooms. Some resemble restaurants in both service and decor. Others will remind you of a college cafeteria serving home-cooked meals.[17]

The services that are offered to residents are truly amazing. Most retirement communities have stores, theaters, libraries, and medical facilities. There are also exercise facilities, walking trails, tennis courts, swimming pools, garden plots, beauty shops, plus an endless schedule of activities ranging from aerobics to study clubs.

Should you consider living in a retirement community? Be advised: older people feel very strongly about such places. Either they love them, or they hate them.[18] Those who love them, however, are effusive in their praise:

I can't really think of any way this place could be improved. My only regret is that there's so much to do here, I just can't do it all.

Bob Maucker, Leisure Village, Fort Myers, Florida[19]

If I had a million dollars, I would not live anyplace else. My husband and I looked from the Canadian border to the Mexican border before we chose this place, Rosa Villa. I can't remember one disappointment.

Deila I. Whitman, Rosa Villa, Portland, Oregon[20]

People sometimes ask me if it gets depressing when you see your friends die. Your friends are going to die regardless of where you live. In the meantime, this is about as close to heaven as you will ever get while on earth.

Marjory Kernkamp, Sun City, Arizona

I cannot sing enough praises for retirement community living. It is a very quiet and relaxing place to live.

Ray Mendenhalls, Green Valley, Arizona[21]

There's very little crime here, and we have so many friends. And the only traffic jams are caused by golf carts.

Beverly Bradshaw, Sun City West, Phoenix, Arizona[22]

Perhaps one of the best things about a retirement community is the possibility of establishing new friendships. As one retired executive commented:

When we left our home on Long Island, we worried most about leaving our friends behind. But what has been best about our move to Florida is that we have met terrific new friends. And our old ones visit us every winter.

As mentioned earlier, the recreational facilities are outstanding. At Sun City there are seven swimming pools (indoor and outdoor), as well as air-conditioned shuffleboard courts. In addition, there are exercise rooms designed to help residents improve their physical fitness. As Mildred Gladwell, of Leisure Village in Lakewood, New Jersey, says: "I am still a healthy seventy-nine and swim all summer in our pools or do a daily walk."[23]

Most retirement communities provide a safe and secure living environment. An added bonus: if you decide to travel, a daily check of your home will be made upon request.

The main reason retirement communities are so popular, however, is that they symbolize *carefree living*. Social activities are planned. Transportation needs are met. Nursing services are available twenty-four hours a day. As Mrs. Whitman of Rosa Villa, Portland, Oregon, says: "You name it, we have it. Our medical program is second to none. A jiggle of our phone and it will bring a nurse."[21]

Knowing that you have competent nursing and medical care at your fingertips is one of the most valued features of a retirement community. Marjory Kernkamp, my former colleague who retired to Sun City, Arizona, commented:

> The biggest advantage to me is that I know I can receive outstanding medical assistance. These people (at Sun City) really want to help you. When I became ill they took me to the hospital. When I was discharged, my physician prescribed swimming therapy for me, but I was too weak to walk to the pool. No problem. I just called the office and they had a young man in a golf cart assist me to the swimming area. I have a cord in my apartment that summons emergency

help. Once I had to pull it. I had help here in two minutes.

Will an investment in a retirement community pay off? In general, homes have *increased* in value. In Green Valley, Arizona, for example, town houses bought for $39,000 in 1977 were going for more than $70,000 in the 1980s. In Oceana, a condominium community in California, home values soared from about $14,000 to $28,000 in 1971 to $45,000 to $80,000 in the 1980s.[25]

Of course no one can predict how inflation will influence future property values. But if you purchase a home in a popular retirement community, your investment will likely increase.

What are the drawbacks to life in a retirement community? Entrance fees are stiff. The average cost for entering a Type A retirement community (which tends to offer the most services) averages from approximately $68,000 for a one-bedroom apartment to $87,000 for two bedrooms (1990 figures). If you want a larger unit, such as a cottage or penthouse, entrance fees average $109,000.

Then, too, there are the monthly fees. For one-bedroom apartments, the average monthly fee is $965 in Type A facilities; for two-bedroom units it is $1,149.

Keep in mind that entrance and monthly fees will be considerably higher if you are married. At the Washington House in Alexandria, Virginia, couples pay an entrance fee of $120,000 for a large two-bedroom apartment, but only $99,000 for a single person. The couple in a two-bedroom unit would pay a monthly fee of $2,090, but a single person would pay $1,600.[26]

If such fees sound prohibitive, you might wish to consider Type B and C retirement communities, which offer fewer services. If you shop carefully, a $50,000 investment will put you into a lovely garden apartment. For further information on costs refer to Table 14.

There are other drawbacks that should be noted. Some people complain about the dense living conditions. Others miss not being around young people. Then, too, there are the rules and regulations. A home owners association might tell you how long your guests can stay, which facilities they can use, and what color you can paint your house. A small number of communities even ban visits by minors, which means that you would have to travel in order to see your grandchildren.[27]

In spite of these limitations, retirement communities offer an intriguing option as to how to spend your retirement years. However, before making a decision ask a lot of questions (see Table 15). If the retirement community is publicly held, obtain a copy of the annual report as well as the more detailed 10K report the firm must file with the Securities and Exchange Commission. Contact the consumer department in your state capital and determine whether any complaints have been filed against the builder. Don't be alarmed over a few complaints. But if there is a long list of grievances, proceed with caution.

After narrowing your choices to two or three retirement communities, evaluate each home owners association. Request a copy of the association's constitution and bylaws. Pay careful attention to fees and whether they have been raised in recent years. Make sure there is a financial reserve for unexpected expenses. And find out whether the association is assessing residents for annual maintenance expenses.[28]

If you have difficulty determining whether the retirement community is financially sound, have an accountant look over the home owners association balance sheet. "When a home owners association gets into financial trouble, services get cut or your monthly dues are raised, or both," warns Susan Brecht, director of the retirement housing practice in the Philadelphia accounting firm of Laventhol and Horvath.[29]

TABLE 14
Retirement Villages: What It Costs to Move In

Here are prices for new homes in some of the nation's most popular retirement communities, each of which boasts several golf courses, pools, and other amenities. If you bought a comparable home from an existing owner in the same development, you'd likely pay between 5% and 15% less. Also, remember that most of these communities are surrounded by similar projects, where homes may cost less.

SUN CITY SUMMERLIN, Las Vegas, Nev.: The 1,086-square-foot, two-bedroom single-family homes start at $86,500, while the upscale homes with 2,500 square feet can cost as much as $195,000. Two-bedroom units in duplexes start at $92,300, while the units in the fourplexes start at $81,000.

SUN CITY VISTONOSO, Tucson, Ariz.: Prices for two-bedroom, two-bath single-family homes with 1,038 to 2,328 square feet range from $96,300 to $184,000. The high-end homes have formal dining rooms and family rooms. A two-bedroom unit in a fourplex costs about $90,000.

SUN CITY WEST, Phoenix, Ariz.: A basic two-bedroom, two-bath single-family home with a bit more than 1,000 square feet of living space sells for $72,000. A more luxurious model with

TABLE 14 (*Continued*)

2,800 square feet goes for $194,000. A 1,165-square-foot, one-bedroom unit in a fourplex starts at $76,000.

LEISURE RIDGE, Lakehurst, N.J.: A two-bedroom detached home with skylights, patio, and formal dining room goes for $190,000. A similar unit in a duplex sells for $174,000.

LEISURE VILLAGE OCEAN HILLS, Oceanside, Calif.: A two-bedroom, two-bath single-family home with a formal dining room and spacious living room among its roughly 2,000 square feet of space sells for about $300,000. Only furnished models are left in the popular duplexes. They sell for nearly $370,000, although units on the resale market can be purchased for much less.

LEISURE VILLAGE SEVEN LAKES, Fort Myers, Fla.: There are no detached homes in the sprawling complex, but $100,000 fetches a unit in a duplex with about 1,700 square feet of living space, including two bedrooms and two baths, a large screened porch, and a formal dining room.

Source: David W. Myers, "Seniors on the Move," *Personal Investor,* January, 1990, page 72.

TABLE 15
Questions to Ask Before Joining a Retirement Community

A. *Entrance fee*
   1. What does my initial lump sum pay for?
   2. Prior to moving in, is my initial fee escrowed, and do I receive interest on earnings?
   3. If I change my mind prior to moving in, what amount, if any, do I forfeit?
   4. If I decide to leave the community during the first five years, what refunds are made?
   5. Who is the principal lender to the retirement community, and are principal interest payments current? (You don't want to buy a property in a community that may be going bankrupt.)
   6. What evidence is there of internal auditing?
      Is an external audit done each year?
      What firm does the external audit?
      Can I receive a copy of last year's audit?
   7. What is the financial background of the officers of the retirement community? Is the policy-making

TABLE 15 (*Continued*)

board fiscally competent to assess the health of the community?

B. Operating budget and control of income and expenses

1. What is the monthly fee? What kind of increases have there been in the monthly fee over the past five years? Are any increases anticipated for next year?

2. Are there any activities or projects supported by the community that are in financial trouble, such as a golf course, swimming pool, recreation facility?

C. Management issues

1. Who is the chief manager of the facility and what experience does he or she bring to the job?

2. What is the turnover rate of residential units? Why do people leave the retirement community? Will the turnover of residential units support debt service (interest and principal)?

Adapted from: Michael Sumichrast, et al., *Planning Your Retirement Housing.* Copyright © 1984. By permission of HarperCollins Publishers. Pages 226-227.

If the retirement community has condominiums or town houses for sale, make a careful analysis before investing any money. The homes that will appreciate the fastest are those close to the golf course as well as those that have a beautiful view. If you want to save money and don't mind a little walk, you might enjoy the privacy of a home off the beaten path.

If the home you are considering is new, find out if there is a warranty against defects. If no warranty exists, your purchase offer should be contingent on the unit passing a housing audit conducted by a building inspector. You will have to pay the fee for this service, but if the inspector discovers a problem your money will be well spent.[30]

But remember: Before you sign on the dotted line, make sure that your future home is in the geographical setting that you like. Be cause if you have to sell later, it could cost you a lot of money. As Bill Brennan states: "We saw a lot of our friends move down to Florida because it was the popular thing to do. But after a couple of years, they discovered they really didn't like sitting on beaches. They missed the change of seasons. So they moved right back where they came from, and it cost them a bundle."[31]

In summary, most retirement communities

offer these benefits: planned recreational activities, nursing services, a secure living environment, and the opportunity to make new friends. The drawbacks include a high entrance fee, dense living conditions, and rules and regulations that you might not like.

In spite of these limitations, if you are looking for an environment where your needs for housing, recreation, and companionship can be met, retirement communities present an attractive option.

APARTMENTS FOR SENIOR CITIZENS

Many retired adults can't afford an expensive retirement community. But they do want to move out of their big home and into a smaller residence.

If this has appeal, consider the advantages of renting an apartment designed for adults aged fifty-five or over. One thing is sure: most apartment owners will give you a warm welcome. Why? "People who are fifty-five and older treat their apartments like they own them," said Gene Rerat, a partner of Pointe Development Corporation, which manages three senior communities in Minnesota and Colorado. "For example, they're the only residents who will tell us the maintenance person left the sprinkler system on too long, and we're wasting money. They take a very active interest in the upkeep of the entire complex."[32]

Today's apartment buildings are very different from those built fifteen or twenty years ago. There are lounges and libraries, swimming pools, and exercise areas. If you don't want to cook, there are apartment buildings with warm, romantic dining rooms. If you don't want to clean, there is maid service. If you are worried about your health, there is twenty-four-hour nursing care. In addition, many apartment complexes have planned social activities and a van that will take you to your favorite theater or shopping center. "I'd recommend this place to anyone," says Loretta Lewis, who lives in North Ridge Apartments, a two hundred-unit congregate housing complex in New Hope, Minnesota; it is connected to the 560-bed North Ridge Nursing Center. "I just don't have time to participate in everything they offer. I exercise three times a week. I go shopping three times a week. We have movies here once a week. They bring in entertainment. There are church services. And there are card games going on practically all the time. I'm very happy here."[33]

Those who prefer a more tranquil and contemplative life might explore apartments owned by a religious denomination. Such facilities sponsor study groups, chapel services, trips to theaters and concert halls. That's not to say the residents don't have fun. I often dine with my father, who lives at Covenant Manor, a retirement community in Golden Valley, Minnesota, sponsored by the Covenant church. I am always impressed with the laughter around the dining room tables and the quiet humor as residents share their lives and experiences with one another.

In selecting an apartment, note its location. Ideally you should be able to walk to a bank, post office, restaurant, and bus line.

If you are undecided on apartment living, ask for a "test drive." Many managers will rent you a fully furnished apartment for a month or two. This will give you time to assess whether you really want to sell your home.[34]

CONDOMINIUMS

If you like the idea of *owning* a smaller residence, a condominium may be the answer to your housing needs. The amenities found in apartment buildings are also found in condominium complexes. There are, however, three significant differences between apartment and condominium living.

First, condominiums offer tax advantages if you are taking out a mortgage to pay for the residence. Second, the management of the condominium will assess a monthly fee for the main-

244

tenance of common areas such as sidewalks, elevators, roofs, recreational facilities, and so on. And third, repairs to the interior of the unit will be your responsibility.

If you don't like the "apartment look" of old condominium buildings, consider a spanking new condo. The architecture of today's condominiums represents a stunning departure from units built only a decade ago. Today there are low-rise garden apartments, town houses that resemble row houses, and even attached houses — all sold under the title of "condominium." And some boast a wide array of amenities. For example, one of Florida's three Century Village Developments in Deerfield Beach, north of Miami, has a huge clubhouse that is used every night by 3,000 to 4,000 residents, a 1,600-seat theater that would be the envy of many Broadway houses, and a large social staff that caters to the interests and needs of residents.[35]

One of the advantages of purchasing a condominium is the cost. It is still possible to purchase such a unit for under $40,000 in many sections of the country. Of course the sky is the limit when it comes to what you might pay for a luxury condo penthouse on New York's Park Avenue or a unit within walking distance of the Pacific ocean near La Jolla, California.

Before purchasing a condominium, *be mindful that the number one complaint of condominium owners is the quality of construction.*[36] Therefore hire an independent building inspector to evaluate the property.

Be mindful, too, of financial assessments. If the pool leaks, all owners must pitch in for repairs — regardless of whether you like to swim. The best way to guard against unexpected costs is for the ownership to have an emergency fund equal to 1 to 3 percent of the property's replacement value.

If you want to keep the cost of condominium ownership low, purchase a unit near a major retirement complex. Since you do not pay for all of the amenities associated with a large retirement community, your costs will be dramatically lower. To make things even better, if you have good friends in the larger retirement facility, you may be able to use the recreational and other facilities as a guest for a minimum charge.[37]

Finally, never purchase a condominium that offers services you don't need. If you are not an athlete, there is little need for a fancy exercise room. If you do not golf, why pay for the maintenance of the greens? Your best bet is to purchase a unit with *only* those services you will use on a regular basis.

ASSISTED LIVING COMMUNITIES

What should you do if your health isn't the best and you need some nursing assistance? Assisted living communities come fully equipped with all the care you could possibly need. While some have the traditional look of a nursing home, the newer models resemble condominiums and have the cozy feel of a home. Others even resemble a plush resort hotel.[38]

Models built during the past decade usually come with library, whirlpool, exercise room, and lounges for social gatherings. Monthly fees cover the cost of your apartment, utilities, housekeeping, and meals. Nurses will assist with your personal care, monitor your medications, and if needed, summon emergency help.

Assisted living facilities have dramatically changed their philosophy from an "illness model" to a "wellness orientation." In the past, assisted facilities were useful when your health deteriorated. But the newer organizations will help you stay in good health — regardless of your medical situation.

If you are in need of assisted living, check out the costs, for they vary. To obtain a listing of assisted living organizations in your community, contact your state legislative office.

Useful references include: *National Continuing Care Directory* (AARP Books, 400 S. Edward St., Mount Prospect, IL 60056); *A Consumer's Guide to Life-Care Communities* (National Consumers League, 815 15th St. NW, Washington, DC 20005); "Communities for the Elderly," *Consumer Reports,* February, 1990.

DRIVING YOUR HOME

When a friend told me that he celebrated his retirement by purchasing a recreational vehicle (RV), I had to admit to some skepticism. Sell your house? Live in a "trailer"? Frankly, I didn't understand it.

But after talking with RV owners, I have caught a glimpse of what makes them so happy. They travel where they want. They set their own schedule. They meet new friends. They breathe clean air. They see beautiful sights. And many choose to sell their house, eliminating the costs and obligations of home ownership.

In the winter RV owners can open the door of their motor home and see the silver globe of Epcot Center shining brightly through the trees. In the spring, they can point their RV toward picturesque lakes in upstate New York or the Rocky Mountains in British Columbia.[39] "It's hard to beat," says Robert Cramish of Roseville, Minnesota. "I've been retired only four years, but I have seen thirty-six states and covered 100,000 miles. We have met new friends and seen new sights. We have thoroughly enjoyed the freedom that comes from owning a recreational vehicle."

There are over 7.5 million RV's on the road, 30 percent of which are owned by adults fifty-five and older. Today's sleek vehicles are easier to drive than ever before. And they are fuel efficient, with some models getting over thirty miles per gallon.

You will have all the comforts of home in most RV's. They have conventional/microwave ovens, coffee makers, sinks with garbage disposals, vacuum cleaners, plush furniture, and superb audio systems. You can even purchase a motor home with a garage inside. Niersmann Bischoff, of North American, headquartered in Beaumont, Texas, offers a home with a garage that can hold a small vehicle, such as a two-door Ford Escort.[40]

How much do they cost? The least expensive units are light-weight folding camping trailers, which start at $3,500, sleep four people, and are pulled by a car or truck. Type A motor homes are the most luxurious, can cost up to $300,000, are twenty to thirty-five feet long, and can sleep up to eight people. U-Haul, which is the largest RV rental company, sells two- to three-year-old RV's that once sold for $42,000 for approximately $28,000.

Where do you travel, once you have purchased an RV? Most communities have RV clubs that plan motor coach tours. Names of such organizations can be obtained from your local RV dealer. In addition, consult *Vacation Places Rated: Find the Best Vacation Places in America.* This book ranks 107 vacation areas according to natural beauty, outdoor recreation, restaurants, accommodations, history and culture, and overall entertainment value.[41]

Is a recreational vehicle for you? Can it really meet your retirement housing needs?

If you are tired of the costs of home ownership, and if you like to travel, an RV might be for you. But before you make a decision, *rent* a vehicle, take it on a trip or two, and see if driving your home appeals to you. You can rent RV's through four hundred rental chain outlets and three hundred local dealerships. Many have excellent emergency road service networks. There is even a Loners on Wheels program that arranges get-togethers for single campers. They do have one rule: if a get-together leads to marriage or a traveling relationship, it is a cause for immediate expulsion! For further information, write Loners on Wheels, 90 Lester St., Poplar Bluff, MO 53901.

* * *

What housing options should you consider? Much depends upon your lifestyle and what you hope to get out of your retirement years. If you like to garden or if you enjoy puttering in the yard, a single-family home is tough to beat. If you are weary of household chores, an apartment might be an attractive possibility. But if you want never to worry about the expenses of nursing home care, and if you like the thought of meeting new friends and starting new avocations — you ought to investigate a retirement community.

CHAPTER SEVEN

Twelve Great Retirement Locations

We're not simply changing houses. We're changing a lifestyle.
        Barry Lindaman, sixty-five
        Orlando, Florida

In the last chapter we noted the many housing options available to retirees. But *where* should you live? Should you sell your home and move to Florida or southern California? Would you be better off in a dry desert climate, such as Arizona? Or should you take a gamble, and move to a completely unknown part of the United States — or even the world?

The purpose of this chapter is to describe twelve beautiful retirement locations. But before we take mental flight to various parts of the country, let's take a close look at how to evaluate a new location.[1]

How to Evaluate a New Community

I can't emphasize this point enough: Before

253

making a move, you need to make a careful analysis of the advantages and disadvantages of a new location. Here are the critical issues to address:

First, does the community have a high-quality medical system? If you are in the peak of health, it may seem strange to suggest that your first consideration should be medical and hospital services. But at some point you and/or your spouse may need them. When that time comes, you won't want to worry about the quality of care you are receiving.[2]

Dr. Arthur Kaufman, a Maryland physician who coauthored a medical consumer's guide titled *The People's Hospital Book* stated: "If I were selecting a retirement community, I'd never locate more than thirty minutes' driving time from a major medical center, preferably a teaching hospital affiliated with a good medical school."[3]

Of course, a big teaching hospital does not guarantee quality care. Therefore, in seeking to understand a community's health care system, visit a physician and a hospital representative. Among the issues to address are:

* How many physicians are there in this community? *Note:* There should be at least one doctor for every 750 residents.

* What percentage of the hospital's staff is board certified? *Note:* Better hospitals will have at least 50 percent of their physicians board certified, which means that they have additional specialized training.
* Is the hospital's emergency room staffed by a physician at all times?
* Is the hospital accredited? Were there any deficiencies mentioned in the last accreditation assessment? Have they been corrected? *Note:* The hospital should be accredited, generally for two years. If the deficiencies are not being addressed, think twice about the community, particularly if there are no other nearby hospitals.
* Is the hospital's bed occupancy at least 50 percent? *Note:* If it isn't, the hospital may be having difficulty surviving financially.
* If the hospital cannot manage a particular problem, does it have a relationship with a larger hospital? If so, which one, and how far away is it?
* Will your insurance cover medical and hospital costs?
* Does the hospital have a relation-

ship with a home health care agency or a long-term care organization, such as a nursing home?[4]

It is particularly important to analyze the medical system if you have health problems. For example, if you have heart problems, does the community have physicians specializing in cardiovascular health? If you have arthritis, are there physicians specializing in rheumatology? And what kind of help will you receive in an emergency?

If you are contemplating a move to a new city, check out the medical care system *first*. Frankly, the last thing you need in retirement is to make a move, become ill, and then discover that the medical system is inadequate.

Second, can you pursue your recreational interests in this community? Most people don't want to retire to an endless sit on the beach. They want to do something, whether it be fishing, golf, garden, or horseback riding.

In selecting a retirement location, consider places where you can carry out your hobbies and avocations. If you are a writer, you probably want to be near libraries, museums, and theaters. If you are an artist, consider Santa Fe, New Mexico, which has over two hundred art galleries. If you like jazz, you can't beat New Orleans, with Preservation Hall,

Tipitinas, and Benny's, where rhythm and blues can be heard every night. And if you like the challenge of catching world-class muskies, one of the best places to retire is near the Chippewa Flowage in northwestern Wisconsin.

Remember this: *the setting for your retirement should enhance your lifestyle.* Consider John and Betty Kittredge, who retired to Chapel Hill, North Carolina; and Henry and Jane Veatch, who chose Bloomington, Indiana. Why did these couples choose university communities for their retirement? Because an academic community supported their values, interests, and lifestyle. "We wanted a temperate climate with fewer people than the New York area has," said Mr. Kittredge. "But what we especially wanted was a place that offered a wide choice of cultural events as well as good shops and restaurants, and a college town was perfect."

Adds Mr. Veatch: "The move to a small, welcoming college town made sense to us. I use the university library all the time, and we attend opera, theater, and concerts."[5]

Retiring to a college town might not appeal to you, but it is important to identify your avocations, whether they be cross-country skiing, gardening, golfing, mountain climbing, scuba diving, snorkeling, snowmobiling, or waterskiing. Then ask yourself: what geographical location would further my interests?

Third, is the cost of living reasonable? Most of us need to cast a watchful eye over our retirement dollars. Therefore it is important to assess the cost of living in various parts of the country.

Housing costs vary enormously, depending upon where you live. A single-family home selling for $59,300 in Louisville, Kentucky, will cost $92,900 in Charlotte, North Carolina, and $269,400 in San Francisco.[6] In addition, it is possible to reduce your state and local taxes by 50 percent by carefully planning where to retire. In New York you will probably pay more than $10,000 in state and local taxes if your income is between $75,000 and $100,000. But if you retire to picturesque Wyoming, your tax bill will be less than $2,000.

Where can you find current information on state and local taxes? *The Statistical Abstract of the United States,* found in most libraries, is a useful resource. If you want to obtain the latest cost-of-living trends, consult the *Consumer Price Index* (CPI), which is published by the U.S. Bureau of Labor Statistics. Or use a very reliable indicator: travel to two or three locations and compare the price of products and services you frequently use.

Fourth, is the area safe from crime? While

258

all parts of the country have crime, it is possible to retire to an area where the chances of being harmed are greatly reduced. When I visited with David Smit, he made special note of how secure he feels in Sun City, Arizona:

> I feel very comfortable when I take walks in the evening. We have volunteers known as the "sheriff's posse" who patrol the streets of our community. And our neighbors keep an eye on our home when we are away. It really is a safe, comfortable, and secure place to live.

It makes sense to check out an area's crime rate before you relocate. Again, a helpful library resource is *The Statistical Abstract of the United States,* which enables you to compare crime rates in various parts of the country. You can also discover the number of law enforcement officers employed per 1,000 population. But remember: the fact that a community has many police officers doesn't mean that it is safe. It might imply that crime is out of control.

Fifth, is the community economically prosperous? You don't want to move to an area in which there is economic decline, especially if you are purchasing a home.

259

What are the signs of a prosperous community? The population should be growing, not declining. The tax base should be expanding so that the community can afford education, safety, and fire protection services. In addition, tax dollars should be allocated to recreation centers, public transportation services, and adult education programming — all interests of retirees. And there should be a low unemployment rate, which signals a healthy, vibrant economy.

To assess the economic strength of a community, visit with a stockbroker, banker, or city manager and determine the local government's bond ratings. A high bond rating means that the community is fiscally sound, while a low one suggests a possibility of default.[7]

Six, is the climate conducive to your lifestyle and your health? Most retirees are drawn to a geographical location because of climate. "I like the change of seasons," said one sixty-six-year-old. "That's why I retired in Grand Rapids, Michigan." Said a sixty-eight-year-old Sioux Falls, South Dakota, man, "I could hardly wait to get away from the blizzards. The day I retired, my car was packed. Two days later I was in sunny New Mexico."

It is particularly important to analyze the climate if you have certain health problems.

If, for example, you have hay fever, arthritis, asthma, heart disease, allergies, bronchitis, pulmonary hypertension, or emphysema, climatic conditions (temperature, altitude, humidity) can *significantly* affect your well-being.

In analyzing climatic conditions, compare city to city, not state to state. The reason for this is that climatic conditions can vary between two communities in the same region of the country. In Miami, the average humidity count is 76.25, while in Orlando it is 72.0. Sixty-six inches of rain falls each year in Tallahassee, while Tampa receives slightly less than forty-three inches. In Arizona and New Mexico there are a variety of climatic conditions depending upon whether you are living in the higher table lands or in the river valleys.[8] Table 16 provides temperature data, humidity and precipitation rates, and *the average number of sunny days per year* for cities in each of the fifty states. Check it out thoroughly before making a move. If you have a medical problem, talk with your physician and learn how temperature and humidity might influence your condition.

Seven, after all the facts have been gathered, where would you REALLY like to live?

If you are thinking about retiring elsewhere, take time to learn everything you can about the community. Go to the local library and ask for a history of the region. Attend a city council meeting and determine the key issues the community is facing. And schedule a visit with a physician, clergyman, banker, or stockbroker. Learn everything you can, so that there will be no surprises if you decide to move.

But after all the information has been gathered, listen to your heart and trust your intuition. That's what Bill and Laura Smithson did, and they have never regretted moving to the Oregon coast:

When I turned fifty-five we started to plan for our retirement. Each summer we visited a different part of the country. Seven years later we settled on two potential locations for our retirement: San Diego, California, and Seaside, Oregon.

We took out a piece of paper and compared the advantages of each. San Diego had the better climate, the better medical care system, and certainly had more cultural events. By any objective criteria, we should have retired in San Diego.

But I love the rugged Oregon coast. I like the people and the slower pace of life. Our heads told us to retire to San Diego. But our hearts told us to go to this little community located on the Oregon coast.

We followed our hearts, and we have never regretted it. This place feels like home. Every morning I walk up a hill overlooking the ocean. From there I can see our community, and even our home. I always conclude: This is the perfect place for our retirement.

Now there is one other point that should be emphasized: Before deciding on a retirement location, check it out during various seasons of the year. The reason? Your impressions may be quite different depending on the month you visit.

To illustrate, let me share an experience my wife and I had as we visited Hilton Head Island, which is located off the South Carolina coast. We left our Minnesota home in a blinding snowstorm. The temperature was -4 degrees, and the streets were covered with ice.

When our plane touched down in Savannah, Georgia, we were greeted by a warm tropical breeze, a bright sun, and 71 degrees of warmth. Ninety minutes later we were on Hilton Head Island, walking underneath palm trees, strolling by the ocean, and eating on the veranda of a charming restaurant. I must tell you: we thought we were in paradise!

A week later we were convinced that we had found the perfect place for our retirement. I went to a real estate company and discovered several lovely town houses in our price range.

That evening, however, my wife suggested that we delay our purchase. "We've only been here a few days," she noted. "Maybe we should return for a longer visit."

Her suggestion made sense and we returned to Hilton Head Island the following August. This time the island was loaded with tourists and traffic. We had difficulty locating an open tennis court, and there was an hour's delay before we could be seated in some of the restaurants. The shops were so crowded with tourists that it took some of the fun out of browsing in the beautiful specialty stores.

In addition, the temperature and humidity were high. Sometimes it was too hot to play golf or even lounge by the swimming pool.

We were now seeing Hilton Head Island in a different light. We came to realize that the island had many advantages over other retirement locations. But there were some problems we had not foreseen.

Now mind you, we are still high on Hilton Head Island as a place to retire. But before making a final decision, we will visit the island one more time. We will schedule our visit during the time of year when the humidity is the

TABLE 16
Where's the Best Retirement Weather for You?

Location	Eleva-tion	Average Temperature (Winter)	(Summer)	Avg. Sunny Days	Avg. Humid-ity	Average Precipitation (Rain)	(Snow)
ALABAMA							
Montgomery	183	55.1	76.0	233	71.8	47.1	0.0
Birmingham	620	51.3	73.3	207	72.7	52.5	Trace
ALASKA							
Juneau	114	25.8	49.1	100	77.2	53.7	150.2
Fairbanks	436	0.7	49.5	161	61.5	8.1	80.9
ARIZONA							
Phoenix	1117	60.5	96.4	289	33.5	10.87	0.0
Yuma	194	61.8	84.6	310	36.5	3.28	0.0
ARKANSAS							
Little Rock	257	41.3	82.1	212	69.3	43.08	4.0
Fayetteville	1270	46.2	72.8	196	70.8	46.43	8.9

TABLE 16 (Continued)

Location	Eleva-tion	Average Temperature (Winter)	(Summer)	Avg. Sunny Days	Avg. Humid-ity	Average Precipitation (Rain)	(Snow)
CALIFORNIA							
Los Angeles	270	60.6	72.5	293	63.3	6.54	0.0
San Francisco	52	52.7	59.6	211	76.0	20.79	Trace
Eureka	43	48.9	55.3	149	77.9	39.7	3.5
COLORADO							
Denver	5280	36.3	63.5	210	55.0	16.87	83.2
Grand Junction	4843	37.7	69.5	237	45.0	7.33	20.7
CONNECTICUT							
Hartford	169	33.7	64.0	165	71.0	64.55	58.2
Stamford	8	37.5	64.8	196	70.5	73.8	24.0
DELAWARE							
Wilmington	74	41.1	76.1	181	69.5	48.13	9.5
FLORIDA							
Tallahassee	55	68.5	77.1	232	76.25	66.06	0.0

TABLE 16 (Continued)

Location	Eleva-tion	Average Temperature (Winter)	Average Temperature (Summer)	Avg. Sunny Days	Avg. Humid-ity	Average Precipitation (Rain)	Average Precipitation (Snow)
FLORIDA (Continued)							
Tampa	19	66.5	79.8	233	75.25	42.18	0.0
Miami	7	72.1	79.7	252	76.25	63.11	0.0
Orlando	108	67.9	80.7	231	72.0	51.35	0.0
GEORGIA							
Atlanta	1010	50.2	71.5	206	70.8	50.61	Trace
Macon	354	55.2	74.7	220	72.5	46.83	0.0
Savannah	46	58.3	75.8	212	73.8	48.57	0.0
HAWAII							
Honolulu	7	72.9	79.6	244	68.8	26.90	0.0
Lihue	103	72.4	78.3	211	77.5	43.54	0.0
Kahului	48	71.9	77.4	250	74.0	15.71	0.0
IDAHO							
Boise	2838	34.5	62.3	216	57.5	11.43	21.4

TABLE 16 (Continued)

Location	Eleva-tion	Average Temperature (Winter)	(Summer)	Avg. Sunny Days	Avg. Humid-ity	Average Precipitation (Rain)	(Snow)
IDAHO (Continued)							
Pocatello	4768	29.5	59.5	209	55.8	10.85	37.4
ILLINOIS							
Springfield	588	35.3	67.8	176	74.3	32.03	26.2
Chicago	607	32.1	65.1	161	69.8	41.19	61.9
INDIANA							
Indianapolis	792	36.4	66.9	159	72.3	40.27	18.1
Fort Wayne	791	33.4	64.2	157	73.8	40.78	28.9
IOWA							
Des Moines	938	29.1	62.3	176	73.5	36.02	36.7
Dubuque	1056	25.9	63.1	167	68.0	39.78	58.4
KANSAS							
Topeka	877	37.7	68.4	180	69.8	31.21	26.1
Wichita	1321	38.9	70.5	194	67.0	23.31	16.7

TABLE 16 (Continued)

Location	Eleva-tion	Average Temperature (Winter)	Average Temperature (Summer)	Avg. Sunny Days	Avg. Humid-ity	Average Precipitation (Rain)	Average Precipitation (Snow)
KENTUCKY							
Louisville	477	42.4	69.5	177	69.0	49.38	10.4
LOUISIANA							
Shreveport	254	54.2	77.4	231	73.3	46.96	Trace
New Orleans	4	59.7	77.5	234	78.8	63.98	0.0
MAINE							
Portland	43	28.6	58.1	178	74.8	48.62	123.7
MARYLAND							
Baltimore	148	41.8	67.7	186	69.0	52.33	13.0
MASSACHUSETTS							
Boston	15	36.5	64.3	175	68.3	53.11	40.7
Worcester	986	30.5	60.5	170	69.0	71.66	88.9
MICHIGAN							
Lansing	841	29.4	60.0	149	74.5	37.38	76.7

TABLE 16 (Continued)

Location	Eleva-tion	Average Temperature (Winter)	Average Temperature (Summer)	Avg. Sunny Days	Avg. Humid-ity	Average Precipitation (Rain)	Average Precipitation (Snow)
MICHIGAN (Continued)							
Sault St. Marie	721	19.8	55.2	142	78.8	35.45	190.5
MINNESOTA							
Duluth	1428	15.2	53.9	165	74.0	39.61	110.2
MISSISSIPPI							
Jackson	310	55.0	77.4	226	76.0	50.03	Trace
Gulfport	15	56.3	80.8	205	69.3	58.58	Trace
MISSOURI							
Kansas City	1014	38.7	70.6	194	66.8	27.75	15.9
St. Louis	535	39.3	69.9	178	74.5	33.74	12.5
MONTANA							
Helena	3828	27.1	55.1	169	57.0	8.22	40.0
Billings	3567	29.3	59.3	187	56.3	18.17	71.5

TABLE 16 (Continued)

Location	Eleva-tion	Average Temperature (Winter)	(Summer)	Avg. Sunny Days	Avg. Humid-ity	Average Precipitation (Rain)	(Snow)
NEBRASKA							
Omaha	977	32.6	66.3	185	71.8	35.56	27.1
Grand Island	1841	32.6	66.7	195	63.3	25.74	36.4
NEVADA							
Las Vegas	2162	52.4	80.1	297	28.8	4.85	0.4
Reno	4404	37.0	60.8	245	48.3	5.52	Trace
NEW HAMPSHIRE							
Concord	342	27.7	58.8	167	77.0	42.07	100.3
Mt. Washington	6262	10.8	40.8	108	84.0	121.61	449.3
NEW JERSEY							
Lakewood	64	34.7	66.7	175	74.8	45.06	10.8
Trenton	56	40.2	66.8	193	70.6	47.13	17.2
NEW MEXICO							
Albuquerque	5311	44.0	69.4	271	42.3	10.11	6.4

TABLE 16 (Continued)

Location	Eleva-tion	Average Temperature (Winter)	Average Temperature (Summer)	Avg. Sunny Days	Avg. Humid-ity	Average Precipitation (Rain)	Average Precipitation (Snow)
NEW MEXICO (Continued)							
Roswell	3612	48.1	71.8	280	48.8	16.50	9.9
NEW YORK							
Albany	275	30.0	61.3	145	70.3	47.18	102.3
Buffalo	705	30.9	61.6	111	75.5	41.63	120.1
New York City	132	39.9	67.8	232	67.8	67.03	22.9
NO. CAROLINA							
Asheville	2140	45.5	66.1	207	78.8	48.02	15.4
Charlotte	736	48.1	70.3	210	69.0	44.23	4.2
Greensboro	900	41.7	75.1	207	72.5	41.36	8.6
NO. DAKOTA							
Bismarck	1647	19.9	58.8	171	67.0	15.16	45.6
Fargo	896	17.4	60.8	177	69.5	17.78	61.6

TABLE 16 (*Continued*)

Location	Eleva-tion	Average Temperature (Winter)	Average Temperature (Summer)	Avg. Sunny Days	Avg. Humid-ity	Average Precipitation (Rain)	Average Precipitation (Snow)
OHIO							
Akron	1208	33.8	62.9	135	73.3	43.88	43.7
Toledo	669	32.7	62.3	150	71.0	38.41	35.7
Cincinnati	869	38.2	66.3	158	71.8	45.30	21.4
OKLAHOMA							
Oklahoma City	1285	45.2	74.0	226	65.5	27.63	14.6
Tulsa	650	44.9	74.3	219	67.5	35.54	13.0
OREGON							
Pendleton	1482	39.4	65.4	193	54.0	11.65	23.6
Portland	21	44.4	63.6	156	61.0	38.82	6.5
PENNSYLVANIA							
Harrisburg	338	38.8	66.8	191	68.0	59.27	33.4
Philadelphia	5	40.2	67.9	174	70.5	49.63	12.1
Pittsburgh	747	38.5	69.0	169	73.6	41.16	27.3

TABLE 16 (Continued)

Location	Eleva-tion	Average Temperature (Winter)	(Summer)	Avg. Sunny Days	Avg. Humid-ity	Average Precipitation (Rain)	(Snow)
RHODE ISLAND							
Providence	51	35.8	63.4	179	71.0	65.06	30.4
SO. CAROLINA							
Charleston	40	56.2	74.7	226	75.5	42.86	0.0
Columbia	213	53.1	73.1	216	75.5	55.51	0.0
SO. DAKOTA							
Aberdeen	1296	21.8	62.3	178	71.0	20.39	42.1
Sioux Falls	1418	23.7	61.7	181	71.3	26.43	27.1
TENNESSEE							
Nashville	590	47.4	71.8	198	71.8	54.41	2.5
Memphis	258	48.0	73.9	211	65.0	58.95	0.4
TEXAS							
Amarillo	3657	39.9	76.0	225	67.5	20.50	2.5
Dallas	481	54.1	79.4	233	63.5	24.36	0.9

TABLE 16 (*Continued*)

Location	Eleva-tion	Average Temperature (Winter)	Average Temperature (Summer)	Avg. Sunny Days	Avg. Humid-ity	Average Precipitation (Rain)	Average Precipitation (Snow)
TEXAS (*Continued*)							
Houston	96	59.0	77.4	199	78.3	50.80	Trace
UTAH							
Salt Lake City	4220	37.5	67.2	211	51.3	15.74	76.8
St. George	2880	34.6	73.6	258	61.0	7.65	0.0
VERMONT							
Burlington	332	25.5	59.2	151	73.0	38.10	121.6
VIRGINIA							
Richmond	164	45.9	66.8	188	73.5	59.34	14.3
Roanoke	1149	44.4	66.2	197	67.8	51.64	12.8
Norfolk	24	47.1	72.3	202	74.3	46.23	1.8
WASHINGTON							
Seattle	400	42.9	69.4	151	72.5	48.36	22.2
Spokane	2356	33.4	60.1	187	61.8	13.53	31.3

TABLE 16 (Continued)

Location	Eleva-tion	Average Temperature (Winter)	(Summer)	Avg. Sunny Days	Avg. Humid-ity	Average Precipitation (Rain)	(Snow)
W. VIRGINIA							
Charleston	939	42.9	66.1	128	71.3	51.15	26.5
Huntington	827	41.9	65.9	131	74.5	46.72	21.7
WISCONSIN							
Madison	858	25.2	60.8	163	75.5	30.96	50.2
Milwaukee	672	26.5	60.6	163	74.8	36.68	50.2
Green Bay	682	20.2	61.0	161	71.5	25.27	42.8
WYOMING							
Cheyenne	6126	31.8	74.6	204	53.3	15.04	48.6

Source: "Finding the Right Place for Your Retirement," © 1991 Retirement Living Publishing Co., Inc. Reproduced with permission.

highest and the tourist population is the greatest. If we like it then, our retirement home will have been found.

Retirement Hotspots: Twelve Gorgeous Locations

Here are some of the very best retirement locations in the United States. Each has been selected on the basis of quality-of-life indicators such as climate, medical service, recreational possibilities, restaurants, shops, and safety. None is perfect and all have limitations. Because of space limitations, I have left out many regions of the country that might appeal to you. Nevertheless, here are some of the very best retirement communities, whose geographical setting and charm may captivate you.[9]

RETIREMENT ON THE EAST COAST

Amherst, Massachusetts. If one of your goals in retirement is to learn new things, explore new concepts, and be on the cutting edge of new knowledge, this community might be for you. Amherst, with a population of 36,000, is the home of Amherst College, Hampshire College, and the University of Massachusetts. Mount Holyoke College and Smith College are nearby.[10]

Amherst is located 87 miles west of Boston

and 157 miles northeast of New York City. It combines the tradition of a small New England town with the cultural vitality of a major educational center. Set among fertile farmlands and wooded hills, the community enjoys a cosmopolitan ambience seldom found so close to the peace and beauty of nature.

Amherst has an attractive downtown shopping area where customers can avail themselves of a full range of retail services ranging from handicraft and specialty shops to food markets and deli stores. These shops have garnered a reputation for quality and service at affordable prices. The many restaurants in the community provide a wide range of choices from traditional Yankee dining to international cuisine.

Amherst's location in the heart of the Pioneer Valley makes it an ideal setting for recreational activities. The community is surrounded by hills and rivers and within its borders has nineteen conservation areas comprising over 700 acres of land with trails designated for hiking and cross-country skiing enthusiasts. Ice skating, golfing, horseback riding, and fishing are also popular activities for citizens of Amherst.

Retiring in a college community such as Amherst has many advantages over other locations. There are sporting events and theatrical activities that can keep you busy every night of the year. There are discos if you like to dance and inexpensive restaurants if you like to dine. There are seminars, lectures, and college courses in which to enroll. And college students and retirees often form meaningful friendships. "When the Connecticut River flooded in 1986," says Lynn Hoffman, sixty-three, "the university kids helped the senior citizens move into dorms. It illustrated the real alliance here between younger people and older people."[11]

Amherst is particularly mindful of the needs of retirees. A cable television channel lists social activities for seniors, and a free van service transports retirees to their personal appointments. For those with poor sight, there are over 1,850 large-print books in the 90,000-volume public library.

One of the appealing characteristics of Amherst is that it has a crime rate about half that found in a typical metropolitan city.

What are the disadvantages? Amherst won't provide you an average winter temperature of 68.5, as does Tallahassee, Florida. You won't have 289 sunny days per year, as does Phoenix, Arizona. And you have to be prepared to foot some pretty high housing bills: the median house price is now over $190,000. To make matters worse, apartments are hard to come by. If you are fortunate enough to find one, the cost per month of a two-bedroom apartment can be over $500.

Nevertheless, if you like the idea of being but a short drive from concerts at Tanglewood and dance performances at Jacob's Pillow, and if you would like to further your education by taking college classes — Amherst might be the spot for you.

Chapel Hill, North Carolina. Chapel Hill is a *marvelous* college town. It has more retired people in it — approximately eleven thousand — than any other college community. "If the students weren't here, every other head would have gray hair," states Jerry Passmore, director of the county's Department of Aging.[12] The University of North Carolina is located in Chapel Hill. Duke is but a short ten-minute drive away in Durham, and North Carolina State, in Raleigh, is only thirty minutes away.

Retirees in Chapel Hill enjoy a multitude of cultural events without the hectic pace and the harsh winters (February temperature averages 42 degrees). "Between UNC and Duke, you can go to concerts three or four times a week, and most are free," states Edwin Jackson, seventy-seven, a former Connecticut librarian.[13]

If you like sports, you will find few settings that will provide as many opportunities. The

280

athletic programs at North Carolina and Duke Universities are among the best in the nation. If you like golf, you will be in paradise, for North Carolina has over four hundred golf courses, including sixty in the Pinehurst area, which is a short ninety-minute drive south of Chapel Hill. If you like mountain climbing, the Blue Ridge Mountains are but three hours away.

But one of the best features of the Chapel Hill area is its medical care system. In Durham, North Carolina, there are seven doctors per thousand residents, which is nearly quadruple the national average. One of the largest cardiac rehabilitation programs in the United States can be found at Duke University, where doctors perform fifteen hundred open-heart operations a year.[14]

Disadvantages? The summers can be hot and sticky. The average temperature is 77 degrees and the average humidity is 71 percent. But when tulips and daffodils push up, you can't ask for a better climate in which to retire.

There is one other location in North Carolina that should be mentioned, and that is a little community (population 4,000) called Tryon. It is located in the western end of the state in the Appalachian highlands. It's off the beaten track, but it isn't in the sticks. About half of its residents are retired, with individuals migrating to Tryon from all parts of the United States and the world.

The town is situated in a marvelous climate. It is sheltered from the cold by mountains to the north and the east. But the warm air from the south bathes the community throughout the year. And if you like to garden, you can be tending your flowers and vegetables during a two-hundred-day growing season.

One of the advantages of Tryon over other communities is that you can still find affordable housing. Small houses sell for $40,000, although if you want a marvelous view of the mountains, you probably will pay $200,000 or more. The average home sells for $80,000.[15]

Jekyll Island, Georgia. Would you have an interest in retiring to a small community where you can get to know your neighbors? If so, consider Jekyll Island, which is a community of about twelve hundred people off the Georgia coast. It is one of three state-owned islands known as the "Golden Isles."

Because of its beauty, the island is designated as a public park. A modest house will cost $80,000, although you will have to sign a lease of ninety-nine years for the land under the home. If you want to test out the area, you can rent a $400 home (per month) in off-season.

The medical services in nearby Brunswick

282

are excellent. The weather is moderate. The cost of living throughout Georgia is 10 percent below national norms.[16]

RETIREMENT ON THE WEST COAST

The Oregon coast. Shortly before writing this section, I traveled to Cannon City, Oregon, for I had heard many wonderful things about retirement on the West Coast. I want to tell you, it lives up to its billing. The scenery is gorgeous. The people are friendly. And it represents one of the most economical areas in the country in which to live.

Peter A. Dickinson, an authority on retirement havens, had this to say about the rustic Oregon coast: "The four hundred-mile drive along Oregon's coast is the most scenic and dramatic I've ever seen. It's wilder than Cornwall and more picturesque than Maine — rolling sand dunes, craggy cliffs, white-water rapids, jutting headlands, deep inlets, proud meadows, magnificent forests, exotic wildflowers, and leaping waterfalls — one of the scenic wonders of the world."[17]

The coastal towns are small and charming. The best way to see them is to head to Astoria, Oregon, located in the northwestern corner of the state, and make a picturesque journey south on Highway 101. You will go through such communities as Seaside, Rockaway

283

Beach, Tillamook, Lincoln City, Florence, Reedsport, Nesika Beach, and Pistol River.

Frankly, I could retire in any of these communities, for each has its own charm and its own history. Gold Beach, for example, has its name derived from a prospector who found a small quantity of gold mixed in with the beach sands.

If a community of five hundred to three thousand residents is too small for you, consider Coos Bay-North Bend, sister cities located in the southern part of the state, which have a combined population of 25,000. These two communities offer all the services you need, since they are the trade center for a 150-mile region.[18]

In many coastal communities it is possible to rent a one-bedroom apartment for as little as $150 a month, while two-bedroom townhomes with free TV and cable TV cost $250. If you want to splurge, you can find a three-bedroom house to rent for $250 per month, and many of the homes for sale are listed for under $60,000.

What type of retiree would enjoy living on the Oregon coast? One who loves the ocean, appreciates cool summer breezes, and enjoys walks and drives through lush mountain parks. And if you get a kick out of beachcombing, you couldn't find a better place to live, since the ocean's currents bring in all types of treasures, some from as far away as Japan.[19]

For those who like to fish, the Oregon waters provide endless possibilities. Not only can you go deep-sea fishing, but there are many picturesque mountain streams that are home to rainbow and brown trout. And some of the best salmon fishing in the world comes out of the Pacific northwest. For further information, call the visitors service center at 1-503-378-4423.

San Diego, California. Twenty-three years ago, my wife and I were married in this lovely city, so I must admit to a strong, positive orientation towards it! For me, San Diego is one of the most beautiful cities in the world. And I can think of few places that I would recommend more highly for your retirement.

Why do retirees flock to this area? For one thing, you couldn't ask for a better climate. On average, there are only three 90-degree days and no freezing days. Storms are infrequent, although a heavy fog often rolls in at night. According to the National Weather Bureau, the weather conditions are the best of any city in the continental United States.

The city is filled with marvelous restaurants and picturesque parks. It is possible to garden year-round. The fishing piers are free, and you do not need a license to embark on your search for a trophy catch. A senior citizen identification card gets you discounts for the San Diego Symphony, the zoo, theaters, movies, beauty shops, restaurants, sporting events, and much, much more.[20]

One of the nicest features of San Diego is its public transportation system, which can connect you to tourist attractions, city parks, and major shopping centers. An added benefit for considering San Diego is that there are more than one hundred senior citizen organizations, which have a membership of 100,000 people.[21] These organizations offer recreational and educational programming as well as services to help meet your medical needs.

The downside to living in this paradise? It costs a bundle — more than double that of most retirement places around the country. Houses rarely sell for under $100,000, and rental apartments start around $500 per month. One way to save, however, is by renting a mobile home, where monthly costs are approximately $350 per month.[22]

If the high cost of home ownership in San Diego is prohibitive, consider El Cajon, Alpine, Lakeside, Ramona, and Julian, which are suburbs of San Diego. Land in El Cajon (population 85,000) is cheaper, and the lots are considerably larger than in San Diego. Escondido, thirty miles northeast of San Diego (population 79,000) has a major hospital, an outstanding senior service center, a community college, and an adult education program that is free of charge for anyone sixty years of age or over. Since rents average $100 less a month than in San Diego, retirees are increasingly gravitating to this thriving city.

Santa Cruz, California. Santa Cruz is located near some of the most beautiful real estate on the North American continent. Monterey, Carmel, and Pebble Beach are less than a hour's drive south, while San Francisco lies seventy-four miles to the north. Santa Cruz County features a magnificent blend of redwood forests and Pacific coastline.

The county has rebounded impressively after incurring significant damages in the October 17, 1989, earthquake, and it continues to be a major tourist attraction because of its beautiful beaches and the Santa Cruz beach boardwalk.

Santa Cruz has more than one hundred churches, fourteen libraries, twenty parks, and three golf courses. Housing prices in Santa Cruz County have escalated rapidly, as the area has appeal for the many people employed in the nearby Silicon Valley and those who work at the University of California at Santa Cruz. The median cost of a house is approximately $250,000. Housing expenses are highest in Scotts Valley, Aptos, West Lake, and some areas of Capitola, the city of Santa Cruz, and some of the more exquisite beach communities on Monterey Bay. If you would prefer a smaller community but with the amenities of living near Santa Cruz, consider Moss Landing and Castroville. Or you might wish to find a mountain hideaway where housing costs range from economical to expensive, dependent upon location.

If one of your main criteria in selecting a retirement community is a mild climate, you would be hard-pressed to find a better location. States John Howell, author of *Retirement Choices:* "The exceptionally mild climate and relatively low cost of living are two commonly given reasons for going to Santa Cruz. Like many beach areas on the Pacific Ocean, summer days are often overcast until afternoon, thus shielding the beaches from the onslaught of the sun. Summer rain is all but unknown. Then, from September on, the sun makes its presence known, beaming warmth to keep the chill off the air, making Santa Cruz a truly twelve-month resort."[23]

While the costs of housing are relatively inexpensive, I don't want to mislead you: Santa Cruz is located next to the Monterey/ Carmel area and San Francisco, which are two of the most expensive places in the nation in which to live. But if you look carefully, you can rent older homes and small beach apartments, sometimes for as little as $500 per month.[24]

RETIREMENT IN THE SOUTHWEST

Bisbee, Arizona. When a good friend told me that he was planning to retire in Bisbee, Arizona, I had to confess that I had never heard of the town. The next day he showed me a picture, and I was immediately struck by the beauty of this Arizona community.

Bisbee is located a few miles north of the Mexican border, tucked into a canyon in the southeastern part of Arizona. When you enter Bisbee, note winding, narrow streets and Victorian architecture dating to the 1890s.[25]

A walk through downtown Bisbee is like a return to a kinder, gentler era. As author John Howell notes: "The pace is slow and quiet. Since the town is off the standard tourist track, relatively few visitors disturb the ghosts of yesteryear. Night sounds are muted and after midnight the streets are all but deserted. Still there are several excellent restaurants, set in authentic period decor."[26]

At one time Bisbee, Arizona, was a thriving, bustling mining city of more than twenty thousand people. It had first-class hotels and was filled with prosperous commercial enterprises.

But in 1975 it came into hard times when a large mining company ceased to operate. Unemployed miners left their homes, businesses closed, and Bisbee resembled a ghost town. Houses could be purchased for under $500.

Bisbee's fortunes changed in the 1960s and 1970s when it was discovered by artists, intellectuals, and adventurers. In the 1980s retirees who had grown weary of congestion, smog, and crime in northern cities migrated south. Many could scarcely believe their good fortune in finding Bisbee, a relatively unknown gem located but a short drive from the Pedregosa Mountains and the Coronado National Forest.

Today there are 8,500 people living in Bisbee, including a large population of retired adults. The chief drawing cards are the beautiful climate and affordable housing. But retirees also point to the fact that Bisbee is a lively cultural center, featuring classical concerts at the Bisbee Women's Club (1902), gallery openings featuring local and southwest artists, dinner theater, and even Old West melodramas.

Not surprising, a host of national publications have consistently rated Bisbee high on their list of favorite retirement communities. Crystal clear air, golfing, low crime rates, and active senior organizations are but a few of the benefits of this charming community.[27]

Prescott, Arizona. Peter Dickinson, author of *Sunbelt Retirement,* has studied over eight hundred potential retirement spots and has chosen Prescott, Arizona, for his retirement home. "I paid $117,000 for a three-bedroom house on a third of an acre with a spectacular view of the Thumb Butter Ridge of the Bradshaw Mountains," he says. "The house and land are comparable to what I own in Larchmont, New York, worth $500,000. My property taxes will be $900 a year versus $6,000 in New York. I can live on 50% to 70% of my New York income and have the same lifestyle. I just have to give up the New York ballet. But Phoenix is only 102 miles away, and it is home to Ballet Arizona, an up-and-coming troupe."[28]

While low-cost housing represents an important advantage of Prescott, most retirees point to the clean and healthful living conditions as the prime reason that they relocated here. The elevation is 5,354 feet, and if you have respiratory problems, the climate may be helpful. Summer temperatures average 70 degrees, with a maximum of 87 degrees in the afternoon. In winter, the average maximum temperature is 58.6 degrees and the average minimum is 32 degrees. The humidity is usually around 45 percent *year round,* which makes life comfortable.

Prescott has affordable housing in the average price range of $60,000 and up, including patio homes, town houses, condominiums, mobile homes, and apartments. Rentals are available in houses and apartments ranging from $175-$350 for a one-bedroom apartment to $575-$850 for a three-bedroom house.

A third of Prescott's population is retired, and a third is made up of students attending three colleges — Yavapai, Prescott, and Embry-Riddle. Retirees can enroll in courses at Yavapai for $21 to $41, while full-time students are charged $295 a semester.

Albuquerque, New Mexico. Approximately 500,000 people reside in the Albuquerque metropolitan area, which includes the city of Albuquerque, the surrounding areas of Bernalillo County and the communities of Rio Rancho and Corrales in neighboring Sandoval County. Albuquerque is by far the largest city in New Mexico, since almost one-third of the state's residents live in the Albuquerque metropolitan area.

Albuquerque's elevation ranges from 4,900 to nearly 6,500 feet above sea level. The Sandia Mountains, which rise five thousand feet above the east side of the city, have a major effect on the city's climate, keeping most of the extremely cold Arctic air masses from entering the community.

Snowfall ranges from less than ten inches per year near the Rio Grande to more than one hundred inches on the crest of Sandia Peak. Snowfall in the city is usually light and quickly melts. As one local puts it: "Most of the snow falls in the mountains where it belongs."

Because Albuquerque is well watered from abundant underground aquifers, beautiful vegetable and flower gardens can be found throughout the city. In fact, the areas adjacent to the Rio Grande have been farmed for hundreds of years by the Pueblo Indians and Spanish settlers.

If you have a bent for history, you will enjoy the state of New Mexico. Just forty-nine miles northeast of Albuquerque is Santa Fe, which is the oldest capital city in the United States and was discovered in 1610 by Pedro de Peralta. In Santa Fe you can see the oldest private house in the United States as well as the oldest public building in the country, the Palace of the Governors.[29]

If you are a ski enthusiast, Albuquerque will offer you eleven facilities. Sandia Peak, located fifteen miles northwest of Albuquerque, has lifts that soar over ten thousand feet. If you don't ski but like to fish and hunt, streams and woods are but a few miles from your door.

The air is dry in Albuquerque, and the temperatures are mild. Seldom will you experience a 100-degree day, and only on rare occasions will temperatures plummet to zero. In addition, residents enjoy over 270 sunshine-filled days each year.

The average cost of a single-family home is just under $97,000, although new and older homes can be bought less expensively. The average rent for a one-bedroom apartment is $350 a month; $450 for an apartment with two bedrooms.

RETIREMENT IN THE SOUTHEAST

Sarasota, Florida. The retirement capital of America is Sarasota, Florida, on the west coast. One-third of the population of Sarasota (244,364) is made up of individuals sixty-five and older, many of whom have migrated to Florida from northeastern cities.

Retirees rave about this part of the world, and for good reason. Beautiful golf courses, tennis, and boating facilities can be found everywhere. The beaches are wonderful — particularly Lido Beach, which is reported to have the whitest, finest sand in all of Florida. And the temperature averages 62 degrees in the winter and 86 degrees in the summer.[30]

Residents take great pride in this city. But

what sets it off from other retirement cities in Florida is the cultural events. "Art and theater lovers, in fact, have nearly as much to choose from here as they do in Baltimore, more than three times the size," state authors Richard Eisenberg and Debra Englander.[31]

There are numerous opportunities to study and to be challenged by new ideas. At the Longboat Key adult education center you can enroll in courses on physical fitness, religion, and architecture. The Sarasota Institute of Lifetime Learning presents programs on literature, politics, religion, and history. The cost is reasonable: for only $20 you can attend an unlimited number of seminars.[32]

For those who love major league baseball, springtime in Sarasota is hard to beat. The Chicago White Sox train in a lovely new 7,800-seat stadium in Sarasota, and the Pittsburgh Pirates can be seen at McKechnie Field in Bradenton, which is but a short fifteen-minute drive north.

Ocean Springs, Mississippi. Ocean Springs (population 17,000) is located on the Gulf coast and is affectionately known to residents as "America's Riviera." Like Sarasota, tropical sunshine and cooling breezes will give you an enjoyable year-round climate.

In the nineteenth century Ocean Springs was a health resort frequented by tourists who drank from the area's health-giving springs. The streets are lined with pecan and moss oaks, even as they were generations ago. And as you walk through the community, you will see century-old homes neatly tended to by their owners.

It is possible to purchase a lot for your retirement dream home for only $7,500. Construction costs are a modest $35 to $40 a square foot. There is also low-cost senior housing, notably Villa Maria Apartments, which were built by the Catholic Charities Housing Association of Biloxi.[33]

Mobile, Alabama. Mobile, Alabama (population 210,000), is a gardener's delight. If you like the charm of a city filled with magnolia blooms and a gorgeous climate (average minimum temperature in January is 43.2 degrees), Alabama's Mobile Bay might be for you.

Mobile is famous for its southern charm. But until recently it has not been considered a major player in retirement housing. That is fast changing, however, not only because Mobile is blessed with a wonderful climate, but because of agencies that creatively meet the needs of older adults. Through these agencies retirees are offered a multitude of services, including transportation, legal counsel, home health care, and hot-meal programs. In addition, the Senior Citizen Service, a private, voluntary organization, has had success in finding senior citizens jobs in local department stores.

Mobile has seven general hospitals, a private mental health hospital, a public mental health center, and a diagnostic clinic and rehabilitation center. Some 495 doctors reside in the area, providing you with a wide range of medical specialties.[34]

Who should consider Mobile, Alabama, as a retirement location? Those who want to be associated with a thriving, economically viable, middle-size American city. In Mobile you have the advantages of big-city life. You can attend concerts, go to plays, and manage your money in sophisticated financial establishments. But you are only minutes away from small coastal communities where the cost of living is less and the pace of life is slow.

Thirst for Adventure? Retire Abroad!

Some people reading the above paragraphs might say: "Well, those places sound interesting. But I want to find a more exotic place to live."

If so, consider living in a foreign country. Why? Housing expenses are affordable. Domestic help is reliable. American dollars are valued. And there is an opportunity to make new friends with a people of a different culture.

One of the best foreign places in which to retire is Mexico.[35] The reasons? English is widely spoken. Violent crime and drugs are less of a problem than in the United States. Consumer products ranging from cereal to car parts are readily available in most metropolitan areas. United States newspapers can reach you the same day they are published, and cable television brings you a full range of U.S. programming.

You can live comfortably in Mexico on $1,500 a month. If you are willing to live in smaller towns, such as Zacatecas and Oaxaca, it is possible to purchase an attractive home for $30,000 that would fetch over $200,000 in a modest Los Angeles suburb.

Nevertheless, housing costs are on the rise. In the 1980s you could have purchased a home in Cuernavaca, near Mexico City, for $40,000. Today the same home sells for $100,000.

There are of course, inconveniences in living in a foreign country. Mail service in Mexico is slow. The tap water isn't always the best. A trip to the supermarket might cost you 30 percent more than what you would pay in a United States store. And if you don't like the local food, your restaurant choices are limited.

Nevertheless, many retirees are sold on Mexico as their retirement haven. Guadalajara, for example, is the home to some 30,000 foreign retirees, primarily individuals from the United States and Canada. There are bridge clubs, library lending services, and outstanding restaurants. Domestic help, including maids and cooks, costs about $5 per day.

If the idea of living in a new culture sounds intriguing but you are worried about the cost, may I suggest that you take a close look at Costa Rica, Greece, Ireland, Portugal, and Spain. An annual income of $5,000 to $20,000 can provide you with an *outstanding* retirement in most of these locations. In Spain, for example, where 6,400 Americans are now retired, it is possible to live in Costa Del Sol (Sun Coast), which overlooks the blue Mediterranean waters, for $12,000-$16,000 per year, which includes the cost of domestic help.[36]

If retiring in a foreign country has appeal, heed the following suggestions offered by Jane Parker, a foreign-travel advisor.[37]

First, retire in an area that has a sound health care system. The community should have several English-speaking, board-certified physicians. In addition, there should be a well-equipped hospital with an intensive-care unit. The hospital should have an emergency room, and it should be staffed with a physician twenty-four hours a day.

How do you locate a community with a good health care system? Talk to other Americans, preferably those who have lived in the country for several years. Visit a local hospital and ask to see a list of physicians and their specialties. Inquire how patients pay for their medical bills. And contact your insurer and determine how you would be reimbursed in the event of a medical emergency.

Second, check out the climate at various times during the year. You couldn't find a more beautiful place to retire than northern Italy. But the icy winds that cut across Lake Como in the winter are some of the coldest you will ever experience. In short, a beautiful summer climate doesn't necessarily mean a worry-free winter.

Third, ask a travel bureau whether they offer trips for retirees. Some travel companies sponsor trips designed for older adults. For example, a company called Retirement in Mexico (RIM), conducts thirteen-day tours from Mexico City to various communities, including Guanajuato, San Miguel de Allende, Morelia, Guadalajara, and the Lake Chapala area. Seminars lasting four hours are held in Mexico City and Guadalajara. The manager of Barvi Tours of Los Angeles, which represents RIM, states that the emphasis is on showing Americans what it is like to retire in Mexico. "We take people to the bank to show them the way to make investments, we take them to the hospital, we take them to the American societies."[38] In Mexico City, for further information contact Barvi Tours, 11568 Gateway Blvd., Los Angeles, CA 90064 or call 800-824-7102.

Fourth, select a community that is close to a major airport so that you can travel without hassle. New Zealand and Australia are marvelous countries in which to retire, but transportation costs to the United States will be significant. On the other hand, if you retire in Caribbean countries, you are usually but an hour or two away from Miami. Once at the Miami International Airport, you will have little difficulty in making connections to most United States cities.

Fifth, know what you want to do in retirement. If you like to swim, communities along the Caribbean sea are hard to beat. If you like classical music, you will be in heaven in Vienna. And if you are a college professor, think about the great reference libraries in Germany. Not only are the libraries accessible, but you will be in close proximity to the original documents.

Sixth, consider becoming a permanent resident. Residents often have tax advantages, and there are fewer hassles with visas and other paperwork. Your foreign tax bill might be diminished. And the Social Security Administration will mail your check to you — as it does to 350,000 individuals who live outside the United States.

Finally, and perhaps most important, determine whether the country welcomes Americans. The last thing you need in retirement is to worry about your security. Nor do you wish to fret over the stability of a government or whether the currency will be devalued.

How do you assess a country's attitudes toward Americans? Inquire at the American embassy. Talk with community leaders. And interview Americans living in the country. You will quickly discover whether you will be considered a friend or tolerated as a tourist.[39]

In summary, never select a retirement location in haste. Visit during different times of the year. Talk to retirees who have migrated from other areas of the country. Check out the services in the community, particularly the health care system. Examine the tax rates and assess the community's economic viability.

Then trust your intuition. If a smile comes to your face whenever you think about your retirement Eden, pack your bags and get ready for one of the best periods of life.

PART III
HEALTH WISDOM

Strategies for Long Living

The purpose of this section is to help you stay in top mental and physical condition throughout your retirement years.

Chapter 8, Retirement Blues: Stop Worrying and Start Living, takes aim at one of the myths associated with retirement, which is the notion that your leisure years will be all joy and no worry. But as most attest, retirement is not always glamorous. There are anxieties about the present and concerns about the future. And the prospect of a worry-free retirement often recedes as personal issues cloud our lives.

Chapter 8 will help you evaluate your outlook on life. If discouraged, you will learn how to reverse the blues. And if depressed, you will discover tools that will enable you to recapture a positive spirit.

Chapter 9, Ten Tips for a Healthy Retirement, focuses on strategies that will enhance your physical well-being. We will discover the powerful effect that exercise and nutrition have on health. And we will discover how to stay in shape, regardless of age.

This section concludes by taking a fresh look at health and long-term-care (nursing home) insurance. With the costs of health care skyrocketing, you don't want to be without adequate protection. Chapter 10, Health Costs: Protecting Yourself from Financial Ruin, will help you evaluate your insurance needs and will provide practical advice on how to obtain the best insurance coverage at the lowest possible cost.

CHAPTER EIGHT

Retirement Blues: Stop Worrying and Start Living

I really looked forward to retirement. But I have had one bad thing happen after another. How do you stay hopeful, when you feel sad?
Alma Barkowsky, sixty-two

I want to be candid with you: when I first started this book, I had no intentions of writing about the dark side of retirement. After all, since retirement is supposed to be the best time of life, why focus on those who are unhappy?

But as I visited older adults, it became clear that many were not content. Some had financial troubles. Others were worried about health. And some had legitimate concerns about children and grandchildren.

I do not want to minimize these issues. But if your life is clouded with worry, read this chapter carefully. For no matter how discouraged you may feel, there are things to do *right now* that will put a smile on your face and a new bounce in your step.

How do you reverse the blues? How do you stay mentally healthy? Before examining specific strategies, let's consider one of the biggest myths surrounding retirement, which is the notion that your "golden years" should be worry free.

Surprise! Retirement Can Be Stressful!

For a moment, imagine you are an energetic sixty-five-year-old person. You had a successful career. You have few financial concerns. And you are in love with your spouse.

Sounds good? But suppose four months into your retirement you don't feel particularly good. Your spouse gets on your nerves. You can't break your handicap in golf. And the winter months are fast approaching — with no golf, few friends, and little to do.

One evening you feel emotionally overwhelmed. You miss your colleagues. You miss the daily routines that provided a comfortable rhythm to life. Worse yet, you can't seem to identify anything that provides the same joy as your former job.

If this description sounds familiar, you are not alone. The transition into retirement *is* stressful. In fact, according to Dr. Thomas Holmes, professor of psychiatry at the University of Washington, retirement ranks *tenth* in importance in terms of forty-three stressful events that happen in life (behind death of a spouse, divorce, marital separation, a jail term, the death of a close family member, personal injury or illness, marriage, fired at work, marital reconciliation).[1]

What makes the transition into retirement taxing? Often stress is created by having unrealistic expectations. For example, on my desk I have a number of travel brochures designed for retired adults who want to see the world. One brochure shows an energetic, suntanned sixty-year-old playing golf at a prestigious country club. Then there is the picture of a beautiful, mature woman being courted by a handsome silver-haired man seated in an expensive restaurant. Finally, there is a snapshot of a retired couple on a Cayman Island beach, enjoying their favorite drink, serenaded by local musicians.

Such pictures are delightful to behold, and if you are like me, your first impulse might be to call a travel agent and book the first flight south!

But in truth, most of us retire on modest budgets. We play golf on public links, not at the country club. We have aches and pains and are rarely courted by handsome suitors! And a trip on a luxury cruise might be a once-in-a-lifetime event, rather than a routine winter activity.

In reality, most people have concerns as they plan for retirement. And once retired, they often experience disappointments, especially if expectations are not realized.

Now, the question is, How do you keep negative thoughts under control? And how do you keep your expectations reasonable, so that you don't have a pile-up of disappointing experiences?

Here are six strategies that can restore a positive spirit. No strategy by itself will produce contentment. But these tools will resolve problems that threaten peace of mind. And they will keep life moving in a forward, positive direction.

Strategy One: Stay Positive! If there is one thing that gerontologists are agreed upon, it is this: A *positive mental attitude* can do wonders in ensuring that your retirement years are lived to their fullest. But a negative outlook will greatly diminish your happiness.

Are you optimistic about life? Are your attitudes conducive to a successful retirement?

The following quiz will help you answer these questions. Read each of the following twenty-eight statements. Circle the number that best represents your point of view. Be honest, but don't agonize over any statement.

308

TABLE 17
A Self-Inventory

Unlike Me Like Me	Self
1 2 3 4 5 6 7 8 9 10	1. I have a strong and positive self-image.
1 2 3 4 5 6 7 8 9 10	2. I am satisfied and at ease with my physical appearance.
1 2 3 4 5 6 7 8 9 10	3. I am satisfied with my emotional health.
1 2 3 4 5 6 7 8 9 10	4. I usually feel happy and satisfied with life.
	Spirituality
1 2 3 4 5 6 7 8 9 10	5. I have a spiritual side of life and I am satisfied with it.
	Health
1 2 3 4 5 6 7 8 9 10	6. I am in good physical health for my age.
1 2 3 4 5 6 7 8 9 10	7. I manage stress well.
1 2 3 4 5 6 7 8 9 10	8. I eat nutritious meals.
1 2 3 4 5 6 7 8 9 10	9. I exercise for mobility and flexibility as well as good cardiovascular health.

TABLE 17 (*Continued*)

Unlike Me *Like Me*	*Relationships*
1 2 3 4 5 6 7 8 9 10	10. I understand my feelings and I'm at ease in communicating them to others.
1 2 3 4 5 6 7 8 9 10	11. There is stability and strength in my interpersonal relationships.
1 2 3 4 5 6 7 8 9 10	12. I am able to communicate openly and effectively with partner and/or family about money.
1 2 3 4 5 6 7 8 9 10	13. I have friends who give me emotional support.
1 2 3 4 5 6 7 8 9 10	14. I have friends with whom I can share my concerns.
	Finances
1 2 3 4 5 6 7 8 9 10	15. I understand my present financial position reasonably well.
1 2 3 4 5 6 7 8 9 10	16. I do a good job of managing my personal day-to-day financial affairs.

TABLE 17 (*Continued*)

Unlike Me Like Me	Finances (Cont.)
1 2 3 4 5 6 7 8 9 10	17. I understand my (former) employer's pension program.
1 2 3 4 5 6 7 8 9 10	18. I understand my Social Security benefits.
1 2 3 4 5 6 7 8 9 10	19. In the event of death, my financial assets would protect my loved ones for a reasonable length of time.
	Home
1 2 3 4 5 6 7 8 9 10	20. I feel safe and secure in my home.
1 2 3 4 5 6 7 8 9 10	21. I am satisfied with the physical environment and location of my home.
	Self-Management
1 2 3 4 5 6 7 8 9 10	22. I have clear goals for the future.
1 2 3 4 5 6 7 8 9 10	23. I can make plans and bring about changes in my life.
1 2 3 4 5 6 7 8 9 10	24. I use my time creatively.
1 2 3 4 5 6 7 8 9 10	25. I am able to accept change and deal reasonably with loss.

TABLE 17 (*Continued*)

Unlike Me Like Me	Career
1 2 3 4 5 6 7 8 9 10	26. I have satisfying plans for my future.
1 2 3 4 5 6 7 8 9 10	27. If I needed a job, I would know how to find one.
1 2 3 4 5 6 7 8 9 10	28. I know how to communicate my goals and needs to any employer I might have.

Total Score _____.

Source: Adapted from: Jim Vetsch, "What Are You Doing With the Rest of Your Life?" *Active Senior Lifestyles,* Nov. 1989, © Training by Finesse, Minneapolis, Minn.

If your total score is over 200, you probably are enjoying life. This does not imply there are no worries. But it does suggest that your priorities and values are focused.

However, even if your score was over 200, there may be statements which you rated 5 or less. And if your total score was under 200, it is likely there may be entire sections (e.g., health) where you averaged 5 or fewer points. These questions and sections represent your psychological "hot spots" — areas of worry, but also areas where growth can occur.

For example, if you averaged less than 5 on the health section, you may not be exercising. You may feel lethargic and mentally dull. You may even feel guilty for not taking better care of yourself. Here is a plan that will help turn the situation around.

First, choose a goal. ("By May 1st I will be five pounds lighter and be able to walk two miles without being winded.")

Second, state why you want to achieve this goal. ("I want to feel energetic. I want to be able to bounce out of bed in the morning without feeling fatigued.")

Third, visualize how you will feel when you've accomplished the goal. ("I will feel great! My spouse will find me even *more* sexy!")

Fourth, determine how you are going to get started. ("I'll have a complete physical examination. Then I will walk four blocks every day.")

Fifth, stipulate a deadline. ("I will loose fifteen pounds by July 4th.")

Sixth, find someone who will encourage you. ("My neighbor takes a walk every day. I'll see if I can join him twice a week.")[2]

Now, a word of caution is in order for those who scored 200 points or less. This is only a reflective test, and your answers may change dependent upon your mood. Therefore you may find it helpful to take this test at three-month intervals. Not only will you get a good reading of your feelings over a period of time, but you will also be able to identify problems that threaten peace of mind.

Strategy Two: Think Young!

The first step in improving mental health is to examine your outlook. The second is more difficult, and for some a bit more threatening. In this step you need to take a hard look at your attitudes about aging.

How do you feel about growing old? Do you find yourself worrying about the receding hairline, the stretch marks in the skin? Do you regret the loss of youth and the vigor you felt ten, twenty years ago?

If you do, you are not alone. Many people regret growing old. And some feel that once they turn sixty-five years of age, the game of life is essentially over.

Why the negative attitudes? In spite of all you read about the "graying of America," we continue to live in a youth-dominated culture. For example, when Ronald Reagan ran for president, he was asked whether he was mentally "fit" for the job. The implication was that since he was over sixty years of age, he might be senile. After repeated questions Mr.

Reagan was forced to tell the press that he was not suffering from any disability and that if he were to become senile, he would resign.

The fact that senility was raised as a political issue appalls gerontologist Dr. Robert N. Butler, former director of the National Institute of Aging: "I doubt that anyone in Germany ever asked that question of Adenauer, or of de Gaulle, in France. It has to be an American cultural disease, part of the idea that senility is an inevitable concomitant of aging."[3]

Ageist attitudes are everywhere. For example, Jack Mathews, of the *Los Angeles Times*, highlighted some of the attitudes young Hollywood executives have of older people. His nominees for "The Most Ageist Movie Executive of the Year" include:

* The executive who asked a seventy-year-old if she thought she could write a love scene.
* The young development executive who asked George Sherman (producer/director of hundreds of films): "Why do you think a network would accept you? I've been in the business eight years, and I've never heard of you."
* The young producer who reacted to a veteran TV writer's reference to

Shakespeare by saying he hadn't read any of the classics: "No history, no literature, nothing that happened before I was born is relevant to my life today."[4]

Negative attitudes about growing old are deeply embedded in society. Consequently, fortunes are made promoting consumer products that promise to delay the signs of aging! If you are growing bald, try Minoxidil, which might keep your hairline from receding. If wrinkles appear, there is Retin-A, which smoothes them out. And if you don't like cellulite, liposuction will restore a shapely figure.

To repeat: many adults have a visceral, negative reaction to the idea of growing old. But I am convinced that the real fears are not the thinning hair, the wrinkles, or even the bulging thighs. The real fear is more basic, more harrowing: life may be drawing to a close. The options are narrowing. The future is uncertain.

Frankly, some of the saddest interviews I had were with those who believed life was over. Often they had trouble identifying negative thoughts. And if they could define them, they felt powerless to change their attitudes.

I think, for example, of a sixty-six-year-old

man who complained that he was always tired. "I guess it goes with growing old," he lamented. Then there was the fifty-eight-year-old salesman who upon looking at his pension statement said fatalistically: "I'll be poor until I die." And then I think of an older man who no longer had sex with his wife: "Well, at our ages, what can you expect?"

I can tell you what to expect about sex: no matter the age, the need for intimate relationships continues. In a nationwide survey of sexual practices of men and women over sixty-five, respondents were asked: "Does sex change after retirement?" Most respondents indicated that it did not change. And for many, sex became *better* with age.[5]

George Burns has perhaps the best perspective on how old age affects sex:

Physician: When did sex stop for you?
Burns: At 3 this morning.

There generally is no physiological reason to stop loving, whether you are sixty or ninety. But there is every reason in the world to confront negative attitudes about aging. Because if not conquered, negative thoughts will not only affect your mental well-being but may also influence your physical health. One gerontologist put it this way: "Most of my patients owe their physical problems to emotional and psychological ones. They've been told by their bosses, their younger co-workers, their neighbors, and their children that the game of life is over. They feel worthless, shoved aside, and they get the big hint society has been giving them: Go home and die. The ones who buy the old idea that retirement means dropping out often do that — they succumb to all these ailments and diseases."[6]

If you feel that your options in life are closing in because you are retired, remember this: you're never too old to think young. As authors Albert Myers and Christopher Anderson write: "Youthfulness is not a period in life, but an *attitude* toward life."[7]

You are never too old to learn. States gerontologist Edgar J. Munter: "Even at eighty your brain can learn at the speed of a thirteen-year-old's, and that's damn fast!"[8] And the great fear that you will become senile is grossly exaggerated: senility is diagnosed in only about 1 percent of people over sixty-five years of age.[9]

Legendary baseball player Satchel Paige hit the nail right on the head when he asked: "How old would you be if you didn't know how old you are?"

How old would *you* be, if you didn't know how old you are? A good answer given by a seventy-year-old man: "I do not feel old inside — I feel no great change. I'm simply appalled at how old my children are."[10]

The best way to fight ageist attitudes is to remember that you are never too old to make a contribution. For example:

* Oliver Wendell Holmes was in his sixties when he first became a member of the United States Supreme Court, and served that body for *thirty* years.
* At seventy-four Kant wrote three great books, and Tintoretto painted the *Paradise.*
* Verdi wrote *Othello* at seventy-four, *Falstaff* at eighty, and "Ave Maria" at eighty-five.
* At seventy-eight Grandma Moses started her painting career, never having had an art lesson.
* At eighty-three Tennyson wrote "Crossing the Bar."
* At ninety-eight Titian painted the *Battle of Lepanto.*
* James Michener began his writing career at forty.
* Churchill was a failure until age sixty-six, when he became Prime Minister of England.

* George Bernard Shaw was ninety-four when one of his plays was first produced.

Remember: The greatest enemy of happiness is the belief that because we are growing old, we have nothing to contribute. And nothing to learn. And the second greatest threat to happiness stems from making our problems bigger than they are.

Strategy Three: Stop the Negative Thoughts!

Shortly before writing this section, I went to my mailbox and picked up the current issue of *Fortune* magazine. On the cover were the following words in bold print: WILL YOU BE ABLE TO RETIRE? Underneath the headline were pictures of four couples and two single adults. Next to each was a dollar figure showing how much money they would need if their retirement were to be successful.

How much would they need? The least amount would be $1,100,000. And one couple would actually need $9,800,000 if their lifestyle were to be maintained.

Immediately I thought about those who would see the cover picture and throw up their hands in despair. After all, most of us don't retire with a million dollars in the bank. Nevertheless, the message was clear: unless you have a lot of money (and I mean *a lot!*) you will not have a good retirement.

Nonsense. As we saw earlier, there are millions of people who have little more than a Social Security check and a modest pension yet enjoy life to the fullest.

But what *does* threaten a successful retirement is negative thoughts — thoughts which, according to psychologist Thomas Borkovec, "race out of control."

How do thoughts race out of control? Imagine a driver going five miles over the speed limit. A car swerves in front of him and he sharply applies his brakes. After the crisis a thought crosses his mind: "How good are my brakes? Do I need new ones?"

He becomes worried and envisions his brakes failing and his car hitting a young child. He sees himself in court, facing a hostile lawyer. He loses the verdict, faces financial ruin, and ends up on welfare.[11]

Now this example might strike you as amusing. But in reality, most of us have worries that on occasion get out of control. "Worrying is circular," says Elwood Robinson, a psychologist who heads the worry treatment program at North Carolina Central University in Durham, North Carolina. "It builds, so you feel

321

worse and worse."[12]

Studies indicate that 30 percent of us do not worry, 15 percent are chronic worriers, and the rest of us fall somewhere in between. States Royland Folensbee, a psychologist who heads a Houston worry clinic: "Some people are not worriers at first but *become* worriers. They find that their worry incubates. While they might once have worried about paying a bill, they'll eventually worry about paying for things they haven't even bought yet." Interestingly, Dr. Folensbee reports that some of his patients are so prone to worry that they decide not to undergo treatment because the prospect worries them too much![13]

The key to getting worry under control is to stop negative thoughts. How do you do it? One of the best ways is to "image" positive outcomes. Let me illustrate by telling you about my father's open-heart surgery.

Frankly, it was one of the most frightening things we as a family have ever been through. I was with my father when the cardiologist informed him that he needed surgery — preferably the next day. The reason? The aorta valve was simply giving out. The prognosis? Not very hopeful.

I slept very little the night before his surgery. My own heart was racing with anxiety. Finally, after turning and tossing for much of the night, I made some hot chocolate and sat alone with my thoughts at the kitchen table.

My wife sought to comfort me and suggested that I write down reasons for optimism. Frankly, it was the last thing I wanted to do, but I followed her suggestion. Here is what my list looked like:

1. My father is optimistic. He has a meaningful faith that will sustain him. He also has many friends who will encourage him.
2. I have confidence in my father's surgeon. He has *successfully* completed this operation many, many times.
3. The hospital has an *outstanding* cardiovascular unit. My father will receive outstanding care.
4. My father's medical bills will be paid for by his health maintenance organization.
5. My father has been through difficult experiences before. He is a survivor.

I reread the list and then with a touch of irony, I added a sixth point: "While I am sitting here stewing at 2:00 A.M., my dad is probably getting a good night's rest!"

I would like to report that my anxiety disappeared after writing these statements. It didn't. But I was comforted by rereading my list. And I was able to put my fears on a short leash.

My father survived the surgery with his health and wit intact. Three months later we were fishing together on our favorite lake.

The moral to the story? No matter what you may be experiencing, keep your fears contained. How to do it?

First, *recognize distorted thinking*. Few individuals are able to think objectively all the time. Even the most logical, rational thinker has moments in which feelings threaten objectivity.

If you analyze your emotional turmoil, states David M. Burns, M.D., you will probably discover negative thinking. Usually the thoughts are irrational. And to make things worse, the twisted thinking is often the *exclusive cause* of psychological suffering.[14]

Here are some of the most common perceptual mistakes — errors that not only cause psychological pain but keep you from thinking clearly on important issues.[15]

Type of Error	*Example*
1. Personalizing	"My children didn't call on my birthday. They don't care about me."

2. Magnifying	"Being forced to retire is the worst thing that can happen."
3. Minimizing	"My monthly Social Security check increased by \$23. That doesn't help."
4. Either/or	"I'll never be able to stand these winters unless we move to Florida." (Note: The respondent has survived the Minnesota winters for fifty-nine years!)
5. Jumping to conclusions	"I know the lump is cancerous."
6. Over-generalizing	"No matter what I do, I never seem to succeed."
7. Comparing	"If we had as much money as the Smiths, we, too, could have a good retirement."
8. Catastrophizing	"Until my child is happy, I can't be."

If you want to diminish worry, identify your cognitive distortions. But also *answer your negative thoughts with an affirmative response.* For example:

Negative Thought	Response
1. "No one is going to remember my birthday."	"If no one calls, I will telephone a couple of friends."
2. "I'm not sure that I will survive this surgery."	"Thousands of people have had better lives, thanks to this surgery."
3. "I will never be able to find anyone to love."	"Many people remarry after the death of a spouse."
4. "My son is a failure."	"True, he has had some bad luck. But he has always paid his bills. And he has always found a new job."
5. "I'll never be able to apply the concepts discussed in this chapter."	"Once I master these, I will be able to get my worries under control."

Once you answer negative thoughts with an affirmation, take *constructive action:*

Apparent Situation	*What I Can Do*	*True Situation*
"I don't know where to retire. I fear making a mistake."	Visit three retirement communites. Prioritize the strengths and weaknesses of each.	"In twelve months I can discover a nice location. If I make a mistake, it's not the end of the world."
"I'm broke. I will never have a good retirement."	Find part-time employment. Reduce expenses. Rent a smaller apartment.	"True — I have little money. But I am not broke. I can pay my bills."

It is particularly important to use powerful, positive words in determining your future. Use "I will" instead of "I'll try," or "I choose to" rather than "I have to . . ." The more you can frame actions in terms of powerful

327

phrases and sentences, the more quickly you will be able to break the power of negative thinking.

Finally, remember that there is nothing wrong with engaging in a *little* worry. Willard Scott, the weatherman on the "Today" show, apparently decides whether or not to wear his toupee depending on whether there is a high or a low over Utah. He is a realistic role model: some days you feel up, some days down; sometimes you feel young, other times old.[16]

Of course, some worry is normal. But experts suggest that if you are plagued with fears and regrets, you might benefit by designating thirty minutes each day as your "official worry time." Studies on individuals who spend thirty minutes a day in "enforced worrying" find that their worries are reduced by nearly 50 percent.[17]

What should you do in your enforced worry time? First select a location in which you will not be interrupted. Second, never sit in a favorite reading chair, for it might become associated with all your cares and concerns. Third, write down the major issues that irritate you. Fourth, identify distortions in your thinking. Finally, *focus on issues where constructive action can be taken.* As Dane Gibson, director of activity therapy at Sheppard and Enoch Pratt Health System says: "If something is worrying you, decide whether you can do anything about it. If you can, then do it. If it's out of your control, then let it go. Don't waste your time and energy worrying about things that you can't do anything about."[18]

What should you do if you can't shake the blues? See a physician and/or a professional counselor. This is particularly true if any combination of the following symptoms persists for two weeks or more:

* Frequent or unexplainable crying spells
* Unexplainable jumpiness or anxiety
* Physical pains that are hard to describe
* Difficulty in concentrating or remembering
* Appetite loss or overeating
* Lack of interest in family and friends
* Loss of self-esteem
* Attitude of indifference ("Nothing matters")

These symptoms may indicate that you, like an estimated thirty million other Americans, are suffering from a depressive illness. If so, remember this: depression can be diagnosed. It can be *successfully* treated, and a new sense of purpose and direction can be developed.

Strategy Four: Pep Up Your Life!

Former representative Claude Pepper once remarked: "Life is like riding a bicycle. You don't fall off until you stop pedaling."[19]

Pepper is correct. The surest way to get yourself into a blue mood is to sleep late, turn on the soaps, pour yourself an alcoholic drink, and watch four hours of evening television. As George Bernard Shaw once observed: "A perpetual holiday is a good working definition of hell."[20]

For retirement to be successful, life must be *focused*. This does not imply that you should never sleep late. Nor does it suggest that life can't be lived at a more relaxed pace. But there must be something to do that provides a sense of accomplishment.

If you feel blue, take out paper and pencil and write down *everything* you could conceivably do tomorrow. For example, you might be able to:

Walk in the woods
Work in the garden
Go fishing
Play golf
Go to the zoo
See a movie

Browse in a bookstore
Telephone a friend
See a high school athletic event
Attend a college theater production
Enroll in a college class
Revive interest in an old hobby
Discover a new hobby
Buy tickets for a concert
Play tennis
Read a novel
Make plans for a winter vacation
Start dieting
Write in a diary
Attend a worship service
Volunteer at a shelter for the homeless
Rent a rowboat
Purchase a new rod and reel
Work on income tax materials for next year
Organize your files
Establish a budget
Subscribe to a new magazine
Take a drive in the countryside
Meditate
Rent a movie
Talk to a neighbor
Plant a shrub
Clean the garage
Discover a new restaurant
Purchase some fresh flowers
Treat yourself to an evening on the town

Now review *your* list and put a star next to every item that you truly enjoy. Then jot down at least *two* activities for each of the following seven days. At the completion of the seven days a new list should be defined for the following week.

What does this exercise accomplish? It focuses your energy. It provides structure for the day, and it changes the rhythm of life.

Dr. Bernie Siegel, author of *Mind, Medicine and Miracles,* puts it this way: "Each person has to figure out how they want to contribute to life. It doesn't matter what it is, just that they decide to do something. If you like to baby-sit, be a baby-sitter. If you're a judge and you don't like it anymore, retire. I tell people no matter what age you are, ask yourself what you want to be when you grow up. Take a course. Learn to sing. Stay active — that's what keeps you young."[21]

Strategy Five: Take a Few Risks with Your Life!

And the trouble is, if you don't risk anything, you risk even more.
Erica Jong
A Woman's Notebook[22]

Going to a restaurant, working in the garden, attending a major league ball game will relieve stress and reduce tension. But these activities will not necessarily bring happiness. Why? Because their positive effects end when the fun is over.[23]

For example, one of my students at the University of Minnesota was having difficulty adjusting to college life. He came from a small Iowa town and missed his family. He wasn't enjoying his courses and was having difficulty sleeping.

A roommate gave him a ticket to a University of Minnesota football game, thinking it would cheer his spirits. I asked if he enjoyed attending the contest. "The game itself was terrific," he commented. "But midway into the fourth quarter I started to think about how much I missed my family and friends." He then paused and his eyes welled with tears: "You know, it is possible to be with 46,000 people and still feel incredibly alone."

Football games, concerts, plays, movies provide momentary pleasure. But they do not necessarily address the existential issues you may be facing. Nor do they provide a focus for your energy or a blueprint as to how you should spend your life.

Unfortunately, we have been conditioned to believe that happiness comes when we purchase a car or a bigger house. We believe that once the kids get through college or the mortgage is finally paid — then we will be truly happy.

That's not necessarily the case. In fact, once the last child leaves home, there is often sadness. Said Betty Fortane, fifty-two:

Our last child left for college two weeks ago. I love my children. But I always looked forward to the day in which my husband and I would be free of all the responsibilities of raising a family. But the house is quiet and I miss their laughter. And I never thought I would admit this — but I sometimes even miss their rock music.

What does it mean to be happy? To repeat, happiness should not be confused with pleasure. Pleasure is represented in activities which provide a momentary high. Happiness, on the other hand, is a deep feeling of contentment. It's a belief that your life has importance and what you are doing with your time matters to yourself as well as to others.

Understanding the distinction between happiness and fun can have a liberating effect, states author Dennis Prager. It liberates *time*, because you place your energy into those things that have lasting value. It liberates *money,* because you are less tempted to purchase an expensive car or mortgage your future for a bigger house. And it liberates us from *envy.* Just because a neighbor has more money or a friend has more prestige does not imply that they are happier.

What brings happiness? What can be done to create contentment?

The answer is to take some risks. As actress Sissy Spacek notes: "When I'm pushing myself, testing myself, that's when I'm happiest. That's when the rewards are greatest."[24]

What kinds of risks produce happiness? Without a doubt, some of the most energized people I know are taking risks in their *relationships.* They are striving to make good marriages better. They are learning new ways of communicating with their spouse. They are addressing problems that threaten their relationship. And they are finding new ways of expressing their love and tenderness.

Others are forming new friendships. I think for example of widows and widowers who join support groups. Or I think of divorced individuals who refuse to be lonely and are organizing social activities for themselves and others.

Of course some find that true happiness comes by *helping others.* Consider a Columbus, Ohio, executive who works ten to twelve hours a day. But every Tuesday night he is at a shelter for homeless people, cooking food and washing dishes. "Life has been good to me," he comments. "It's my way of putting something back into my community."

You are never too old to volunteer. Vince Meyer is eighty-three years old and is a Peace Corps volunteer in the Central American Republic of Belize. For sixty-six years he worked as a plumber. But then he decided to take a risk and joined the Peace Corps. Now he is training others with notable results. "Young men trained by him are finding gainful employment all over Belize City," states fellow volunteer Kathy Peery. "Employers speak glowingly of their competence but also of the work attitudes they learned from Vince's disciplined, professional approach."[25]

Why is Vince in Central America, working hard, when he could be spending leisurely days in his hometown of Chicago, Illinois? "I knew I had to give (something) to the world for all the good things that came to me over the years."

In spite of all that you read about this being the age of narcissism and indifference to moral issues, eighty-nine million Americans are donating their time and energy to worthwhile causes, including 44 percent of those aged fifty to sixty-four. Why? Because helping others provides a strong feeling of self-worth. It provides an avenue to use your talents. And it makes your community a better place in which to live.

Of course, sometimes the biggest risks you can take are *financial*. I think of Brent Kippleton, a sixty-eight-year-old former schoolteacher whose entire retirement savings amounted to $51,500. During the first two years of his retirement, he moped around the house, depressed over his paltry pension. "Why didn't I have enough sense to save more money?" he would ask himself. But then he decided to take a financial risk.

I had a choice to make. Either I could be depressed over my lack of money. Or I could try and expand our savings.

I went to the library and read everything I could on mutual funds. I subscribed to the *Wall Street Journal*. I talked with stockbrokers who probably thought I was worth a couple of million dollars!

Then I went to the bank and withdrew $7,500. I invested the money in three aggressive growth mutual funds. The first six months my little portfolio was down by 17 percent and my wife thought I had lost my mind.

But I exchanged two of the funds for

even riskier ones. The first year my $7,500 was worth $9,000. The second it was worth over $11,000. And three and a half years later, it has climbed to over $14,000.

All my life I have been a history teacher, with little interest in finances. But this financial adventure has opened up a whole new world for me and has made my retirement exciting.

How am I going to celebrate? Yesterday I withdrew $3,500 from one of the funds. I went to a travel agent and purchased two tickets to England. Tomorrow night I am putting the tickets in a special Valentine's Day card for my wife. It's time for a second honeymoon.

Now some may say that this gentleman is just plain lucky. I don't think that is the case. What Brent Kippleton did was take a risk. But it was a *calculated* risk. He didn't throw his money away. As he indicated, "The worst thing that could have happened was that I would lose half of the $7,500. It would have been tough. But we would have recovered."

The key to his success was that he identified a new avocation. It was something that gave purpose and direction to his life. And when the risk paid off, he shared his good fortune with the person he loved the most.

Of course, some of the most content people I have interviewed are those taking *intellectual risks*. These are individuals wanting a deeper meaning in life. And they want answers to tough, perplexing questions.

When Betty Crompton retired after a successful thirty-seven-year career in sales, she decided that it was time to turn inward.

I never took the time to explore religious issues. But shortly after retirement, I felt a void in my life. I needed a challenge — something that would help me grow and expand my interests.

I found four women who also wanted to grow spiritually. We meet at least twice each week.

We have read books on Zen, Buddhist, and Jewish theology. We have read the great existential writers — Camus, Sartre, and Kierkegaard. We have also been touched by the meditations of Christian writers. It has been fascinating. For the first time in my life I am getting some of my deepest questions answered. And my faith has become more meaningful.

Now the question is: Are *you* a risk taker?

If you answer no, don't feel bad. After all, we have been conditioned to believe that as we grow old, our lives should be lived more conservatively.

But if you feel blue, or if you sense that your life needs a spark of excitement, perhaps you ought to reexamine your attitudes toward risk. Do you like to take risks? Do you seek out adventure? Do you like to be challenged by new ideas? Here is a brief test that measures your attitudes toward risk. Circle the number which best reflects your personality and interests.

How Much of a Risk-taker Are You?

1. I like to read books on many different topics.

NO   1 2 3 4 5   YES

2. I have started a hobby within the past five years.

NO   1 2 3 4 5   YES

3. I withhold judgment when hearing a controversial idea.

NO   1 2 3 4 5   YES

4. I like to take different types of vacations.

NO   1 2 3 4 5   YES

5. I like someone to challenge my point of view.

NEVER   1 2 3 4 5   ALWAYS!

6. I have taken some financial risks during my life.

NO   1 2 3 4 5   YES

7. I like to socialize with people who have values different from my own.

NO   1 2 3 4 5   YES

8. I can spend my money on "foolish things" and not feel guilty about it.

NO   1 2 3 4 5   YES

9. I wouldn't mind retiring in a different region of the country.

NO   1 2 3 4 5   YES

10. If I fail at something, I chalk it up to experience.

NO   1 2 3 4 5   YES

Total Score_____.

If your score was 15 or less, you tend to be a *risk avoider*. Risk avoiders have their own motto: Do not make a mistake. Stick to what is safe and predictable. Do not initiate new projects unless success is guaranteed.

Risk avoiders feel comfortable with friends who have similar values. They tend to be conservative with their money, keeping most of it in a savings account or under the proverbial mattress. Most of the activities that risk avoiders pursue are designed to create a safe and secure life.

If you scored between 16 and 34, you are

a *risk evaluator*. As the name implies, you check the temperature before jumping into the water.

Risk evaluators are more assertive than risk avoiders in how they use their money as well as their time. They might, for example, vacation on a foreign island. But first they go to the library and obtain all the relevant information on the place, including the daytime and nighttime temperatures, currency exchange rates, foods available, and diseases endemic to the country. Then they make reservations at the Holiday Inn!

Risk evaluators enjoy meeting new people. But if they had their choice they would spend a quiet evening with fellow Republicans, Democrats, Methodists, or Rotarians — but probably not Unitarians, who might challenge their thinking!

Risk evaluators are slightly more aggressive than risk avoiders with their investments. They tend to put their money in growth and income mutual funds and may have a portfolio of conservative stocks.

One of the positive attributes of risk evaluators is that they make wonderful managers. They are perceived to be "down to earth" and "solid." Unfortunately, they may not obtain the big promotion because they do not have an "entrepreneurial flair" — a willingness to take big risks in order to gain commensurate rewards.

If your score was between 35 and 50, you are a *risk seeker*. You like adventure. You enjoy meeting new people, especially those who have points of view different from your own. You like to travel, and you enjoy reading on a wide variety of topics. You attend plays, concerts, and lectures. If a friend calls you and suggests a new adventure, you don't think twice: "Let's do it!" would be your response.

One of the best attributes of risk seekers is their attitude toward failure. They see failure as a necessary part of life. When they fail they lament the loss. But they seek to learn from the experience. "I'll know what to do next time" is a frequent response of risk seekers.

It should be pointed out that risk seekers can be conservative. They are not apt to blow their life's savings on financial whim. Nor will they enter into new hobbies, avocations, or business ventures without evaluating the downside. They know the value of negative as well as positive thinking ("What's the worst that could happen?").

But fundamentally, risk seekers *love life*. They enjoy meeting new people, experiencing new sights, challenging old ideas. They love putting their mind to work on challenging problems. And they would concur with Aleksandr Solzhenitsyn's observation that a decline in courage is the first symptom that vital life is about to end.

Now the question is, Should you be taking more risks with your life? Should you, for example, extend yourself to the less fortunate? Is it possible to deepen your friendship with your spouse and adult children? Can you renew ties with old friends, and establish new ones? And what about your finances? Is there "lazy money" sitting in a low-interest savings account that could be more assertively managed?

Only you can answer these questions. But if there is one thing that I am convinced of, it is this: many older adults believe that they lived their life too conservatively. Consider, for example, how one woman would live if given a second chance at life:

If I Had My Life to Live Over

I'd dare to make more mistakes next time. I'd relax. I would limber up. I would be sillier than I have been on this trip. I would take fewer things seriously. I would take more chances. I would take more trips. I would climb more mountains and swim more rivers. I would eat more ice cream and less beans. I would perhaps have more actual troubles, but I'd have fewer imaginary ones.

You see, I'm one of those people who live sensibly and sanely, hour after hour, day after day. Oh, I've had my moments, and if I had it to do over again, I'd have more of them. In fact, I'd try to have nothing else. Just moments, years ahead of each day. I've been one of those persons who never go anywhere without a thermometer, a hot water bottle, a raincoat, and a parachute. If I had to do it again, I would travel lighter than I have.

If I had my life to live over, I would start barefoot earlier in the spring and stay that way later in the fall. I would go to more dances. I would ride more merry-go-rounds. I would pick more daisies.

Nadine Stair, eighty-five years old
Louisville, Kentucky[26]

Strategy Six: Keep Your Sense of Humor!

Older audiences usually nod with approval when I suggest that the key to good mental health is having a sense of humor. But after a recent presentation a woman confided: "I'm finding it *very* hard to be hopeful." She then described the difficulties in caring for her husband, who had a chronic illness.

There are times in life when it is difficult to laugh. But as Hawkeye Pierce, Trapper John, Klinger, and the rest of the M★A★S★H gang knew, it is important to laugh, even in the midst of tragedy. For when you laugh at something frightening, you have a wonderful moment of relief. And it keeps overwhelming and frightening thoughts outside the door.[27]

"A merry heart doeth good like a medicine," writes an Old Testament author. "Laughter is the best medicine," suggests *Reader's Digest*. A growing number of physicians, nurses, and psychologists are discovering that laughter truly is the best therapy. And they are using laughter to diminish pain, reduce pain, and brighten their patients' outlook on life, regardless of how grim the prognosis.[28]

A number of hospitals, for example, are sending "laughter wagons" to patients' rooms, stocked with joke books, humorous tapes, toys, and games designed to amuse patients. A few hospitals have even set up "humor rooms," where patients and their families look at funny videotapes, including movies featuring Woody Allen, Bill Cosby, George Burns, Rodney Dangerfield, and Mel Brooks. Staff members frequently join in for a hearty laugh.[29]

Why is laughter such a good therapy for

our blues? Why can it be used in fighting depression when things go wrong?

Dr. William F. Fry, a psychiatrist affiliated with Stanford University, has studied humor for three decades. He suggests that laughter stimulates the production of "alertness hormones" called catecholamines. These hormones trigger release of endorphins in the brain. Endorphins, in turn, foster a sense of relaxation and well-being. They also dull the sensation of pain.

How does one develop a sense of humor — especially if life is clouded with worry? Perhaps a good starting point would be to go to your neighborhood video store and rent several "Candid Camera" tapes. Or you might want to bring home from the library an armful of *Doonesbury* or *The Far Side* cartoons. Or attend a few movies to brighten the spirit.

But never take yourself too seriously. While Joanne Izzo and her husband were vacationing in Las Vegas, Nevada, Rodney Dangerfield was the featured comedian in their hotel. During the Izzos' breakfast in the coffee shop, Mr. Dangerfield came in and sat down in an unoccupied section of the restaurant. A waitress approached him and said: "I'm sorry, Mr. Dangerfield, but this area is closed." As the comedian moved to another section, Mr. and Mrs. Izzo heard him mutter, "No respect. . . ."[30]

★ ★ ★

If you are feeling discouraged, remember this: the transition into retirement can be stressful. While some sail into retirement in sunny weather, others report dark clouds and even a few storms.

If you are encountering heavy weather, assess your thoughts. Identify cognitive distortions. Pep up your life through joyful activities. And never go to bed without a blueprint for how you will organize tomorrow's time.

CHAPTER NINE

Ten Tips for a Healthy Retirement

We know that disease and illness aren't inevitable consequences of aging. There are things that people can do at almost any age that will make their lives healthier and possibly even longer.

J. Michael McGinnis, M.D.
Deputy Assistant Secretary, Department of
Health and Human Services

Have you ever wondered how the rich and famous stay healthy and why they always appear in such marvelous shape? Here are the secrets of their success:

Kirk Douglas, seventy-one: "I go to the gym every day and I walk a lot. And when I go into a building, I never use the elevator. My kids get mad at me because I bug them to stay in shape."

Barbara Walters, fifty-eight: "I don't take vitamins, I've never been a good athlete, and I adore pasta. So for years I've gone for an early morning workout at a gym in New York, where a trainer directs me through a session of warm-ups, stretches, and bends. This is followed by a ring and trapeze routine that develops flexibility and helps keep my body supple."

Tony Randall, seventy: "I eat very simply. For breakfast, it's one egg, soft-boiled. At other meals I eat only broiled foods — say a pork roast with apple sauce, carrots, and potatoes, and a bottle of red wine. Also, I believe in regular sleeping habits. I'm asleep almost always before twelve and up at seven to get a jump on the day."

Bea Arthur, sixty-six: "I was always heavy, but after 'Maude' ended in '76, I gained ten pounds. When I saw myself in the mirror I was not pleased, and I decided to do something about it. On a diet my doctor prescribed, I took off thirty pounds and have kept them off. Now I feel thirty years younger."

Carol Burnett, fifty-three: "I start every morning with hot cranberry juice and then an herb tea with whole-wheat toast, a soft-boiled egg, and a slice of papaya. At other meals I prefer such vegetables as jicama, followed perhaps by a kiwi fruit."

Sophia Loren, fifty-five: "Every day I reserve a quiet time to relax. All people, especially those over forty, need the rejuvenation that a few moments alone can provide."[1]

These statements attest to an important principle that will affect the quality of your retirement years: if you want to live in optimal health, *you need to develop a healthy lifestyle.* This does not suggest you become a vegetarian. Nor must you become a compulsive jogger. But as Carol Burnett, Tony Randall, Kirk Douglas, and others attest, good health can be preserved. And from this, illness can often be prevented.

How do you stay healthy? Here are ten tips that will not only energize your life but also increase the odds that your retirement will be lived in good health.

Tip #1: Take Responsibility for Your Health!

If you want to have a long and healthy retirement, take control of your health. How do you do it?

The first step is to take a close look at how

your lifestyle may be influencing your health. On the following pages you will find a test that measures the extent to which you are living a healthy life (Table 18). Try to answer each question thoughtfully and honestly.

If the results indicate that your lifestyle is conducive to optimal health, congratulate yourself. If there is room for improvement, however, do not be disheartened. As we see, it is never too late to get into optimal physical condition, regardless of the aches or pains we periodically experience. Nor is it too late to take constructive action to better our mental outlook.

How do you improve health? What can be done to give you more energy and a sense of optimism about your medical future?

The starting point is to get in shape, for as a former president of the American Medical Association said: "Exercise is the master conditioner for the healthy and the major therapy for the ill."[2]

In a nutshell, here are the benefits of engaging in a program of regular exercise:

If You Exercise
* You will be more cheerful, less depressed, and *more confident of the future.*
* You will have *additional endurance*

TABLE 18
How's Your Health?

Here is a brief test that will give you some solid clues as to the state of your health. Circle the correct answer to each question.

Exercise, Fitness, and Health Maintenance:

1. How often do you get 15 to 30 minutes of vigorous exercise (swimming, running, aerobics, brisk walking, tennis, dancing)?
   a. Three or more times a week
   b. Once a week
   c. Once a month or less

2. How often do you get 15 to 30 minutes of exercise that will tone your muscles (push-ups, yoga, calisthenics, weights)?
   a. Three or more times a week
   b. Once a week
   c. At least once a month

3. How often do you see a physician?
   a. Monthly
   b. At least once a year
   c. Hardly ever

4. When it comes time to make a doctor's appointment, do you
   a. Call and schedule an appointment immediately?
   b. Have someone else in your family make the appointment for you?

TABLE 18 (*Continued*)

Exercise, Fitness, and Health Maintenance: (Continued)

   c. Fear what the doctor might tell you and procrastinate, delay, and postpone for as long as possible?

5. Of the more common 50-plus medical conditions — heart disease, diabetes, arthritis, circulatory difficulties, emphysema, backache — how many affect your health?
   a. One or more
   b. Two to five
   c. More than five

6. Have you ever been hospitalized for a serious condition?
   a. Never
   b. In the past five years
   c. In the past year

7. How do you assess your overall health?
   a. Excellent
   b. Good to fair
   c. Fair to poor

Eating Habits

1. How often do you get well-balanced meals? (Nutritious meals include the four basic food groups: (a) fruits and vegetables — four or more pieces or half-cup servings per day; (b) breads, cereals, and other grains — four slices or one-cup servings per day; (c) milk and milk products — two eight-ounce servings per day; (d) poultry,

TABLE 18 (*Continued*)

---

fish, meat, legumes, nuts, and seeds — two three-ounce servings per day.)

   a. Every day
   b. Three times a week
   c. Rarely

2. Are you careful about your intake of fats, saturated fats, and cholesterol by limiting the following foods in your diet: fatty meats, eggs, butter, cream, and shortenings?

   a. Always
   b. Occasionally
   c. Never

3. Are you careful about your sodium intake? Do you limit your consumption of salt when cooking, seasoning, or snacking?

   a. Always
   b. Occasionally
   c. Never

4. Do you watch your sugar consumption? Do you consciously avoid candy and nondiet soft drinks?

   a. Always
   b. Occasionally
   c. Never

5. Do you maintain your recommended weight?

   a. Yes

TABLE 18 (*Continued*)

Eating Habits (*Continued*)

If not, are you

b. 5 to 20 pounds from normal (overweight or underweight)?

c. More than 20 pounds from normal weight?

Alcohol and Drugs

1. How many prescriptions do you currently take?

 a. None

 b. One to five

 c. More than five

2. Do you always follow your doctor's or pharmacist's instructions when you take these drugs? For example, do you take medications for their full prescription length? Do you discard prescriptions after the expiration date on the label has passed?

 a. Always

 b. Occasionally

 c. Never

3. Do you avoid drinking alcohol when taking drugs that could cause harmful interactions (tranquilizers, barbiturates, and antihistamines, for example)?

 a. Always

 b. Occasionally

 c. Never

TABLE 18 (*Continued*)

Alcohol and Drugs (*Continued*)

4. Do you use painkillers to excess or without regard to specific doctor's instructions?
   a. Never
   b. Occasionally
   c. Often

5. How many alcoholic drinks, including wine and beer, do you consume on a daily basis?
   a. None to one
   b. Two to four
   c. Over five

Smoking

1. Do you smoke fewer than 10 cigarettes a day?
   a. I don't smoke.
   b. I smoke fewer than 10 cigarettes a day.
   c. I smoke more than 10 cigarettes a day.

2. Do you smoke low-tar cigarettes, cigars, or a pipe?
   a. I don't smoke.
   b. Yes, I smoke low-tar cigarettes.
   c. I smoke regular cigarettes, cigar, and/or pipe.

Stress

1. How often do you get a good night's sleep?
   a. Every night
   b. Only occasionally
   c. Rarely, I suffer from insomnia

TABLE 18 (*Continued*)

Stress (*Continued*)

2. Do you devote any part of your day to re-laxing and daydreaming?
   a. Always
   b. Occasionally
   c. Never

3. Do you feel these statements are accurate? I enjoy my work. I am relaxed. I enjoy being with people.
   a. Yes.
   b. I share only some of these feelings.
   c. No, these descriptions don't fit me.

Safety

1. When you drive, do you wear your seat belt and obey traffic rules and the speed limit?
   a. Always
   b. Occasionally
   c. Never

2. Do you avoid driving under the influence of alcohol and drugs?
   a. Always
   b. Occasionally
   c. Never

3. Do you smoke in bed?
   a. No
   b. Sometimes
   c. Yes

TABLE 18 (*Continued*)

Scoring: Give yourself 4 points for every question you answered "A," 2 points for every question you answered "B," and 0 points for every question you answered "C."

80-100 points: You are healthy, active, and obviously know how to take care of yourself.

70-85 points: You are concerned about your well-being and are only a few steps away from getting into tiptop shape. See your doctor, hit the track, watch your diet — you're almost there.

55-70 points: There is room for improvement in your lifestyle. If you are concerned about your health, think of ways in which you could improve your daily habits.

Below 55 points: Trouble ahead. See your physician in order to determine a healthier course for your life.

Source: Adapted from Edwin Kiester, Jr., "Set the Pace for Good Living," *50-Plus,* January 1985.

and stamina. You will be able to do more in less time and with less strain.

* You will have a *quicker reaction time in processing information.* In one experiment, the thinking ability of an older, physically fit person was greater than that of a twenty-five-year-old person who was not fit.

* You will have *lower cholesterol levels.* You will have lower blood pressure and be less prone to diabetes mellitus.

* *You might live longer.* Based upon a study of 17,000 Harvard graduates, Dr. Ralph Paffenbager, Jr., professor at Stanford University, concluded: "If you want to live longer, exercise. It's that simple."[3]

Frankly, there is no medication on the face of the earth that can provide as many benefits as does exercise. But, you might ask, if the rewards are so great, why don't we do it?

Well, exercise is a bit like dieting. Many of us know the benefits of shedding a few pounds. But when we are tired, it's easier to plop in front of the television set than walk around the block.

Nevertheless a brisk walk will be better for you than slouching in an easy chair. And a trip to the swimming pool might provide an unexpected bonus: in a study of competitive swimmers, those in their forties and sixties had sex lives that resembled those of individuals who were in their twenties and early thirties![4]

How do you get in shape, especially if you are not in the habit of exercising? First, get a complete medical checkup. Ask to take a stress test, which provides an evaluation of your cardiovascular health.

If your physician gives an all-clear signal, select an activity that you enjoy. Among the options: walking, jogging, swimming, mountain climbing, biking, canoeing, rope jumping, basketball, tennis, volleyball, stationary bicycling, golf, ice skating, racquetball, bowling, backpacking, softball, weight training, table tennis, calisthenics, and roller skating.

Start slowly. If you aren't in shape, a walk around the block might be a good place to begin.

But as your fitness improves, exercise at least three times a week for twenty minutes a time. Then expand your program so that your routine focuses on 1) cardiovascular fitness, 2) muscular strength, 3) flexibility, 4) balance, and 5) coordination and agility.[5]

1. *Cardiovascular fitness.* Strengthened cardiovascular endurance reduces fatigue, increases energy, and reduces the risk of having a heart attack. Activities that improve cardiovascular endurance include walking, jogging, rope jumping, and swimming.

2. *Muscular strength and endurance.* If you want to mow the grass, shovel the snow, or be able to go up a flight of stairs without feeling winded, focus on improving your muscular strength as well as your general level of fitness. Activities that help include weight lifting, push-ups, and general calisthenics.

3. *Flexibility.* You stand a good chance of avoiding muscle tears, strains, and sprains if you like to bowl, play tennis, or dance. You need only fifteen minutes of stretching exercises a day to keep your muscles loose and relaxed.

4. *Balance.* It is important to retain your sense of balance, since most of life's pleasures are dependent upon it. For example, if you like to ski, you need to keep your poise as you head down the slopes. Dancing, calisthenics, or even hopping on one foot can improve balance, even after a few sessions.

5. *Coordination and agility.* The one thing you don't want to lose as you grow older is your sense of coordination. Coordination is basic to swinging a golf club, casting a lure,

baking a cake, or even driving a car. Golf and table tennis help preserve eye-hand-foot coordination. Swimming enhances breathing and arm-leg coordination. But dancing is one of the best bets for improving your overall coordination.

Which physical activity provides the most benefits with the fewest risks of injury? The answer is *swimming*, which according to a recent Gallup poll is the number one favorite recreational activity of Americans. Swimming won't hurt your joints. It provides relief if you have arthritis. And if you are overweight, the water's buoyancy will keep your body as well as your spirits afloat.

Now you might be thinking: "I've never liked to swim. I don't like to jog. And I can't imagine lifting weights." If this is the case, why not take a spirited walk?

Tip #2: Walk Your Way to Good Health.

Feeling depressed? Lethargic? Wishing that a creative idea might strike? Forget about jogging or running a marathon. Slip into comfortable shoes. Find a scenic stretch of land. And go for a walk.

Why walk, when there are more physically demanding ways to exercise? It won't cost you a cent, outside of the purchase of a good pair of shoes. You never have to wait in line at an exercise club. And you can do it anywhere — on a street, around a lake, in the woods, or in a shopping mall.

Does walking *really* enhance health? It all depends. If you take a quiet stroll with your lover on a moonlit night, the answer is "no." Your heart might beat faster — but it won't come from the exercise!

But if you take *brisk* walks, your cardiovascular fitness improves. The heart beats more efficiently. Tension headaches go away. Excess weight is lost. Sleep comes more readily. And your chance for living longer increases.

How much longer? In a study of Harvard alumni, subjects who walked five to ten miles a week reduced their mortality rate by 10 percent. The death rate of those who walked twenty to twenty-five miles a week plummeted by almost 40 percent.[6]

Ease into any walking program, especially if you aren't a regular exerciser. Your pace should initially be about one to two miles per hour, and you should be able to speak comfortably to anyone who walks with you.

Gradually increase your speed. Set a goal; within a month or two you should be able to walk four to five miles an hour, thirty to forty-five minutes a week, without feeling winded.

Supplement your formal exercise program by taking short walks to various destinations. A good rule of thumb: if you can walk, don't drive. Vern Hildebrandt, who lives in Gary, Indiana, walks one and a half miles to his regular breakfast spot each morning and another two and a half miles for his noon lunch. Walking is "keeping me alive," says Hildebrandt, sixty-four, who had open-heart surgery in 1982.[7]

If your walking program gets boring, change locations. Or join a walking club. The Fifty Plus club in Sauk Village, Illinois, meets almost every weekday morning to walk one mile or twenty-five laps around a gym. "It's better to walk with a group," states Jan Valzsquez, sixty-seven.[8] To find a walking club in your community call the YMCA or YWCA.

Remember: No matter how modest the program and no matter how late in life it is initiated, an exercise program will enhance your health. Adults over the age of sixty are able to improve their aerobic capacity by 40 percent.[9] And ninety-year-olds can strengthen their muscle strength by an astounding 300 percent through simple calisthenics.

If you need encouragement, pair up with another walker or subscribe to *The Walking Magazine*, P.O. Box 56651, Boulder, CO 80322.

Tip #3: Eat the Right Foods. Drink the Right Beverages.

There is no question about it: As we grow older our bodies change. Bones lose their density. There is an increase and a redistribution of fat cells. And there is a decline in cardiovascular and immune response.[10]

Until recently, all of these changes were chalked up to "growing old." But that isn't necessarily so. States Dr. Jeffrey B. Blumberg, of Tufts University: "The manner in which the body declines is more a cumulative effect of diet and lifestyle rather than the inevitable result of passing years."[11]

Why should you be concerned about nutrition? Because a well-balanced diet can prevent bone loss, improve gastrointestinal performance, and provide added energy. In addition, it may prevent certain forms of cancer, since nutritional inadequacies contribute to approximately 35 percent of all cancer deaths.[12]

How can you improve nutritional health? Here are some practical suggestions for healthy adults.[13]

BREAKFAST

Choose more often:
* Skim milk, low-fat yogurt, low-fat cheese like farmer, cottage, and ricotta

* Apples, bananas, apricots, oranges, pears, papayas, tangerines, peaches, and berries
* Muffins, rolls, bagels, pumpernickel and bran breads
* Whole wheat, bran, corn pancakes, waffles
* Oatmeal, shredded wheat, bran, and other whole-grain cereals

Choose less often:

* Whole milk, cream, coffee creamers
* American, Swiss, cheddar, and cream cheese
* White breads, French toast, sweet rolls, doughnuts, Danish pastries, coffee cakes
* Bacon and pork sausage

LUNCH AND DINNER

Choose more often:

* Fish, chicken, and lean meats (Flounder, sole, haddock, red snapper, halibut, cod, bluefish, and ocean perch are particularly good.)
* Shrimp, crab, clams, mussels, and scallops
* Chicken, turkey (skinned)
* Beef, lamb, pork, and veal cuts trimmed of fat
* Lentil, pea, or minestrone soup;

three-bean salad
* Skim milk, sherbert, ice milk, low-fat yogurt
* Fruits
* Carrots, broccoli, cauliflower, tomatoes, kale, and spinach
* Leafy green salad, beans
* White and sweet potatoes, eggplant, squash, turnips, and corn
* Rye, whole wheat, pumpernickel breads, whole wheat pastas, unbuttered popcorn, and whole grain crackers

Choose less often:
* Beef, lamb, pork, and veal cuts with marbled, untrimmed fat
* Hamburger, rib roasts, corned beef
* Meat sauces, gravies, stews
* Potato chips and other fried snacks
* Ice cream, cream sauces, cream soups

Remember: eating is one of life's great pleasures. You do not need to abandon your favorite snack, nor do you have to become obsessed with counting calories. Nor should you follow every food fad that comes along. But as C. Everett Koop, M.D., the former U.S. Surgeon General noted, adopting a healthful diet is the most important step anyone can take toward a long and healthy life.[14]

Tip #4: Protect Your Bones!

We have all heard stories of people who were all set for retirement, when something suddenly went wrong. Sometimes it is a heart attack. But often it is an accident, such as a fall in the backyard while chasing the dog or a slip on the ice. The result: bumps, bruises, broken bones. And sometimes death.

What causes such accidents? Often times it is *osteoporosis,* which is a preventable bone disease. How does it come about? In the fourth decade of life, our bone reaches its maximum strength. But beyond age forty, both men and women begin losing bone at approximately 1 percent per year. When women enter menopause, bone loss doubles. If preventive measures aren't taken, the bones weaken and can easily break. When this happens, physicians call the problem "osteoporosis." But patients call it an end to their retirement dreams.

How can you keep bones strong? Many exercises, such as tennis, bowling, golf, jogging, and running, will help prevent bone loss. But you also need to take in calcium. The normal daily adult requirement for calcium is 800 to 1,000 milligrams for men, premenopausal women, and women taking estrogen. But as you grow older, 1,000 to 1,500 milligrams may be needed. This is particularly true for Caucasian and Oriental women after menopause.

There are numerous ways to obtain calcium. You can go to your drugstore and purchase without a prescription tablets labeled "calcium carbonate," "calcium gluconate," or "calcium lactate." But you are better off eating and drinking foods rich in calcium. Among the best: milk (one eight-ounce glass of skim milk contains 300 milligrams of calcium), cottage cheese, yogurt, canned sardines, spinach, kale, cheese with crackers, and ice cream. Remember, an apple a day may keep the family doctor away. But calcium will do a better job of keeping the orthopedic surgeon at bay.[15]

Want to learn more about osteoporosis? You can obtain a free copy of *Preventing Osteoporosis* by sending a stamped, self-addressed envelope to the American College of Obstetricians and Gynecologists, 600 Maryland Avenue SW, Suite 300 E., Washington, DC 20024.

Tip #5: Give Your Doctor a Checkup.

There are many things you can do to improve health. You can eat a diet rich in vegetables, fruits, and lean meats. You can exercise in a hundred different ways. And, as we will soon see, you need to sleep restfully.

Nevertheless, there are times in which you need the services of a skilled physician — someone who can treat your aches and pains and, when appropriate, refer you to a specialist.

Permit me to ascend a soapbox, for I feel very strongly about what follows in this section. It is very important to enter your retirement years knowing that you have competent medical help. Because realistically, at some point in your retirement, you will need a physician. When that times comes, you want to be certain your doctor will provide the best possible care.

Regrettably, many older Americans are not receiving adequate medical help. This is particularly true for some cancer patients; according to one federal study, state-of-the-art treatments are not being received by:

* 60 percent of rectal cancer patients,
* 25 percent of small-cell lung cancer patients,
* 37 percent of premenopausal breast cancer patients,
* 20 percent of Hodgkins disease patients.[16]

Why aren't patients receiving the best possible help? Sometimes physicians fail to keep up with the latest research in their discipline. Sometimes they refuse to refer patients to more knowledgeable doctors. And sometimes advanced technology is not readily available.

To ensure that you are getting the best possible care, the starting point is to evaluate your physician. Ask yourself whether your physician:

* Listens to you
* Appears calm
* Lets you speak without interrupting
* Returns your telephone calls promptly
* Explains the tests that are ordered
* Explains the risks, benefits, and side effects of medications
* Respects your modesty
* Takes a medical history when conducting a physical examination
* Reacts supportively when you request a second opinion
* Provides you with a telephone number where you can obtain medical help regardless of the time of day
* Follows up to determine whether medications are working
* Arranges for subsequent appointments

* Confers with colleagues to sharpen his or her knowledge
* Seems interested in you as a person

If you can answer yes to most of these questions, the chances are good that you are receiving competent medical assistance. If you can't, find a new physician.

One of the easiest ways to approach this important task is to call your state and/or county medical society and explain that you are looking for a physician, *preferably an internist with a subspecialty in geriatrics.* The medical society will give you the names and telephone numbers of several physicians. They will also provide information on the physicians' age and medical training. Sometimes they will inform you as to their hospital affiliations.

Armed with this information, make an appointment with at least two physicians. Consider limiting your selection to physicians who are board certified. A board-certified physician is one who has received extensive training in his or her discipline and has passed a rigorous written and oral examination.

Bring to your appointment a brief one-page history of your medical condition. Included should be the following information:

* Current health problems, if any

* Past health problems, including surgical procedures
* Medications you are now taking
* Medications to which you are allergic
* Steps you are taking to improve health (exercise, eating a well-balanced diet, etc.)

Present the information and then ask each physician the following questions:

1. What is your specialty? Do you have a subspecialty?
2. What is your hospital affiliation?
3. Do you refer patients to other specialists?
4. If I had an emergency, how would I obtain help?
5. What is the average age of your patients? Do you like caring for older adults?
6. How long does a patient have to wait for an appointment?
7. If your appointment calendar is filled, who will I see?
8. Is there a long wait to see physicians once at the office?
9. Do you encourage second opinions?

10. How will I be billed for your services?
11. How will my insurance company reimburse you?

Of particular importance is the physician's answer to the question, "Do you encourage second opinions?" If the physician acts defensive, look elsewhere.

Remember, you *always* want a second opinion on any important medical problem. Consider one study of 700,000 patients at Cornell Medical Center. Of those who received a second opinion, 25 percent were told that they did *not* need the surgery another doctor had recommended. Most refused the surgery and suffered no ill effects.[17,18]

If you're unsure as to whom to contact for a second opinion, call the U.S. Department of Health and Human Services, which will make a referral free of charge (800-638-6833). When you do see another physician, bear in mind a few ground rules:

First, be specific about complaints. Informing your physician that "I have a headache" is not as helpful as stating: "My headache began seventy-two hours ago. My fever is 99.8. And I have a dull pain in my lower back."

Second, be honest. Don't exaggerate or minimize your symptoms. Never forget that the most important factor in receiving an accurate diagnosis is your ability to communicate what it is you are feeling.

Third, ask questions. Discover everything you can about your illness and various treatment strategies. Learn the benefits and risks associated with medications. And if you're concerned about medical costs, don't stew over the bill after the fact. Discuss medical costs with your physician in a forthright manner.

Tip #6: Understand Your Medications.

According to Dr. Sidney Wolfe, director of the Public Citizen Health Research Group, fully 38 percent of adults over sixty are taking five or more different prescription drugs and 19 percent are using seven or more.[19] Unfortunately the medications sometimes do not have the desired impact: between 10 percent and 15 percent of hospitalizations among the elderly are due solely to *drug reactions*. People over sixty-five are approximately three times more likely to be harmed by drugs than are young adults.[20]

Can those little pills really harm you? Here are the troubling facts:

* Adverse side effects, contrary to

376

public opinion, strike more than half of all consumers who take medications. Many of the side effects are relatively minor. But some are severe as evidenced by the fact that 300,000 people are hospitalized each year due to adverse drug reactions.

* Of the one hundred most frequently prescribed drugs, approximately half contain at least one ingredient that reacts badly with alcohol. Consequently, 2,500 people die from the combination, and thousands more are hospitalized each year.

* The rate of medication errors in hospitals is close to 12 percent. Many of these errors are benign. But as one author on medication notes: "If you can forget to give a dose of milk of magnesia, you can forget a dose of an anticancer drug." When you consider that the average patient receives ten medications per day in the hospital, there is a distinct possibility that at some point in your hospitalization you may be victimized by a medication error.[21]

One of the major reasons that we have medication problems can be traced to the cavalier attitude of some physicians. For example:

* Thirty-five percent of us leave the physician's office without *any* information about the prescription that has been handed to us.
* Seventy-four percent of us will not be told about possible side effects of our medications.
* Ninety-four percent of us will leave our physician's office without any written information about the medications we are to take.[22]

Once the pharmacist receives the prescription, a new problem develops: the pharmacist might not be able to read the physician's handwriting. According to one survey, almost 25 percent of the pharmacists make at least one telephone call a day simply to check on an illegible prescription. Unfortunately, only 22 percent of the physicians return the call.

The same survey found that half of the physicians were indifferent to the problem associated with their handwriting, 22 percent were defensive, and 14 percent actually became angry when they were asked to clarify their script. As incredible as it may seem, a few looked upon their handwriting problem as a joke and almost none of them bothered to change.[23]

Equally sobering is the fact that half of the pharmacists indicated that they had dispensed a wrong medication because of misreading a prescription. One pharmacist said that he gave *Librium,* which is a sedative, instead of *Indocin,* which is a drug for arthritis. Another patient received the allergy drug *Periactin* instead of the pain medication *Percodan.*

This may seem like a tempest in a teapot, but not if you are the patient receiving *digoxin,* a heart regulator, instead of the antibiotic *Ceclor.* If you find yourself on the receiving end of such a mix-up, you will not be receiving the medications needed to counteract your illness. Worse yet, there may be complications from receiving the wrong medication.[24]

Let me be very clear as to the main point of this section: *A drug that can help you can also harm you.* Never assume that medications are good for you. Far better to raise questions that might prevent an adverse drug reaction. Here are the key ones to ask your physician:

1. What is the medication expected to do? What are the possible side effects? If I did not take this medication, what might happen?
2. Are there alternative methods of

treating my problem? (For example, if you start a good walking program, you might not need a tranquilizer to relieve stress.)

3. How should this medication be taken? Can it be taken with food and/or caffeine products?
4. How long should I stay on this medication? If there are negative side effects, what should I do?
5. Are there less expensive medications than this one that will have the same impact?

One important task is simply to take the mystery out of drugs. Table 19 will permit you to decipher various prescriptions. In addition, you might wish to examine *The Physician's Desk Reference for Nonprescription Drugs* or *The United States Pharmacopoeia — Dispensing Information*. Both of these volumes, which give clear and concise drug information, are found in most pharmacies and community libraries. Using them might arm you with enough information to allow you to question what seems like an incorrectly filled prescription.

If cost is a concern, be sure to check several pharmacies. "There is enormous variety in price," states Bernard Bloom, a health econ-

TABLE 19
Some Common Prescription Symbols

Latin	Abbreviation	Meaning
ad libitum	ad lib.	Freely, as needed
ante cibos	a.c.	Before meals
bis in die	b.i.d.	Twice a day
capsula	caps.	Capsule
gutta	gtt.	Drop
hora somni	h.s.	At bedtime
per os	P.O.	Orally
post cibum	p.c.	After meals
pro renata	p.r.n.	As needed
quaque 4 hora	q.4.h.	Every four hours
quarter in die	q.i.d.	Four times a day
quotidie	quotid.	Daily
semel in die	semel in d.	Once a day
ter in die	t.i.d.	Three times a day
ut dictum	Ut dict., UD	As directed

Source: A. Hbchp, *F.D.A. Consumer*, Dec./Jan. 1976–1977. Food and Drug Administration, U.S. Public Health Service, Department of Health and Human Services.

omist at the University of Pennsylvania, who compared prices of twenty-one pairs of generic and brand-name drugs at about fourteen hundred pharmacies across the nation. "The same prescription that costs $5 at one pharmacy might cost $30 at another."[25]

One final point: your pharmacist is an important source of information. Unfortunately, while 70 percent of pharmacists indicate that counseling patients is their favorite aspect of their jobs, only 3 percent of patients ask questions.[26] That is a mistake, for your pharmacist is a highly trained professional who can help you stay well.

Tip #7: For Women Only: Obtain a Mammogram.

First the bad news: According to the American Cancer Society, in 1989, 142,000 women developed breast cancer, 90 percent of whom were fifty years of age and older. Of that number, 43,000 died.

Breast cancer can strike any woman, but older women are more susceptible. Only 1 out of every 80,000 women in their early twenties will be diagnosed with breast cancer. But 1 out of every 250 to 350 women in their sixties and seventies will be unfavorably diagnosed.

Fortunately, however, a mammogram (an

X ray of the breast) can prevent many of these deaths by detecting tiny growths. If the cancer is treated at an early stage, there is a good possibility that *total* healing will occur.

Many women don't bother to obtain a mammogram. Some fear radiation. The dose, however, is minimal in mammography and will not affect your health. Furthermore, today's technology is better than ever. In 1974 a typical X ray would discharge 6 rads (a rad is a unit of measurement for radiation), whereas today it is less than half a rad.

Others fear the procedure. True, there may be some discomfort as the female technician positions the breast to get a clear image of the tissue. But as most who've done it can attest, the discomfort is brief and mild. An X-ray picture can be taken in just seconds, and two pictures per breast are usually sufficient for a screening examination.

How frequently should you obtain a mammogram? The American Cancer Society recommends that you obtain one mammogram between the ages of thirty-five and thirty-nine, which will serve as a "baseline" for comparison in future tests. Women forty to forty-nine should have a breast X ray about every two years, depending upon physical condition and previous mammogram results. Those fifty and over should have one every year.

If more women followed this advice, almost one-third of the 44,000 women expected to die of breast cancer this year could be saved. The reason is simple. "The whole point of mammography," states Cori Vanchieri, director of the National Cancer Institute's early-detection program, "is that you can find the breast cancer two years before you can feel it."[27]

If you don't know where to obtain a mammogram, consult your physician or call the Cancer Information Service (800-4-CAN-CER) and request a listing of accredited facilities in your community.[28]

Tip #8: Stop Smoking.

Over eighteen million people over the age of forty-five continue to smoke in spite of the well-known dangers, many because they believe that it is pointless to quit at their age. As one sixty-year-old told me: "It's useless. The damage is done."

Such pessimism is unwarranted. States Dr. Tom Glynn, research director of the National Cancer Institute's smoking, tobacco, and cancer program: "If you quit smoking between the ages of forty and fifty-five, you can expect to add, on average, five years to your life. Moreover, stopping in your fifties, sixties, or seventies will give you increased vitality throughout the rest of your life."[29]

In a recent study, investigators compared smokers and those who had quit. The results were startling: The death rate among smokers was *70 percent* higher than among quitters. Said one of the researchers, "The message is that it's never too late to quit. Older people with heart disease get just as much benefit from quitting as younger people do."[30]

What are the specific benefits of breaking the habit?

* You can reduce your risk of a sudden fatal heart attack. This is especially true if you are overweight or have high blood pressure or elevated cholesterol.
* Your risk of getting cancer of the lungs, mouth, larynx, esophagus, bladder, and pancreas dramatically decreases.
* Your chances of developing age-related conditions such as osteoporosis, fatigue, and even wrinkles are diminished.
* Your risk of developing coronary heart disease is diminished.

Once you quit, positive results are evident

almost immediately. Within twelve hours, the level of carbon dioxide in your blood drops. Circulation improves. Stamina is enhanced. Your sense of taste and smell becomes more acute. And within a month or two, "smoker's cough" disappears.

With every passing month, your chances of getting lung cancer decrease. Ten to fifteen years after quitting, your life expectancy will match those who have never smoked a cigarette.[31]

True, it is difficult to give up cigarettes, especially if you are a pack-a-day smoker. But it can be done. In fact, more than 90 percent of the thirty-five million Americans who have quit smoking have done it on their own. If you want professional assistance, however, call Smokenders (800-828-HELP), which is the nation's oldest commercial program. Since its founding in 1969, it has helped some 600,000 people break the habit. Another option is the National Cancer Institute, which offers no-cost quit-smoking counseling over the phone (1-800-4-CANCER).

Tip #9: Get Your Forty Winks.

When I asked Henry W. Dryer whether he was enjoying his retirement, he replied: "Everything is fine. But I sure wish that I could get a good night's rest."

Mr. Dryer's complaint is shared by many people. In fact, anywhere from one-third to one-half of all older people report sleep problems.[32] Some can't fall asleep at all, while others are wide awake again at 2 or 3 A.M. Still others sleep lightly, mumbling their subconscious thoughts to whoever has to endure their words!

To feel energetic, you must get a good night's rest. But obtaining it, especially if you find yourself tossing and turning most of the night, takes work.

The starting point is to understand that you might not need as much sleep as you think. Babies sleep up to twenty hours a day. Adolescents need somewhere between eight and ten hours a night. But mature adults may find that they need fewer than seven hours of sleep per night. Thomas Edison, for example, slept only three to four hours a night. But he kept a cot in his laboratory, and he catnapped whenever he felt tired.[33]

If you are averaging only five or six hours a night and you feel fine, there is no need to lie in bed, wondering why you aren't sleeping longer. Your body simply doesn't need the rest.

But if you feel tired and long for forty good winks of sleep, do the following.

First, take your exercise regimen seriously. At the very least, get in a brisk walk every day. Don't walk before bedtime, though, since exercise tends to be a stimulating rather than relaxing activity.

Second, don't watch the late-evening news on television. Stories of muggings, robberies, and murders agitate the spirit. Far better to read a comforting novel or drink a cup of decaffeinated tea before settling in.

Third, limit caffeine consumption. Caffeine, which is chemically known as 1,3,7 trimethylxanthine, creates changes throughout our system. After the initial jolt to our cardiovascular system, caffeine goes to work on our muscles, which become tense. Three to five hours later, body metabolism continues to be affected. In fact, the metabolism can be increased anywhere from 10 percent to 25 percent from that earlier "bump" of coffee.[34] After its effects have dissipated, there may be a worn-out feeling as well as a sense of listlessness and weariness.

When considering how much coffee to consume, consider the following: the average cup of coffee contains at least 100 milligrams of caffeine. Only 250 milligrams of caffeine can cause you to exhibit the same symptoms as individuals who are suffering from clinically detectable anxiety.[35]

While caffeine is most commonly associated with coffee, don't forget that it can also be found in tea, cola, and other soft drinks, cocoa, over-the-counter cold remedies, and aspirin. If you stop to think about what you have consumed during the day, you might be surprised to learn that you have had the equivalent of six to eight cups of coffee from several sources.

Fourth, do something fun but not stimulating before you go to sleep. Shortly before retiring I look at my tropical fish. Ten minutes later I feel relaxed. Twenty minutes later, I'm ready for bed.

Fifth, consciously try to relax. Tell yourself that you are getting tired. Think restful thoughts. Meditate. Listen to soothing classical music or quiet jazz. Have someone rub your back. Take a warm, comforting bath.

But if sleep doesn't come, go to another room and read a boring book. Or if you are a professor, like me, look through tomorrow's lecture notes. I guarantee it — sleep will come!

Unfortunately, many people turn to tranquilizers and barbiturates when sleep doesn't come easily. However, barbiturates and tranquilizers can dangerously alter sleep patterns. They often make it almost impossible for the mind to reach the most beneficial stage of sleep, which scientists call the "rapid eye movement" phase (REM).

During REM we dream, rehashing the day's experience, venting frustrations and indulging in fantasy thinking. When we deprive ourselves of this stage for one night, twice as much time might be spent the following night in dream activities. If medications keep us from dreaming, neurotic daytime behavior sometimes erupts. In addition, we may wake up exhausted because the REM time was not sufficient to give us the soothing deep sleep that is needed.[36]

Don't take any drugs without seeing your physician. But if you suspect that medications are compounding your sleep problems, consult your physician or a sleep clinic. Most hospitals associated with major universities have such clinics.

Tip #10: Avoid Fraudulent Medical Practice.

A woman wrote to Ann Landers for advice:

Dear Ann: I just read a news story about a pill for people who hate to diet and exercise and want to lose weight. This miraculous pill was developed by two prominent doctors at a world-famous hospital. It is sold with a guarantee that you can eat anything you want and as much as you want. No calorie counting or exercise. Also there are no hunger pangs.

It is 100 percent safe. All you have to do is take one pill with a glass of water before each meal. It breaks the fat into particles while you sleep. The news story says it is a major medical breakthrough with worldwide patent pending. These pills sound like exactly what I've been looking for. They cost $35 for 180 plus $3 for handling, which is expensive for me, but worth it if they work. What can you tell me about this discovery?

Excited Michigander

As you might expect, Ann burst the balloon:

Says Ann: "What you read wasn't a news story but an advertisement. How these charlatans get away with this stuff is beyond me. If you want to lose weight you will have to change your eating habits and exercise like everyone else."[37]

Today there is an epidemic of medical quackery, which costs Americans an estimated *twenty-seven billion dollars* a year. Approximately nine billion goes for unnecessary food supplements, such as vitamins, pills, and potions. Three billion is spent on bogus therapies for arthritis and heart problems. Cancer "cures" now exceed four billion dollars annually. The rest is spent on various other medical treatments, cures, and equipment.

"It's an outrage," states William Jarvis, professor at California's Loma Linda University Medical School.[38] Unfortunately, however, older Americans continued to be bamboozled by sophisticated con games. Here are some of the most popular scams targeted to the post-fifty generation:

* The most lucrative scams are associated with cancer treatments. Among them are "escharotics," which are salves to "draw out" the cancer from the body. "Krebiozen" is a remedy allegedly obtained from the blood of horses, although scientific analysis has proven that it is mainly mineral oil. Then there is the "spectrochrome," which will "treat disease through attuned color waves."[39]

* Arthritis remedies such as copper bracelets, "immunized" milk, and now "green-lipped mussel extract." According to the Arthritis Foundation, almost a billion dollars is

spent on such unproven remedies.[40]
* Bee pollen, which is promoted as
  a source of youth, vigor, vitality,
  and health. According to the U.S.
  Surgeon General, this one is
  strictly for the bees and the birds![41]
* One of the most believable scams
  has to do with allergy testing. The
  "health technicians" ask whether
  you are tired or have high blood
  pressure or sinus troubles. If so,
  they suggest that you are having an
  allergic reaction to a food. They will
  offer to test your blood for a fee,
  usually between $125 and $240. The
  tests, however, are worthless. The
  New York attorney general's office
  [as a test] sent a blood sample to a
  cytotoxic lab. It got back a reading
  that the patient had a milk allergy.
  The patient, however, was a cow.[42]

*There is no scientific justification for these
products, and there is no empirical evidence that
they work.* Not only will they cost you a lot
of money but, if you put your faith in them
and avoid competent medical treatment, you
will have lost valuable time in arresting your
illness.

Now you might say: "I would never fall for a huckster." Perhaps not. But today's charlatans are sophisticated businessmen who know how to advertise their products and exploit your fears. They also know how to present their credentials so that they sound impressive.

The credentials, however, are neither impressive nor legitimate. Most come out of mail-order diploma mills. One organization boasts that it has issued one and a half million doctoral degrees at twenty-five dollars each through its mail-order program.

How can you spot an imposter? Here is a handy checklist:

* Do the sellers claim that they are battling the medical profession or the federal government, which is trying to suppress the latest advances in science?
* Are you told that the typical medical program involving surgery, chemotherapy, and X rays will do more harm than good?
* Does the seller have a secret remedy or an instant cure?
* Does the seller use testimonials "guaranteeing" his product?
* Is the remedy sold door-to-door by

a "health adviser" or a "health technician"?[43]

If the answer to these questions is yes, beware!

In general, always locate the most competent help you can find, whether you are in need of medical, psychological, legal, or financial services. If in doubt about professional credentials, ask for references. On important issues, obtain a second opinion.

Since 1900 life expectancy has increased by twenty-six years, which is nearly equal to what mankind gained in the preceding fifty thousand years. Consequently, you have a good chance of spending one-fourth to one-third of your life in retirement.

Now the questions are: Can you age in good health? Must we inevitably end up in a nursing home, battling the diseases of old age? Or can you take actions to help prevent cancer, heart disease, and mental disability?

No one can predict with certainty who will become ill. And of course there are limits to what you can do to prevent debilitating illness. But the key point is this: there *are* strategies that can improve health and enhance your retirement years.

The strategies advocated in this chapter are

not complicated, nor will they take up much of your time. But if you forget the specifics, remember these seven commonsense practices.

* Eat breakfast.
* Sleep seven to eight hours a night.
* Do not snack between meals.
* Maintain a reasonable weight.
* Do not smoke.
* Drink alcohol in moderation — if at all.
* Take part in some type of physical exercise program.

The average *additional* life expectancy of those who follow six or seven of these practices (compared to three or fewer) is eleven years for men and seven years for women. Equally important, the sheer *quality* of your life will markedly improve.

CHAPTER TEN

Health Costs: Protecting Yourself from Financial Ruin

If your medical bills are not covered by a former employer's insurance plan and you do not have a medigap policy, you are putting your wealth at serious risk.

Susan Polnaiszek,
Director, United Seniors Health Cooperative

There may come a time when you fall ill. If so, you should make certain that your hard-earned financial assets are not consumed by medical costs.

Frankly, one of the greatest threats to a successful retirement is becoming ill and not being able to cover medical expenses. Worse yet is being admitted to a nursing home without adequate financial resources. States Representative Edward Roybal, chairman of the House Select Committee on Aging: "A year in a nursing home wipes out the income of over 90 percent of the elderly living alone."[1]

The purpose of this chapter is to provide you with practical suggestions for guarding against escalating medical and nursing home expenses. It won't come cheaply, but if there is one thing economists are agreed upon, it is this: Health expenses will continue to rise. And if you don't take measures *now* to deal with future expenses, a major illness could seriously erode your financial security and peace of mind.

How do you protect yourself from unexpected medical expenses? Do you need an insurance policy to supplement what you will receive from Medicare? Does it make sense to purchase long-term care insurance, even though you may never need a nursing home? Here are some thoughts on these and other insurance issues.

Early Retirement: How to Meet Your Health Care Expenses

As I noted earlier in this book, many people aspire to early retirement. But there is a catch: they don't know how to finance the cost of health care on their own. If you are considering an early retirement, be sure to determine how you will protect yourself against the expenses of a major medical illness. Here are the options.

First, ask your company's personnel officer or benefits manager whether retirees can be continued under the company's health insurance plan. By law, your company must offer health insurance protection for up to eighteen months after you terminate employment, but you must initiate the request. And in most instances, you will be forced to pick up the tab.

Second, if forced to retire, find out what is included in your severance package. If you are fifty-five or older, your company might keep you in its insurance program *at their expense*. Don't rejoice too quickly: they might keep *you* in the plan, but not your spouse or other dependents.

Third, if you cannot obtain insurance through your company, consider various "comprehensive major-medical" plans offered by commercial insurance carriers. Be prepared for a surprise: the coverage is expensive. In New York City, Aetna's Comprehensive Medical Plan policy, which has an unlimited maximum benefit, would cost a healthy fifty-five-year-old couple (with a deductible of $1,500 each) about $2,667 yearly. If they lived in Los Angeles, they could pay between $4,188 and $6,159, depending upon where they live.[2]

What can be done to diminish the costs? You can assume more of the risk by purchasing a policy that has limited benefits. This works well provided you don't have a major illness. But if ill fortune strikes, you might be saddled with considerable expense.

A better way to reduce costs is to purchase a policy that has high deductibles but retains a high benefit limit. In the jargon of health insurance, this is a "high-deductible, catastrophic" policy. While you end up paying most of the initial expenses, such as the first day you spend in a hospital, you will be protected from exorbitant bills. A good strategy: put $2,000 in a money market account earmarked for initial medical expenses and purchase a plan with an annual deductible of at least $1,000 and a catastrophic provision of $250,000 or more.[3] To save more, push the deductible to $2,000.

If you already have a medical problem and can't find a company that will insure you, ask your company whether it is possible to take a "phased" retirement. In so doing you will work on a part-time basis, but may retain 100 percent of your health insurance benefits.

Medicare: What It Will and Will Not Pay For

Medicare, founded in 1965, is a Federal health insurance program for people sixty-five or older. It is administered in Washington, D.C., by the Health Care Financing Administration. The Social Security Administration takes applications for Medicare and assists beneficiaries in receiving payments.[4]

Medicare is a complex program whose rules and regulations are often frustrating. In recent years, however, the Social Security Administration has made major strides in improving services. By calling a toll-free number (800-234-5772) you can receive prompt and courteous answers to your questions. In addition, the Social Security Administration provides several helpful publications including *Retirement* (Publication #05-10035), *Medicare* (Publication #05-10043), *Disability* (Publication #05-10029), *Survivors* (Publication #05-10084), *A Guide to Health Insurance for People with Medicare,* and the fact sheet *Should You Buy a Supplement to Medicare?* These publications are free and can be obtained by calling 800-234-5772 or by writing to the Department of Health and Human Services, Social Security Administration, Baltimore, MD 21235.

What health care expenses does Medicare cover, and what must you be prepared to pay? Health care expenses are reimbursed via two programs: the hospital insurance plan (Part A) and the medical insurance plan (Part B). The hospital plan pays for expenses while you are hospitalized, while the medical portion pays for physician and other related costs. Here, in a nutshell, is what you can expect to receive, based upon 1990 dollars:

PART A: HOSPITAL INSURANCE BENEFITS

If you are hospitalized, Medicare pays for all covered expenses through the first sixty days *except for the first $628*. From the sixty-first through ninetieth days, Medicare pays for all covered services *except for $157 a day*.

If you are hospitalized for more than ninety days, it is possible for you to use some or all of your sixty nonrenewable "reserve days." For each reserve day used, Medicare will pay for all covered services *except for $296 a day*.

The term "covered services" includes a semiprivate room, all meals, regular nursing services, operating and recovery room costs, hospital costs for anesthesia services, intensive care, and coronary care, drugs, lab tests, X rays, medical supplies and appliances, rehabilitation services, and preparatory services related to kidney transplant surgery.

PART B: MEDICAL INSURANCE BENEFITS

Medicare medical insurance will assist in paying for your doctors' services and a variety of other medical services and supplies that are not covered under Part A Hospital Insurance. Each year, as soon as you meet the annual deductible ($100), medical insurance pays for 80 percent of the approved charges. Specifically you are covered for:

Doctors' services. No matter where you receive a physician's services in the United States, medical insurance will cover your expenses, including surgical services, diagnostic tests and X rays that are a part of your treatment, medical supplies furnished in a doctor's office, services from the office nurse, and drugs that are administered as part of your treatment and cannot be self-administered.

Outpatient hospital services. Medical insurance will cover outpatient hospital services you receive for diagnosis and treatment, such as care provided in an emergency room or an outpatient clinic of a hospital.

Other medical and health services. Although there are limitations, medical insurance generally covers ambulance transportation; home dialysis equipment, supplies and periodic support services; independent laboratory tests; outpatient physical therapy and speech pathology services; and X rays and radiation treatments.

Some of the services and supplies *not* covered are: custodial care, such as help you may need in bathing, eating, and taking medicine; dentures and routine dental care; eyeglasses and hearing aids and examinations to prescribe or fit them; prescription drugs and patent medicines; most routine physical examinations and related tests and personal comfort items, including a telephone or television set in a hospital room.

Medicare will help pay for care in a qualified Canadian or Mexican hospital; however, *it will not pay for hospital or medical services you receive outside the United States* (Puerto Rico, Guam, American Samoa, the Virgin Islands, and the Northern Mariana Islands are considered to be part of the United States).

What about nursing home expenses? If after a hospital stay you need a skilled nursing facility, Medicare generally pays for all covered services (semiprivate room, rehabilitation services, drugs and medical supplies) for the first twenty days. Then you are responsible for the first $78.50 of daily expense up to eighty additional days. *After the one hundredth day, you are expected to meet all costs of nursing home care.*

In view of the fact that there are many deductibles, partial reimbursements, and exclusions in the Medicare program, don't be surprised to learn that, once retired, you may have to pick up a big chunk of your health care expenses. How best to meet medical expenses? Consider purchasing a supplemental insurance policy.

Medigap Insurance: How to Supplement Medicare Benefits

Medicare has a noble intent and that is to protect the financial assets of those sixty-five and older so that they are not decimated by a major illness. Today thirty-three million Americans receive over $100 *billion* worth of Medicare benefits. These benefits are often the difference between poverty and middle-class comfort.

Nevertheless, the need for supplemental protection is indisputable, since Medicare pays only about 45 percent of enrollees' health care expenses. Therefore it is up to the enrollees to make up the difference. To do so, about 70 percent of the participants, or nearly 22 million people, paid an estimated $17 billion for medigap insurance in 1989.

How do you find a "medigap" policy that is right for you? The most important step is to locate a *quality* insurance company. Table 20 provides a listing of nine companies that market their products to older adults. There are, of course, other insurance companies offering high-quality products. But regardless of the company you select, make certain it has an "A" or "A+" ranking from *Best Insurance Reports,* found in your local library.[5]

When interviewing insurance agents, find out everything you can about the policy. Here are the key questions to ask:

* Is the policy "guaranteed renewable"? In other words, are you protected against cancellation?
* What are the total maximum benefits paid under the plan?
* What preexisting medical conditions of yours are excluded by this policy?
* How long after a claim has been filed is payment received?
* Are the claim forms easy to fill out?
* Can payments be sent directly to your physician's office?
* Will the policy reimburse you for medical expenses incurred in other states or countries?
* What rights do you have if a claim is denied?
* What is the annual cost? How much have the premium costs escalated over the past three years?

The cost of your premiums will reflect whether you want a Chevrolet or a Cadillac

TABLE 20
Medical Plans Which Supplement Medicare

Companies	Plans	Phone Numbers
Bankers Life & Casualty	Planned Insurance Coverage	800-777-5775
Colonial Penn	Medicare Supple-ment Policy	800-523-4000
Equitable Life & Casualty	The New Ultimate	800-633-3480
First National Life	Medicare Supplement	800-356-6271
Golden Rule	Medigap Plus	317-297-4123
Pioneer Life	New Ultimate Protector	800-752-4369
Prudential, AARP	AARP's Com-prchensive Medicare Supplement	913-722-1110
Pyramid Life	Medicare Sup-plement	913-722-1110
Standard Life & Accident	Medicare Sup-plement Policy	405-232-5281

— or a model in between. As a general rule, you will have three choices: A) basic policy coverage; B) optional riders for basic policy coverage; and C) extended basic insurance.

Here is a thumbnail sketch of what each covers:

A. Basic policy coverage. Basic coverage is the least comprehensive and the least expensive. Your coverage includes:

1. 100 percent of Part A hospitalization expenses and some health expenditures that Medicare will only partially pay. Note: Basic policies will *not* cover the $628 Medicare Part A deductible per illness.
2. Pays Medicare Part A skilled nursing care co-payments.
3. Pays the Medicare-approved Part B co-payments.

B. Optional riders for basic policy coverage. Here are some of the most popular riders that bolster the basic plan:

1. Part A inpatient deductible. This extra benefit rider covers the $628 deductible for Medicare-approved hospital expenses.
2. Part B annual deductible. This extra benefit rider will take care of the $100 deductible for Medi-

care-approved outpatient and physician services.

3. Eighty percent or 100 percent of usual and customary expenses. This extra benefit rider is offered at two alternative levels, 80 percent or 100 percent, and pays the usual and customary hospital and medical expenses above those approved by Medicare.

4. Prescription drugs. This extra benefit rider often covers 50 percent of the cost of prescription drugs not covered by Medicare.

C. Extended basic coverage. This is the "Cadillac" of the medigap insurance policies. It is more comprehensive than a "basic" policy, even when you add in the optional riders. In addition to basic coverage, it will:

1. Pay 100 percent of the $628 Medicare Part A deductible per illness.

2. Pay 100 percent of the $100 Medicare Part B deductible.

3. Pay the 20 percent of Part B Medicare-approved charge, plus 80 percent of the usual and customary fees above Medi-

care's approved charge.

4. Have a $1,000 annual limit on money you pay out of your pocket on covered medical expenses, and

5. Provide a lifetime maximum benefit of at least $500,000.[6]

How much does the "Cadillac" cost? In one study of twelve different insurance companies, the lowest premium was $775 annually, while the highest was $1,850. The average was $1,365.[7] How much you ultimately pay will depend upon your age and medical condition.

One important rule to remember: *It is better to own a single comprehensive policy than multiple policies that have overlapping or duplicate coverage.* Unfortunately, 5.6 million older people own multiple policies that are not needed and which may never pay a claim. Take time to examine your insurance situation, preferably with someone who can guide you and help consolidate your policies.

Once you decide on a particular "medigap" policy, answer *all* the questions on the application form. If it can be proved that your medical history has been willfully falsified, the insurance company is not obligated to pay a claim. As Robert A. Gilmour, an authority on insurance programs, states: "[Giving] an incorrect health history guarantees that, even though you may sign a contract and pay premiums, you have absolutely no insurance." Therefore, answer all questions honestly and completely. To do otherwise is to place yourself at enormous risk.[8]

Is "medigap" insurance the best route to take? Not always. If your former employer has a health benefit plan for retirees, you may have the best supplementary insurance program of them all. However, read the fine print. As medical insurance costs rise, your company's benefits might be reduced. They might even be eliminated if your employer retains the right to change the health plan.[9]

Is an HMO in Your Future?

One of the best ways to close the "gaps" in Medicare coverage is to join a Health Maintenance Organization (HMO). An HMO is a private, not-for-profit organization designed to provide health care in an *efficient* and *affordable* way.

When you join an HMO, you agree to use the physicians, clinics, and hospitals affiliated with the HMO's provider network. You pay a monthly Medicare Part B premium plus a small monthly premium to the HMO. Every HMO's rate structure is different, so you must do comparative shopping to determine the most cost-effective HMO in your area.

What are the advantages of joining an HMO? You can save big money — up to 28 percent on yearly expenses compared with traditional health insurance programs.[10] HMO's usually provide prescription drugs, medical equipment, and even eyeglasses at reasonable rates. Because HMO's believe in preventive medicine, you can take advantage of diet counseling, exercise classes, and stress reduction programs. And since the HMO automatically pays your physical, laboratory, and hospital bills, you aren't buried under a blizzard of paperwork.

Nevertheless, HMO's have limitations. You usually give up your right to an unlimited choice of doctors, and you may see a different physician each time you visit. In order to control costs, HMO's may make you wait longer for an appointment, discourage you from entering a hospital, and limit the number and type of diagnostic tests. And if you have an emergency away from home and can't find a doctor affiliated with your HMO, you may have to dig into your pocket to pay a portion of the medical bills.

Perhaps the greatest danger is that your HMO could become financially insolvent and leave you without any insurance protection.

That's what happened to Martha Cohen, sixty-three, who lives in Hobe Sound, Florida, with her husband, Max, sixty-five, a former carpenter. The Cohens belonged to United American Health Care, a local HMO. When Martha was diagnosed as having cervical cancer in February 1987, the couple was comforted by the fact that all her medical costs would be paid for by their $173 monthly premium.

Unfortunately, American Health Care closed because of financial problems. Most of the 13,500 former members were offered Blue Cross/Blue Shield coverage, but insurers wouldn't cover Martha because of her cancer. Fortunately, the state found an insurance carrier to cover her. But it costs the Cohens $8,000 a year in premiums. That's more than 40 percent of their annual income of $19,200. States Max: "We never owed money. Now we're in hock."[11]

Fortunately, such cases are the exception and not the rule. But before joining an HMO, take a careful look at its financial condition and the service it provides. Here are the pertinent issues to address:

* How long has the HMO been in business? If less than three years, look elsewhere.

* How long do subscribers stay with the HMO? Some turnover is normal. But if the turnover is higher than 30 percent, troubles may exist. If the HMO tells you that such records don't exist, be skeptical. States Erling Hansen, general counsel to the Group Health Association of America, the HMO trade organization: "You measure what you care about."[12]
* What medical specialties exist within the HMO? If you have a medical problem, does the HMO have specialists who can address your problem? If not, to whom will you be referred?
* What percentage of the physicians are certified in their specialty? If fewer than 60 percent of the physicians are board certified you may want to look elsewhere for medical care.
* What hospital(s) are affiliated with the HMO? Are these well-established hospitals within your community?
* Are the physicians satisfied with the HMO? To find out, request a listing of physicians affiliated with

the HMO. Interview at least two and ask for their candid evaluation of the strengths and limitations of the HMO.

* What costs will I incur by becoming a member of this HMO? Inquire specifically about costs associated with diagnostic tests and prescription drugs.
* Does the HMO have a grievance system in the event patients encounter problems?

If you want more information on HMO's, a booklet, *Choosing an HMO: An Evaluation Checklist,* is available from the American Association of Retired Persons (Fulfillment Section, AARP, 1909 K Street NW, Washington, DC 20049).

Long-Term-Care Insurance: Who Needs It?

Now we come to one of the most troubling questions asked by retirees: "What will happen to my finances if I enter a nursing home?" The question is pertinent, given the following economic realities:

* Two out of every five Americans sixty-five years or older will need

415

to enter a nursing home.
* Women face the highest risk because of their longevity: 54 percent will enter a nursing home at some point in their lives.
* Costs per year for nursing home care range from $25,000 to $40,000. It takes only thirteen months on average for an elderly person to exhaust his or her savings.
* Less than $2 paid out of every $100 spent on nursing home care is paid by Medicare. *Don't count on Medicare to assist you in meeting long-term care expenses.*

Now the question is: should you begin an immediate crash savings program to subsidize skilled nursing care? Should you purchase a long-term-care insurance policy? Or is it best simply to take your chances and hope that you will never need nursing home assistance?

Let's start with the last question: what are the odds that you will need nursing home care?

As indicated earlier, two out of every five Americans sixty-five years of age or older will be a nursing home resident. But being admitted might not break you financially, because your stay may be brief. *Nearly three-quarters of those who enter a nursing home are discharged within one year.* Only 6.6 percent remain longer than three years.[13]

As a rule of thumb, if you can afford three years in a nursing facility ($75,000-$80,000), think twice before purchasing an expensive long-term-care policy. If your financial assets are less than $50,000 and/or your income is less than $10,000 per year, you may not be able to afford the premium. To help determine whether you can afford long-term-care insurance, consult Table 21.

What if you are in need of skilled nursing assistance and don't have a pot of gold to pay for it? What if your family members have a history of living into their eighties and nineties? And what if you have a chronic illness that is gradually getting worse?

Under these circumstances your best bet is to investigate long-term-care insurance protection. Here is what to look for.

First, select a high-quality insurance company. Today there are over one hundred insurance carriers offering long-term-care protection, triple those existing in 1985. Be sure to find out how long the company has been offering long-term-care policies and the extent to which premiums have risen during the past five years.

Second, purchase a policy that pays a high

TABLE 21
Can I Benefit from Long-Term-Care Insurance?

My Financial Status

A. The current value of my liquid assets:

Cash, checking, and savings	$_____
Certificates of deposit	$_____
Bonds, stocks, and mutual funds	$_____
Cash value of insurance policies	$_____
Other	$_____
Total value of liquid assets:	$_____

B. Current value of my other assets, less any loans against them:

Real estate, not including primary home	$_____
Businesses or limited partnerships	$_____
Annuities	$_____
Total value of nonliquid assets:	$_____

Note: If the total value of both liquid and non-liquid assets is less than $50,000, long-term-care insurance *may* be too expensive to benefit you.

C. My monthly income:

Pension income	$_____
Social Security	$_____
Interest and dividends	$_____
Annuity income	$_____
Proprietary and business income	$_____
Veterans benefits	$_____
Other (including part-time employment)	$_____

TABLE 21 *(Continued)*

C. My monthly income: *(Continued)*
   Total estimated monthly income $_____
   $_____ x 12 months = $_____

Note: If your income is less than $10,000 a year, long-term-care insurance *may* be too expensive to benefit you.

D. Is there someone to whom I wish to leave my estate?

Note: If you do not have heirs and no one to whom to bequest monies, there may be little need for long-term insurance. There are, however, exceptions to this rule. Some individuals purchase long-term-care insurance in order to protect assets that they wish to leave to a favorite charity. Others purchase insurance simply because they never wish to be financially impoverished due to medical and/or nursing home expenses.

Source: Long Term Care Insurance: Is It Right for You?, Metropolitan Senior Federation, 1885 University Avenue, Suite 190, St. Paul, MN 55104.

daily benefit. How much should the policy pay? The best plans will reimburse you for one-third to one-half of the daily nursing home costs.[14]

In selecting coverage, keep in mind that benefits usually remain fixed, even if the cost of long-term care rises. For example, if you purchase a policy today and enter a nursing home ten years from now, the daily benefits will cover a much smaller part of the actual costs than when you purchased the policy.[15] How much will nursing home expenses rise? Here are the projections:

Average Daily Rates for Nursing Home Care

Level of Care	1988	1998	2008*
Skilled care	$ 72	$124	$215
Intermediate care	$ 57	$100	$108
Custodial care	$ 36	$ 62	$108

*Projections assume an inflation rate of 5.6% per year.

Source: Long Term Care: A Dollar and Sense Guide, United Seniors Health Cooperative, 1331 H St. NW, Suite 500, Washington, DC 20005, p. 38.

How much should you expect to pay for long-term-care protection? Premiums can range from approximately $600 to more than

$2,000 a year, depending upon your age. Most insurance companies will not sell a policy to anyone over seventy-nine years of age. And if you are under fifty, you should probably delay your purchase. The reason? As Robert Hunter, president of the National Insurance Consumer Organization states: "I cannot imagine that there won't be some type of national health insurance in twenty years."[16]

Third, what level of care does the policy provide? Nursing homes generally offer three levels of care.

Skilled care is provided by licensed, skilled professionals, such as nurses and therapists working under a physician's supervision. The goal of skilled care is to restore a patient to optimal health, given the patient's medical condition.

Intermediate care requires the skills of a nurse but is generally less complex and intensive than skilled care. Typically, intermediate care is given after surgery. The goal is to help the patient regain health and strength and live a normal life.

Custodial care is provided when individuals have difficulty with such simple tasks as bathing, dressing, and eating. Insurance benefits for custodial care cover room, board, and assistance with daily living.

Ideally, you want an insurance policy that

pays for all types of care: skilled, intermediate, and custodial. It does little good to have a policy that pays for skilled care when what you really need is minimal custodial assistance. Fortunately many insurance companies recognize this fact and provide identical benefits, regardless of the level of care needed.[17]

Fourth, what, if any, restrictions are there in the policy? If an insurance agent tells you that there are no exclusions, look elsewhere. Even the best policies have restrictions defining when care can begin and under what circumstances. Some policies require a stay in a hospital before you are eligible for benefits. Other policies require that you be in a nursing home for twenty or even one hundred days before benefits are paid. And some will not reimburse for "mental disorders." Unfortunately, nearly half of all nursing home patients have Alzheimer's disease or other organically related mental disorders, chiefly multiple infarct dementia, a form of senility. If your policy excludes "organic brain disease," look elsewhere.[18]

Given the disparities in individual policies, it is important to make a systematic evaluation of benefits and exclusions. To assist you in making your decision, refer to Table 22.

Fifth, where will care be delivered? Policies vary as to the amount of freedom you have in selecting a long-term-care facility. Some insurers insist that you stay at a facility designated by them. Others will permit you to stay at the facility of your choice as long as certain guidelines are met. Still others pre-certify a facility you select before purchasing the policy.[19]

Sixth, what is the cost of the policy? Insurance premiums vary considerably, depending upon the type of coverage you select. However, a fairly typical policy will cost a fifty-five-year-old $650 per year and a seventy-year-old $2,300.

These are the ground rules to apply prior to purchasing a long-term-care policy:

* Take your time. Never be rushed by an aggressive insurance agent.
* Ask your insurance agent for a "specimen policy" that will tell you exactly what is and is not covered. Examine the "lifetime" benefit cap, which is anywhere from $12,000 to $200,000.
* Compare the costs and benefits of at least three different plans before you buy.
* Do not purchase more than one long-term-care policy.
* Never pay cash when buying a policy; pay by check or money order.

TABLE 22
Comparing Long-Term Policies

What Does Long-Term Care Cost?

	Policy A	Policy B
1. What kinds of nursing homes are there in your area and how much do they charge for:		
Skilled nursing care?	$_____ per month	$_____ per month
Intermediate nursing care?	$_____ per month	$_____ per month
Custodial/personal care?	$_____ per month	$_____ per month
2. What do home–health–care agencies in your area charge?		
Unskilled care	$_____ per month	$_____ per month
Skilled care	$_____ per month	$_____ per month

How Much Does the Policy Pay?

	Policy A	Policy B
3. What is the maximum amount the policy will pay for:		
Skilled nursing care?	$_____ per month	$_____ per month

TABLE 22 (*Continued*)

How Much Does the Policy Pay? (*Continued*)

	Policy A	Policy B
Intermediate nursing care?	$ _____ per day	$ _____ per day
Custodial nursing care?	$ _____ per day	$ _____ per day
Home health care?	$ _____ per day	$ _____ per day

How Much Does the Policy Cost?

4. How much will the policy cost you over time?

	Policy A	Policy B
1 year	$ _____	$ _____
5 years	$ _____	$ _____
10 years	$ _____	$ _____
15 years	$ _____	$ _____
Lifetime	$ _____	$ _____

TABLE 22 (*Continued*)

How Much Does the Policy Cost? (*Continued*)

5. Can the companies alter your premium over time or under other circumstances?

Yes _____ No _____

If so, under what circumstances?

_____ _____

What Are the Benefits?

	Policy A	Policy B

6. Does the policy provide benefits for the following long-term-care expenses?
If so, check which kind:

	Policy A		Policy B	
Skilled nursing care	Yes____	No____	Yes____	No____
Intermediate nursing care	Yes____	No____	Yes____	No____
Home health care	Yes____	No____	Yes____	No____

TABLE 22 (*Continued*)

What Are the Benefits? (*Continued*)

	Policy A	Policy B
7. For how long will the policy's benefits last?		
Skilled nursing care	_____ days	_____ days
Intermediate nursing care	_____ days	_____ days
Custodial nursing care	_____ days	_____ days
Home health care	_____ days	_____ days
All of the above services	_____ days	_____ days
8. Does the policy cover Alzheimer's disease if you develop it after you purchase the policy?	Yes___ No___	Yes___ No___
9. Does the policy provide benefits if you need care away from the area in which you live?	Yes___ No___	Yes___ No___

TABLE 22 (*Continued*)

What Are the Benefits? (*Continued*)

	Policy A	Policy B
10. Will the policy provide benefits if you have similar coverage?	Yes___ No___	Yes___ No___

What Are the Limits?

11. What is the elimination or deductible period before benefits begin?

Nursing home care _____ days _____ days

12. What is the preexisting-condition limitation period?

_____ months _____ months

13. Can the company cancel or refuse to renew the policy?

Yes___ No___   Yes___ No___

If there are conditions, what are they?

_____ _____

TABLE 22 (*Continued*)

What Are the Limits? (*Continued*)

14a. Is a prior hospital stay required before the policy will pay for:

	Policy A			Policy B		
Skilled nursing care:	Yes___	No___	# days___	Yes___	No___	# days___
Intermediate nursing care:	Yes___	No___	# days___	Yes___	No___	# days___
Custodial nursing care:	Yes___	No___	# days___	Yes___	No___	# days___

14b. Is a prior skilled nursing home stay required before the policy will pay for:

	Policy A			Policy B		
Intermediate care:	Yes___	No___	# days___	Yes___	No___	# days___
Custodial care:	Yes___	No___	# days___	Yes___	No___	# days___

TABLE 22 (*Continued*)

What Are the Limits? (*Continued*)

14c. Is a prior nursing home stay required before the policy will pay for:
Home health care

	Policy A	*Policy B*
	Yes____ No____ # days____	Yes____ No____ # days____

15. Are there other limitations that concern you?

Yes____ No____   Yes____ No____

If so, what are they?____

Source: The Consumers Guide to Long Term Care Insurance, Health Insurance Association of America, 1001 Pennsylvania Ave. NW, Washington, DC 20004.

* When a salesperson tries to sell you a policy, never buy it the same day. Take your time and think it over.[20]

Need help in locating an appropriate insurance company? For a list of private insurers offering products in your state, write to the Health Insurance Association of America, 1001 Pennsylvania Avenue NW, Washington DC 20004-2599.

What, then, are the strategies for protecting yourself from financial ruin due to health care expenses? Become knowledgeable about Medicare, since benefits frequently change. Determine whether health insurance protection can be continued through your employer. If you wish to obtain a policy that will reimburse you for nursing home expenses, inquire about the costs *and* benefits of several plans before making application.

PART IV
LEISURE PURSUITS

Enjoying It All

Have you ever wondered what you are going to do with your time once you've retired? The purpose of part 4 is to focus on two activities that can energize your retirement years.

Chapter 11, *The World Awaits: The Lure of Retirement Travel* is packed with intriguing travel information. We will tell you about ocean liners that transport you to exotic ports of call. We will find out how to arrange a stay in a stunning European villa — *at no cost!* And we will explore the charm of bed and breakfast inns scattered throughout America. Finally, attention will focus on the Elderhostel program, an exciting travel and educational opportunity for those age sixty and over.

After your travels have been completed and your wanderlust satisfied, consider using your experience and talents to better your community.

Chapter 12, *The Joy of Being a Volunteer*, provides timely information on philanthropic activities. In large and small communities, retirees are touching other people's lives in ways beneficial to all. In Massachusetts, older adults are teaching Cambodian children to read and write English. In Florida, retired scientists are helping students learn about engineering, geology, and astronomy. And in California, AIDS victims are comforted by programs staffed with retirees.

If you are tempted to think that your talents and abilities are not needed, read this chapter carefully. The reason? Within a few blocks or miles from your home, there are those who need help. If you provide it, your retirement years will take on a new focus and a new meaning. As Albert Einstein once observed: "There is no higher religion than human service. To work for the common good is the gentlest creed."

CHAPTER ELEVEN

The World Awaits: The Lure of Retirement Travel

I don't think this life is for hibernating and getting ready for the next one. I think you are given it for a purpose and this is to live it. Live while you are alive!

Malcolm Forbes
(1919–1990)

When I asked adults what they *really* wanted to do in retirement, a smile would cross their face. Their eyes lit up with excitement. And they responded with an emphatic "I want to travel!"

If traveling is in your future, you'll enjoy this chapter because, literally, a whole new world of travel opportunities is at your doorstep. If you're worried about high costs, don't be. While some trips cost a financial arm and a leg — many don't. In fact, we will examine numerous ways to keep travel expenses at rock-bottom prices. Where to begin? How about celebrating your retirement on board a luxury ocean liner?

Magnificent Cruises

Charles N. Barnard spent ten days on board the SS *Rotterdam,* one of the *grandes dames* of the sea. Listen to his account of the first day at sea:

The ship is immense at her Florida pier, a towering deep-blue hull with escalators and airport-style jetways for boarding — much easier, I think, than staggering aboard that troopship in 1943 with a helmet cocked on my head and a duffel on my shoulder. What was that rustbucket's name? *The Henry J. Kaiser?* Maybe. Even now, I imagine I hear the music of the '40's.

Young Indonesian stewards in slate-blue jackets, cream pants, and white gloves welcome passengers aboard the *Rotterdam.* A string quartet is playing on the main deck — *that's* what I heard, of course! "Green Eyes!" I'm summoned back to 1941 and the voice of Helen O'Connell: ". . . those cool and limpid gree-een eyes . . ."

Important matters first: A singles party

in one of the lounges — even before dinner. Out of more than a thousand passengers, about 30 of us gather for speculative smiles, introductions, champagne, and peanuts. All ages, all shapes. The string quartet is busy again. *"Beyond the blue horizon, waits a beautiful day . . ."* I say hello to Laura, a physical therapist from Toronto. First Caribbean cruise for both of us. We clink to that! I hear Kay Kyser: *"I'd love to get you on a slow boat to China."*

The first day at sea is for unpacking and learning the ship. Now then, which comes first, boat deck or sun deck? Where is the Laundromat? The beauty parlor? The doctor? Where does one buy laundry soap? And suntan lotion? And where the heck is my cabin? I'm lost already!

We sail through an empty, sunny sea. At 22 knots, the ship never quivers. *Rotterdam* is a steamship; they don't build 'em that way anymore.

"Day at sea" on the itinerary is easy to fill — take your choice: low-impact aerobics, computer lecture, walk a mile (five and a half laps around the deck), bridge lessons, shuffleboard tournament, dancing class, visit the ship's bridge, blackjack lessons, craft class, travel videos, afternoon tea, Bingo! — or find a comfortable deck chair and read your book.

The movie matinee, in a theater big enough for a small town, is a Woody Allen film I missed a couple of years ago. Good, I can catch up. A couple hundred of us surrender to this nostalgic temptation.

For dinner, go calorie-crazy — or eat skinny: Florida oysters, Pacific crab legs, prime ribs. (There are six of us who dine together and become friends at a small oval table.) Then strawberries, eclairs, and coffee with Amaretto. After dinner, a cabaret: Connie Haines is aboard — remember Connie Haines? I do! Vocalist with both Harry James and Tommy Dorsey? Her songs bring back the '40's — and hush the room.

I'll never smile again, until I smile at you . . . I've flown around the world in a plane . . . but I can't get started with you . . . You must remember this, a kiss is still a kiss.

It isn't the Caribbean yet, but the particular magic of being on a big ship at sea is casting its spell.[1]

Does a slow boat to China or Alaska or the

Bahama Islands sound intriguing? As thousands have learned, a cruise offers one of the most thrilling of all vacations. In fact, *cruising has the highest satisfaction rating of any vacation,* whether that be a three-day or a three-month cruise.[2]

How do you find a cruise that is right for you? Here are some exciting possibilities.[3]

TOURING THE CONTINENT

If you want a memorable trip, take a twelve-day cruise between Venice, Italy, and Barcelona, Spain. You will explore the Acropolis in Athens, relax in Venice's magnificent Piazza San Marco, and visit the great museums of Florence. You will see the medieval walls of Dubrovnik, Yugoslavia, and the beaches of Cannes, France. And you will enjoy these magnificent sights and events while based on the twelve-hundred-passenger *Royal Princess,* which is the flagship for the eight-member "Love Boat" fleet. (The television series "The Love Boat" was filmed on Princess ships.) Entertainment and food? Among the best you will find anywhere. Fares are under $300 a day, per person, double occupancy. This *includes* round-trip airfare from major U.S. cities.

If you want to experience the magnificent

culture of Italy, consider the *Sun Viking,* a ship owned by the Royal Caribbean Cruise Line. The ship stops at Livorno (where you can visit Florence and Pisa), Naples (for tours of Capri, Sorrento, Pompeii, and Rome), Gibraltar, Villefranche (for Monte Carlo, Nice, and Cannes) as well as Barcelona and Palma de Majorca. Among the most memorable parts of your trip will be the nightclub and cabaret shows and dancing under the stars.

If you are a history buff, may I suggest a tour to Greece, which is the cradle of Western civilization? The seven-hundred-passenger *Pegasus* will take you to five Greek islands: Crete, whose architectural treasures date back to 200 B.C.; Rhodes, which features its walled city built by the Crusaders; Santorini, which is perched on the rim of an ancient volcano; and the islands of Mykonos and Patmos, frequented by the rich and famous. You will also visit Kusadasi, Turkey, and tour the excavated city of Ephesus, where Antony and Cleopatra's tale of love began and where Alexander the Great made his mark on history. Two days will be devoted to Istanbul, where merchants line the streets with a wide variety of goods. Rates? $1,095-$4,070 without transatlantic transportation.[4]

PACIFIC TRAVEL

If the Far East has long beckoned you, consider the *Ocean Pearl,* a 460-passenger ship owned by Ocean Cruise Line that will whisk you to the idyllic island of Bali and the huge Buddhist temple at Borobudur. You will see the bustling city of Jakarta and tour Kuala Lumpur, the pristine, modern capital of Malaysia. You will also be invited to a beach barbecue on the tropical island of Paula Sepa. Costs run less than $300 per day per person, double occupancy, including precruise and postcruise stopovers in Singapore and Bangkok.

ALASKA!

You don't have to travel to the ends of the world to see beautiful country. Experienced travelers will tell you that some of the world's most spectacular sights are in Alaska.

As your boat cruises through the Inland Passage, you will view snow-peaked mountains framed against blue skies, and ancient glaciers will jut out of the ocean before your eyes. And, in spite of the 1989 oil spill, wildlife is abundant.

Some of the best features of Alaskan cruises are the one-day stops, permitting you to explore the countryside. If you are adventurous, go for white-water rafting on an Alaskan river, or try your luck at fishing for salmon and halibut. If you want a better understanding of Alaskan people, visit some Native American villages and frontier outposts.

One of the most enjoyable Alaska cruises is offered by the Holland America Line, which owns three sleek luxury ships given the exotic names *Nieuw Amsterdam, Noordam,* and *Westerdam.* The seven-day trek starts in Vancouver, British Columbia, Canada, and takes you to Ketchikan, Juneau, and Sitka, Alaska. The cost ranges from $900 to $3,700 per person, double occupancy, depending upon the type and location of your cabin as well as the date of your departure. If you opt for shore excursions, your expenses will be slightly higher.

THE CARIBBEAN

If you're short of cash but still want to cruise, consider a three-day tour out of Miami or Los Angeles offered by NCL, the Norwegian Cruise Line. Prices start as low as $395 per person, two to a cabin. These low rates apply only to three-day trips on specific dates occurring early and late in the season, but they *include* round-trip airfare between more than one hundred U.S. and Canadian cities to your point of departure.

If you want to see Catalina Island and Ensenada, Mexico, take the *Southward*, which sails out of Los Angeles. If you prefer the Bahamas, board the *Sunward II*, whose home base is Miami.

Want a longer cruise? Most travel companies offer seven-day and ten-day Caribbean voyages. But no matter the length of your sailing, you will enjoy the same marvelous service, meals, and entertainment. And best of all: you can carouse to your heart's delight with old and new friends.

To save on costs, keep in mind the following:

* Make your reservation early. You may receive a *deep* discount if you book at least six months in advance.
* Reserve space in less expensive cabins on new, luxurious ships or select middle-range accommodations on older ships. There is nothing wrong with a less expensive cabin, although you probably won't have an ocean view. Be wary, however, if the cabin is located near the galley, disco, or engine room. It can be noisy and hot.

* If you're traveling alone, ask your travel agent or the cruise company to match you up with a like-minded roommate. In so doing, you avoid the costly charges for a single room.
* Ask your travel agent for a complete listing of extra costs called "add-ons" which are expenses associated with inland excursions and entertainment.[5]

According to Shirley Slater and Harry Basch, travel editors of *San Diego Magazine*, here's the best of the best:

Best shipboard service: Seabourn Cruise Line's elegant *Seabourn Pride* and new *Seabourn Spirit*, each with a service ratio of 140 superbly trained European staff members to a maximum of 212 passengers.
Best entertainment: Norwegian Cruise Line's *Norway*, with splashy, full-scale Broadway musicals and star-studded jazz cruises.
Best library: The 12,000 volumes aboard World Explorer Cruises' *Universe*, which cruises Alaska in summer and doubles as a floating university in winter.
Most romantic departure: The American

Hawaii Cruise ships *Independence* and *Constitution* on their Saturday evening departures past the twinkling curve of lights at Waikiki and the dark, dramatic shape of Diamond Head.

Best hors d'oeuvres: The generous help-yourself displays of Beluga caviar on Cunard Line's *Sea Goddess I* and *Sea Goddess II*.

Best soufflés: The cheese soufflé and chocolate dessert soufflé aboard Abercrombie & Kent's *Sun Boat,* on the Nile, in Egypt.

Best seagoing golf course: The computerized system that lets your foursome play Pebble Beach aboard Royal Viking Line's *Royal Viking Sun.*

Best swimming pool: Princess Cruises' new *Star Princess,* with its swim-up bar and waterfall.

Best shore excursions: Holland America Westours, in Alaska, with everything from glacier flights to panning for gold.[6]

To reserve your space on a cruise ship, contact a travel agent, or call the cruise companies direct, toll-free: Holland America: 800-426-0327; Ocean: 800-556-8850; Princess: 800-421-0522; Royal: 800-622-0538; Sun: 800-872-6400; Windsor: 800-258-7245. Bon voyage!

Villas Around the World: How to Rent Your Castle Away from Home

Many retirees have seen Europe's historic cities at some point in their lives. Now they want to settle down — at least for a few weeks — and enjoy the grandeur and splendor of a single city, or perhaps some lush countryside. How do you go about finding a perfect home away from home? Consider renting a vacation villa overseas, or, better yet, taking up residence in a European castle.

Now, you might be thinking you could never afford to rent a home abroad, let alone a castle. Don't be so sure. True, an actual castle on Crete complete with a maid, a cook, and a breathtaking view of the Aegean will cost you $5,000 per week. But the government of Spain, which has renovated its most precious castles and monasteries, will offer you an exquisite room for as low as $70 a night, including breakfast. A room in a castle, monastery, or convent in Portugal costs less than $50.

If a night in a convent or monastery seems austere, may I suggest a cozy eighteenth-century cottage in the English countryside, where you do your own cooking and some gardening, for about $600 a week? Or why not consider a luxurious, picturesque villa on the Algarve coast of Portugal, which will cost approximately $800 a week. What do you get for your money? A private villa, your own swimming pool, and a glorious view of the sea from your living room terrace.[7]

Some of the most popular one-to-three-month rental villas are found in the Caribbean countries and in Mexico, for the simple reason that travel costs won't put a huge dent in your budget. And if you want to fly home for business reasons or to see your grandchildren, you are but a few hours away.

If renting a European villa has appeal, remember one important rule: *be flexible*. As Claire Packman, president of At Home Abroad, in New York City, states: "Americans are very accustomed to going to Mexico or the Caribbean, where everything (staff, driver, or maid service) is included. But it's not the same in Europe. Stoves don't work the same. Costs are different. The phones don't work the same. They often aren't even in the same house."[8]

It is also important to plan far ahead, especially if you want to live in England, Ireland, or Scotland, where rental properties are harder to find. For best results, start your villa shopping *six months* in advance, especially if you are looking to rent between December and May.[9]

To begin the process of locating your foreign Nirvana, consult the travel section of your local newspaper, as well as the ads in large-circulation newspapers, such as the *Los Angeles Times* or the *New York Times*. There you will find the names and addresses of foreign home owners who are looking for renters. In addition, you may find it helpful to consult magazines, such as *European Travel and Life, Travel & Leisure, Southern Living, Sunset,* and *Town & Country.*

Then write directly to the property owners, requesting a description of the property. Don't be surprised by their response. Some will provide a brief sketch of their villa, but then they will request information on *you* to see if you are up to *their* standards! Others will forward a snazzy brochure, colored photographs, and a lengthy description of the property. However, before sending a deposit (often 50 percent of the rental cost), insist on receiving this information:

* A complete description of the home, including the number of bedrooms *and* bath facilities
* Information on how you would obtain assistance in the event of a medical emergency
* Information on where you can go

for your banking and financial needs
* A description of what services are included in your weekly/monthly charge, such as linen, color television, phone service, heat and electricity, firewood, and so on. Remember, services vary from one country to another. In southern France, electricity, heat, telephone, and linens are not always included in the rental price.[10]

Renting directly from home owners certainly has charm, especially if they take an interest in your welfare. But you may prefer to work with an agency specializing in rental housing. As part of their service they will give you a candid assessment of the property. They will provide information on where to do your banking and, if you should need it, where to go for medical help. And if the air-conditioning in your home fails or a pipe breaks, help is but a telephone call away.

Following is a list of seven agencies that can help you locate a property that meets your specifications:

* *At Home Abroad* represents 2,500 villas in the Caribbean, Mexico and Europe. (405 E. 56th St., New

York, NY 10022; 212-421-9165)

* *Castles, Cottages & Flats of Ireland & U.K.* represents one of the few agencies that manages rental properties in Ireland. (P.O. Box 261, Westwood, MA 02090; 617-329-4680)

* *The French Experience* is the only U.S. agency that books 30,000 *gûtes* — rustic cottages — that can be found throughout rural France. (370 Lexington Ave., New York, NY 10017; 212-986-1115)

* *Heritage of England* handles reservations throughout England, Scotland, and Wales. (P.O. Box 297, Falls Village, CT 06031; 800-533-4305)

* *Hideaways International* is an agency and travel club (annual membership fee: $75) that handles 2,000 rentals worldwide. (P.O. Box 1464, Littleton, MA 01460; 800-843-4433)

* *Twelve Islands & Beyond* has rentals on the Greek Islands. (5431 MacArthur Blvd. NW, Washington, DC 20016; 800-345-8236)

* *Vacanza Bella* rents properties in Italy, including unusual farmhouses

in southern Tuscany. (2443 Fillmore St., Suite 228, San Francisco, CA 94115; 415-821-9345)[11]

Home Exchange Vacations

If you're short of cash but would still like to spend time in a foreign country, how about exchanging your home for one abroad? That's what Jan and David Mishel did, trading their Mill Valley, California, home for villas in Paris, London, and Barcelona.[12]

How does a home swap occur? The Mishels bought a map of Paris and identified sections of the city that were conveniently located near tourist attractions. Then they registered with Intervac U.S., one of the oldest organizations devoted to helping people exchange homes. With Intervac's help, they discovered a French couple who wanted to visit California. Jan offered their home, which is situated on an acre of land just north of the Golden Gate Bridge, and, in turn, the Mishels were invited to stay in a luxury two-bedroom apartment in the heart of Paris. "Our location was ideal," states Jan. "We were right around the corner from the Carnavalet Museum, which had a first-rate exhibit on the Revolution, and we were never far from the most charming cafés and markets.[13]

451

"Exchanging homes makes it much easier to meet people — the local butcher or a gate-keeper or neighborhood families. Under other circumstances we might have budgeted ourselves for only four days at a Paris hotel, but this way we could afford two weeks. Trading homes changed our whole notion of what a vacation could be. We may never take a 'normal' trip again."[14]

If interested in exchanging homes, contact a home exchange organization. Three to consider are:

Intervac U.S. (Dept. NC, P.O. Box 190070, San Francisco, CA 94119; 415-474-5170) For a low annual fee, you will receive three directories listing addresses and telephone numbers of 7,000 contacts in the United States and twenty-five other countries. Once a residence catches your fancy, write directly to the home owner for further information.

Home Exchange International (185 Park Row, Dept. NC, P.O. Box 878, New York, NY 10038-0272; 212-349-5340) will manage airline ticketing as well as rentals for those who like to extend their vacations beyond the time limit of the exchange.

Global Home Exchange and Travel Service (P.O. Box 2015, S. Burlington, VT 05403; 802-865-2503) is a personalized search agency that charges a $30 nonrefundable application fee for the first exchange of information on homes. Once a home exchange is agreed to, the fee is $250 for exchanges within the U.S. and $270 for foreign exchanges. Global offers housing in France, Germany, Great Britain, and Switzerland.

When writing to home exchange agencies, describe your priorities as accurately as possible. If a fireplace, golf course, or conveniently located shopping center is essential, indicate your preferences on the application form. And if *your* home has limitations, such as not being near a bus line or being located far from athletic or cultural events, be frank in your appraisal.

Assuming you are adaptable and have made the decision to exchange homes, do not demand perfection in your foreign residence. In Europe, for example, you may be staying in a house that is but a fraction of the size of your home. If you travel to South America, you might not have central air-conditioning, and your host's automobile may not be loaded with optional equipment.

Nevertheless, one of the benefits of going abroad is to see how others live. Enter into your host's living environment with enthusiasm, even if it is slightly less convenient than the one you left behind.

Bed and Breakfast Inns

Sam and Trudy Carson could barely contain their enthusiasm over a Bed and Breakfast Inn located on the southwest tip of Lake Superior:

It's marvelous. You not only have a gorgeous view of the lake, but the staff is attentive to your needs. The food is outstanding. The rooms are spacious. And the three other couples who were in the inn were charming. On Saturday night we played a game called "Murder at the Inn." Now that might sound a little frightening, but it was the most fun-filled evening I can remember. The best part of the experience? Making new friends. We already have decided that we are going to return a year from now and have a reunion.

The Carsons don't have a lot of money. They can't afford a villa on the southern coast of France, nor could they afford a lavish Caribbean cruise. But for $225, they had one of the nicest three-day weekends you can imagine.

If you have never stayed in a B&B, as they are called, you might be missing a sure bet for fun and relaxation. Your day might begin with a sumptuous breakfast, preceded, as you awaken, by the smell of gingerbread pancakes hot off the griddle or an apple–brie cheese omelet bubbling away. If you're in Vermont, the fare of choice may be French toast with *real* maple syrup, perhaps from the farm next door.[15]

After breakfast you can relax in the coziness of the inn or explore nearby attractions. In the afternoon some B&B owners provide a change of pace. A Mississippi River B&B, for example, offers speedboat rides. The owner of a Washington, D.C., B&B takes guests on a Capitol Hill tour. An Iowa hostess prepares a different quiche each day and provides recipes free of charge.[16]

In the evening you can nestle in a comfortable chair with a book. Or you can engage other guests in conversation, a favored aspect of B&B lodgings that many people return for. When sleep beckons, you can be assured of a comfortable and inviting bed.

In the mid-1970s, B&B's were located mainly on the east and west coasts and in a few vacation areas like Cape Cod and Nantucket Island. But today you can find B&B's in almost any American city or resort area. In fact, you can travel across America and stay in B&B's most of the way!

B&B accommodations vary in terms of services and amenities. In New York City, you can rent a penthouse apartment overlooking the historic John Jacob Astor Church. As you awaken and pull the curtains apart, you will have a breathtaking view of the New York harbor. In Estherville, Iowa, a college professor and his wife rent two rooms in their turn-of-the-century, small-town home. The home, furnished in antiques, is located approximately twenty-five miles off Interstate 90, near the Iowa "Great Lakes." If your travels take you to Heraldsburg, California, you will be in the middle of wine-growing Sonoma County. The Grape Leaf Inn, a seven-room hostelry, will serve you a sampling of local wines in the parlor or on the veranda each afternoon.[17]

What are the drawbacks? You will have to carry your own suitcase in most B&B's. There is no Coke machine or ice bucket. Your room may not have a television set or a telephone. And there may be some rules that you might not like, such as no smoking and an 11:00 P.M. curfew.[18]

But if you like homespun service, and if you enjoy the quiet company of other people, you

456

should visit a B&B. "If it's cold, the hostess will lend you a sweater; if it rains, you'll get an umbrella," states Mary McAulay, from Urban Ventures, a firm that represents 500 B&B's in Manhattan and Brooklyn. "She'll tell you how to find the subway and listen to you talk about your visit to the Statue of Liberty. When you come home, you'll have a friend, not just a place to sleep."[19]

To locate a Bed and Breakfast Inn, consult the travel section in your newspaper or obtain the *Bed and Breakfast Guide to the U.S. and Canada*, which is the official publication of the National Bed and Breakfast Association (Box 2394, Washington, DC 20026).

The Delights of Travel: New Friends in the Making

When I asked Grace Reynolds, sixty-two, a widow from Fort Dodge, Iowa, to describe her tour to South America, she didn't talk about the Spanish culture or the picturesque cities of Argentina or Brazil. Rather she focused on one important dividend of the trip: "I met a new friend," she commented. "We hit it off immediately. And I would bet that we will be friends for life."

If you desire new companionship, why not travel with people your own age and see the fjords of Norway or visit the great cathedrals of Europe? Better yet, take advantage of the new group travel opportunities to Eastern Europe to see how democracy is transforming Poland, Hungary, and Czechoslovakia.

To begin, call your local travel agent, who will put you in contact with various tour companies or book you personally. You might want to contact travel organizations that have a particular interest in retirees. Not only do they provide invigorating travel opportunities, but the trips are conducted at a leisurely pace, to ensure that you won't need a vacation to recover once you return home!

Following is information on four agencies that help arrange unique vacations specifically for older adults. Send a postcard with your name and address, and they will forward a current catalog.[20]

* *Saga Holidays* is a British company that provides an expansive selection of travel opportunities to individuals over sixty and their companions aged fifty to fifty-nine. Their tours in the United States include trips to the Northwest and Northeast. They have tours to Europe, Great Britain, Ireland, Mexico, and South America, as well as adventure

travel in Australia, India, and Kenya. (120 Boylston St., Boston, MA 02116; 800-441-6662)

* *Grand Circle Travel* offers individuals fifty-five and over a wide variety of "live abroad" vacations that range from two to twenty-four weeks. They also offer river cruises in Europe, Russia, and Eastern Europe. (347 Congress Street, Boston, MA 02210; 800-221-2610)

* *SCI National Retirees of America* offers a wide selection of trips to senior groups ranging from $25 day trips to luxury cruises. (134 Franklin Street, Hempstead, NY 11550; 516-481-4800)

* *Mt. Robson Adventure Holidays, Ltd.,* provides one-week "gentle" vacations for those over fifty, with various options, depending upon your level of fitness. The programs are based at a secluded camp west of Jasper, Alberta, Canada. After a fun-filled day of exploring the wilderness, your nights will be spent in a heated log cabin. (Box 146, Valemount, B.C., Canada V0E; 604-566-4386)

Make the World Your Classroom

For one of the most exciting ways to spend your retirement years, *join an Elderhostel!* "You don't have to be elderly to participate, you just have to be over 60!" is the frequently cited Elderhostel motto.

What is an Elderhostel, and whom is it for? An Elderhostel vacation provides two or three weeks of study on a college campus. You listen to lectures, participate in discussions, and take advantage of the college's library, cultural activities, and athletic facilities. In addition, you usually take one-day excursions away from campus. At Connecticut College, for example, students cruise down the Thames, visit Eugene O'Neill's house, and take in English country folk dancing.

You sleep in the college dormitory, of course! Says Rose Painier, a three-time participant in Elderhostel programs, "When I tell friends I'm going to Elderhostel, they say, 'No private bath?' But I like being in a dorm — I feel so young!"[21]

What do the 160,000 people who participate in Elderhostel programs study? United States-based programs focus on history, literature, communication, foreign language, dance, theater, biology, ecology, and athletics. Among the international programs are German theology, Japanese culture, Polynesian marine life, English genealogy, Scandinavian history, and Greek civilization.

The titles are intriguing: "Dante: For the Hell of It," "Why Is the Ocean so Close to the Shore?," and "Philosophical Issues in the Films of Woody Allen" are examples of Connecticut College offerings.

Be forewarned: an Elderhostel program differs radically from the kind of treatment you may have received in college. There is no homework, papers to write, or final grades. States Professor Lester Reiss, teacher of the Woody Allen class: "This is an entirely different experience from the undergraduate one. Elderhostelers are so incredibly direct and so alive. They love to argue, love to talk, and love to participate. It makes teaching so easy. I make a few suggestions, and they just roll with them."[22]

There is one main prerequisite for taking part in an Elderhostel program: You must love to learn. And you must be willing to examine new ways of looking at yourself and the world. States Margaret Hazelwood, an Elderhosteler at Connecticut College: "Like the character in Chekhov's *The Cherry Orchard,* I am a perpetual student. I'm curious and I love to read." Adds Lee Kneerim, director of the program at Connecticut College: "People who like to learn never get tired of learning, and a lot of people who never had the time when they were job holders or careerists now, in retirement, finally have the time."[23]

One of the most important reasons for enrolling in an Elderhostel program is that you will meet interesting people who represent a wide diversity of occupational and avocational interests. Sitting next to you might be someone with no more than a high school diploma. But on the other side might be a former college instructor with two Ph.D.'s! The student "fabric" is colorful indeed.

A typical Elderhostel program starts on a Sunday afternoon and ends the following Saturday morning. You can choose one-, two-, or three-week programs. Most of the courses meet for an hour or two each day and are led by a college professor.

Costs are refreshingly reasonable! In the States, prices range from $230 to $275 per person, slightly more in Canada and Hawaii, double in Alaska. This includes six nights' lodging, five days of courses, all meals, and usually some excursions away from campus. The costs for international programs run from $1,610 for a two-week program in Italy to $2,300 for a three-week program in India. These prices include airfare from New York, board, room, excursions, and fees.[24]

If you shop carefully, you can find some terrific bargains — some of which are not associated with Elderhostel. For example, you can stay at McGill University in Canada (summer only) for $13 per day if you are a student registered in the university. The University of London offers rooms for less than $26 per day, and if you want to travel to Australia, the University of Melbourne will provide room *plus three meals a day* for $36![25]

Want more information on cheap places to study? Consult *U.S. and Worldwide Travel Accommodations Guide* (Campus Travel Service, Department P, P.O. Box 5007, Laguna Beach, CA 92652). Or write for a free catalog to Elderhostel, 80 Boylston Street, Suite 400, Boston, MA 02116.

Onc final comment: some of the most interesting educational travel opportunities are offered through professional organizations and foundations. Here are some intriguing options:

* World Wildlife Fund takes expeditions to various parts of the world, including the Amazon River, Brazil, and Thailand and Nepal to see endangered species. (World Wildlife Fund, 1250 24th St. NW, Washington, DC 20037; 202-778-9560)

* The Smithsonian Institution offers 150 domestic and international study tours through its National Associate Program. Among the places visited, a tour of private gardens in Ireland, a Danube River cruise, and an Alaskan landscape tour. (Smithsonian National Associate Program, 1100 Jefferson Dr. SW, Washington, DC 20560; 202-357-4700)

* The American Horticultural Society presents trips to some of the world's greatest gardens, including private gardens in the Canadian Rockies, botanical gardens in the Soviet Union, and historic gardens in Rhode Island. (American Horticultural Society, 7931 E. Boulevard Dr., Alexandria, VA 22308; 703-768-5700)

* The Foundation for Field Research offers you a chance to see a number of their ongoing projects, including a study of how whale-watching vessels affect whales in the St. Lawrence River and a geological study in Spain designed to find the source of pottery that was taken aboard Columbus's ships.

(The Foundation for Field Research, P.O. Box 2010, Alpine, CA 92001; 619-445-9264)
* The National Trust for Historic Preservation offers cruises, such as the "Voyage to Byzantium" from Venice to Istanbul, as well as land tours throughout Europe and America. (National Trust, 1785 Massachusetts Ave. NW, Washington, DC 20036; 202-673-4138)
* The Sierra Club offers approximately 275 backpack, bicycle, burro, family, ski, and water trips in various parts of the world. (Sierra Club Outing Department, 730 Polk St., San Francisco, CA 94109; 415-923-5660)[26]

If you want to travel in retirement, there are many exciting options. You can board a luxurious ocean liner or rent a cozy villa. You can stay in a Bed and Breakfast Inn, or take part in Elderhostel programs.

But if you prefer to be spontaneous and can pack your bags on a moment's notice, here's something to do: Select a country you want to visit. Twenty-four hours before a flight is to leave, contact your travel agent or the airline and see if there are any discounted seats.

Don't be surprised to find a ticket that is 50 percent off the standard price. Why? If there is one thing that tour operators dislike, it's having empty seats. Rather than having a bus, train, plane, or ship half empty, they will sell unsold tickets at a significant discount. It's a fact: you can save from 10 percent to a whopping 60 percent on cruise and other travel costs, simply by making a reservation a few days before the ship is set to sail.

For more information on how to avoid the high cost of foreign travel, contact Spur-of-the-Month Tours and Cruises (4315 Overland Avenue, Culver City, CA 90230); Stand-buys, Ltd. (Box 10291, Chicago, IL 60610); or Moment's Notice, 40 E. 49th Street, Room 72, New York, NY 10017).

CHAPTER TWELVE

The Joy of Being a Volunteer

From now on, any definition of a successful life must include serving others.
President George Bush, 1989

As nice as it is to travel, many retirees indicate that the *very* best way to use leisure time is to help others. A case in point is Jack and Sally Costello of Oakland, California. Jack is a retired credit manager and Sally a home-maker. While they find no shortage of things to do or trips to take, the Costellos donate much of their time to the Center, an orga-nization that helps individuals with AIDS.

Every Monday morning the Costellos plunge into their tasks, as Sally greets people arriving at the Center, and Jack picks up gro-ceries donated by area merchants. Then they pitch in where needed, whether in cooking, cleaning, or tending to the rose garden that adorns the rear of the Center. Their mission? To bring hope and comfort to those afflicted with this horrible disease.

Several years ago the Costellos saw an exhibit called the "Names Project Quilt," which is a memorial to AIDS victims. Each large patch on this enormous quilt is designed, made, and donated in memory of a loved one. "I was overwhelmed by its size and sentiment," states Sally, "and I felt called to do something. It's been tremendously rewarding for both of us." Jack agrees but downplays his role: "I get as much out of it as I give."[1]

If you are wondering what to do in retirement, may I make a suggestion? Consider donating a *significant* part of your time to helping others. If you do, your days will be filled with reward and your retirement filled with memories of glorious accomplishment.

Why Volunteer?

Many nonprofit organizations have a difficult time recruiting volunteers. One minister told me that he makes an average of twenty calls before locating a single volunteer Sunday School teacher. A director of hospital service activities stated: "We used to have hundreds of volunteers. Today, fewer than fifty people have signed up to help."

Why the difficulty in recruiting volunteers? The principal reason is that we have fewer discretionary hours — time that could be spent in volunteer activities. In 1980 American workers enjoyed an average of forty hours of leisure per week. But because of our hectic schedules, we have today fewer than twenty-four hours.[2] The consequence? Altruistic activities get squeezed out of busy schedules.

Compounding the problem is that many housewives who were the backbone of the volunteer movement are now in the labor force. Today over 73 percent of mothers of school-age children are working outside the home. During the day their careers preclude volunteer work. And in the evening, family responsibilities occupy their time.

There is nevertheless a pressing need for volunteers, especially in agencies that serve the poor and the homeless. According to the chairman of the 1989 United States Conference of Mayors, there has been a *dramatic* increase in hunger, homelessness, and poverty in this country. In a survey of twenty-seven cities, emergency shelter requests increased *19 percent* in 1989, while requests for food rocketed by *25 percent*. Unfortunately, most cities could not cope with the requests, and needy people were turned away.[3]

The blunt truth is that the economically disadvantaged do not live in a kinder or more gentle America. Since 1980, federal support for human services has declined a total of $113.4 *billion,* compared to what it would be if the 1980 spending levels had been maintained.[4] The result is that the human face of poverty has changed.

It used to be that the homeless were primarily men. Today's homeless are just as often families with children. In Minnesota, for example, there has been since 1985 a 238 percent increase in the number of children using temporary housing shelters. On any one night approximately one-third of those in shelters are children who, on average, are only six years old.

The future of these children is dismal. They often lack immunizations against disease. They are twice as likely as "normal kids" to suffer from anemia, malnutrition, and asthma. They often have profound emotional, learning, and developmental problems because of the instability in their homes.[5]

Fortunately, there is a ray of hope: in many cities retirees are coming to the rescue, donating huge blocks of time to assist schools, churches, and community agencies.[6] In so doing, they are having the time of their lives. As Margaret Emerson, a spry sixty-two-year-old, said: "I've got the time. I've got the talent. And the good Lord knows the need is there. Why wouldn't I volunteer?"

Now the question is, Should *you* donate a significant portion of your discretionary time to help a nonprofit organization? In my experience, five groups of retirees gain the most when they offer their talents and financial resources to others. Here's who they are. You may belong in one of them.

Who Should Volunteer?

You are a good candidate to be an outstanding volunteer *if you have an interest in solving a particular problem.* Lorena Case devotes over fifty hours a week to NEWS, a Kansas City organization that helps battered women. Lorena's interest in battered women dates back to her childhood, when she witnessed her father abusing her mother.

Today Lorena, age seventy-five, answers the "hotline" at the NEWS center. She makes referrals and gently gives advice. But most of all she listens, not only with her head but also with her heart. At the end of the day she returns home, knowing that she has brought hope to at least a few women trapped in hopeless and abusive relationships.[7]

Six years ago Eliana Shippel, a native of Peru, was fighting alcoholism in an expensive Texas rehabilitation clinic. Unfortunately, Eliana was not getting better because no one spoke her native language, and she was therefore not receiving or giving clear information.

One fortunate day a Spanish-speaking counselor came to the clinic, and Eliana was able to begin using her own words to express her pain. Her recovery began, and a dream began to unfold.

After gaining control over alcoholism, Eliana cashed in her savings account and bought a two-story building in Dallas's inner city. Then she opened an alcohol treatment program called La Posada ("The Inn"), designed to help Hispanic alcoholics. Of particular concern to Eliana are Hispanic women. "It's not acceptable for the female to drink," she notes. "These women die painfully at home, alone."[8]

La Posada has room for sixteen patients. Each pays according to ability. If someone is destitute, a dollar bill will get him or her through the door. Eliana draws no salary, but she is content, knowing that her life is making an impact on Hispanic people: "I'm happy. I'm sober. Being here reminds me of where I was. And if at the same time I can help somebody else, it's a great bargain."[9]

What makes Lorena Case's and Eliana Shippel's altruism rewarding is that they are using their experience in helping others. When a battered woman telephones, Lorena understands the complexity of the issues. And when a Hispanic woman confides her pain, Eliana knows the steps that need to be taken to rebuild a broken life.

In selecting a volunteer activity, think about problems you've experienced. If you had a cardiovascular problem, the American Heart Association could use your help. If you've been diagnosed as having cancer, the American Cancer Society would be delighted to receive your telephone call. If you ever cared for a chronically ill child, think about donating time to an agency assisting handicapped children. And if perchance you once had dreams of being a major league baseball player or Olympic swimmer but didn't quite have the talent — maybe now is the time to serve as a Little League coach or an unpaid assistant in your high school swim program. Think creatively and examine your own range of talents, which may be larger than you suspect.

Whatever activity you select, remember this: if you care deeply about a particular problem, the hours you spend volunteering to correct it will fly by. And those who receive your help will never forget your contribution to their life.

You are a good candidate to be an outstanding volunteer if you are wealthy and can add dollars to your caring. If you are blessed with money, as is Andy Barr, a real estate speculator and millionaire, consider the following. One evening Mr. Barr was watching a television story featuring a Philadelphia woman who fed the hungry and gave hope to the homeless. Deeply touched by the story, he decided to use his financial resources to help the poor. Five nights a week Mr. Barr leaves his suburban home and visits homeless people living on steel grates near the nation's capital. His van is packed with clothing from L. L. Bean — sleeping bags, jackets, pants, gloves — anything that will help protect people from winter's cruel weather.

Why does he do it? "I still spend half a day a week on real estate because I love it," states Barr. "But my aggressiveness is channeled into this now. When you're in your twenties or thirties and you want to make money, you pursue it doggedly. You finally get there, and about 95 percent of the people just go on making more. I'm in the other 5 percent. Rather than doing something I've already proved I'm good at, I try this."[10]

If you are in "the other 5 percent," maybe it is time to channel your financial resources — and your time — into projects that will leave a legacy. True, you could sign your name on a check and send it to a charitable organization. But you double your pleasure when you give both money and time.

William E. Simon, Secretary of the Treasury under Presidents Ford and Nixon, has made a commitment to work at Covenant House, a place of refuge in Times Square for teen-age drug addicts, prostitutes, and runaways. There Simon gives kids an upbeat message: they can make it in America, no matter how bleak their problems or how dark their future.

States Jim Harnett, chief operating officer of Covenant House, "Most of these kids have no idea what a Treasury secretary (like Simon) does, anyway, but Simon provides a layman's enthusiasm that gives the kids a different kind of encouragement from what the professionals offer. Simon could salve his conscience by writing a check. But to him the personal touch is more important."[11]

I have met retired people who have more money than they or their heirs could ever use, people reluctant to part with their wealth for fear that they will be overwhelmed with requests. In addition, they often don't know where their money could make the biggest impact. Should it be given to a college? A hospital? A church? Would it be better spent on programs, or should it be used to establish an endowment? Here are three practical suggestions.

First, go to the human resource department of your former company and find out what types of philanthropic activities they fund. Some companies give to the performing arts, while others donate money to hospitals, social service organizations, colleges, and universities. If your company's charitable priorities appeal to you, inquire whether they will match your contribution. If so, your donation will have twice the impact, simply because you worked for a particular employer.

If you choose not to work through your company, consult with representatives of the United Way or various philanthropic foundations listed in the yellow pages. The advantage of going to various foundations is that most target their monies to a specific cause, such as the advancement of higher education. However, the United Way has a stellar reputation. Monies given to the United Way are used prudently, and you can rest assured that funds will truly reach those for whom they are intended.

Of course, don't overlook members of religious communities since pastors, priests, and rabbis have excellent information on where your charitable dollars can do the most good. In addition, many churches and synagogues have philanthropic programs administered at minimal expense.

Now you might be thinking: "I wish I had money to give others. But I am on a fixed income. There's not much I can do to help."

If this is the case, think again. True, you may not have great wealth to give away. But you are a good candidate to be an outstanding volunteer if you have a *special skill* — a talent that might be more valuable than any gift of money. If so, you too will benefit from volunteer service.

Maurice White is a seventy-two-year-old bachelor who donates time at the Hamilton Elementary School in Boston. What does he do? He teaches Cambodian children how to count change. He helps fifth graders learn math. He cheers a shy Russian girl who stumbles over her first words in English. And he teaches students about computers and how technology betters human life. "Mr. White has been helping me with computers since I was in the first grade," states Toni Haskins, a fifth-grader. "I've been with him so long it's like we're buddies."[12]

Maurice first became interested in helping children while listening to a radio broadcast describing the problems that children were having in school. Since he was a bit bored with his retirement, he decided to pitch in and help.

The school put him through a training program, but his background as a hardware-store owner came in handy in responding to students' questions. Then, too, he has the patience and the perseverance to work with youngsters.

The rewards are numerous: "I had been working with a Cambodian girl who kept mixing up certain letters on the computer keyboard, and, of course, she therefore couldn't get the program to work," states White. "I practiced with her for fifteen minutes every day before she started class. And the first time she got it right, she turned around with such a grin on her face . . . it was as though the world had opened up for her."

Students are not the only ones who benefit from his presence. After a day-long absence from class, Maurice opened the classroom door one morning and he heard a teacher say: "Thank God he's here!"[13]

Regardless of your educational and occupational background, you *do* have valuable knowledge. If you are a mechanic, there are poor people who would be thrilled to have you give their car a tune-up. If you've been a homemaker, church youth groups and scouting programs would welcome you with open arms. If you're good at math, why not serve as a volunteer with AARP's Tax-Aide program, which helps more than a million older adults complete their tax returns each year?

To repeat: *Don't minimize your talents.*

There is an agency in your community in need of your expertise, whether it be helping a youngster learn to read, befriending a prisoner, tutoring an illiterate adult, or serving on an advisory board of a community agency.

Many individuals are not enjoying retirement because they brood over something that happened to them in their career. Some never realized their professional goals. Others were forced out of jobs by cost-cutting administrators. Some worked for punitive bosses, while others were employed in unhealthy work environments and today bear scars created by toxic jobs. Put these disappointments to work; you are a good candidate to be an outstanding volunteer *if you have ever suffered a major career setback.*

Why? It is difficult to get through a thirty- or forty-year career without experiencing disappointments. In retirement you have ample time to think about what occurred. If you're not careful, days can be spent fruitlessly ruminating over the real and/or imagined insults inflicted by your former employer. But time spent stewing over past issues is not productive. Far better to volunteer to help others than brood over past disappointments.

Dr. Richard Blaylock is a former radiologist in a Los Angeles hospital. He had a first-class reputation for being a competent manager and a skilled clinician who cared deeply about his patients. But when the hospital merged with another facility, an administrator many considered arrogant was put in charge. The administrator promptly reorganized the hospital with little consultation from the medical staff, and in the process Rick was stripped of administrative responsibilities.

Rick felt betrayed. His ideas were ignored. His talents were not utilized. When he asked to see the hospital administrator, he was refused an appointment. When he wrote letters asking that the hospital's leadership be sensitive to the needs of an overworked staff, there was no response.

Rick existed in this system for more than five years, but this normally optimistic man became quiet and withdrawn. The bounce went out of his step. And his spirit of optimism gave way to anger and hurt.

The final insult came on the day of his retirement. There was no farewell and no recognition for the twenty-two years of faithful service he had given to the hospital. He went to his office, put his personal belongings in a box, said good-bye to his few trusted colleagues, and headed to his car. In the parking lot he walked by the hospital administrator, who wished him well but never thanked him for his many contributions.

Albert Camus, the French existentialist, once noted that work environments can become "soulless." What is a soulless work environment? It's one where your contribution is not recognized and where your talents are not utilized. It's feeling as if you are a number, and if you walked away, you would not be missed. It's giving notice of your departure, and sensing that no one cares or appreciates the contribution you made.

Frankly, it's hard not to be resentful when treated in such a callous manner. But if you have experienced career disappointments, let go of anger. For if you don't, it will erode your peace of mind. And it might destroy an otherwise successful retirement.

Fortunately Rick let go of his bitterness. "I felt sorry for myself for about a month," he said. "But I knew that I had to overcome my resentment. If I didn't, it would ruin my retirement."

What helped Rick to move past this difficult period in his life? He learned about a rural hospital in need of a volunteer physician. He made an appointment with the chairman of the board of trustees and learned that the hospital was going through tough economic times. They needed someone like Rick — an individual with administrative experience who could also help patients.

Two years later, the vitality has returned to Rick's step. "We started new programs that are generating significant revenues," he says. "We hired some wonderful nurses. This hospital is going to survive."

What Rick doesn't tell you is that he has been the mastermind in helping the hospital avoid bankruptcy. Someday, when Rick leaves, you can bet on one thing happening: the staff will throw him the biggest retirement party it can muster.

If you are frustrated by what transpired in your career, let go of the resentment. But if the disappointments and hurts linger, see a counselor. Then get involved. Find a part-time job. Start a new career. Or, perhaps best of all, donate time to an organization that will value your abilities and support your interests. If you do, the resentment will fade and you will have the retirement you deserve.

How do you go about locating a volunteer activity that will enhance your retirement? How do you locate a nonprofit organization that will value your talents and abilities? Here is a step-by-step guide to finding a credible service organization.

How to Find the Perfect Volunteer Assignment

Step one is to assess your schedule. Before agreeing to help any organization, determine how many hours per week you wish to work. The reason? Many nonprofit agencies are so desperate for help, they have a tendency to overwork their volunteers. You'll need to know your own limits to be effective.

Kelly McGuire used to volunteer four hours a day in a neighborhood school. When the district cut the school's budget, Kelly was asked to double her commitment. Soon she was putting in thirty to forty hours a week — not counting evening P.T.A. meetings!

Kelly's husband, frustrated by her hectic schedule, commented: "I thought retirement was to be our special time. I see you less than when you were fully employed!"

Kelly rearranged her priorities and patched up the problems in her marriage. "But if there is one thing I came to understand, it is that you have to be very firm as to *exactly* how much time you wish to give." Remember: nonprofit organizations should tailor their needs around your schedule — not yours to theirs. If you can't get a good fit, look elsewhere.

Step two is to assess your talents. What is it you enjoy doing? If you like books, why not volunteer to help in a community library? If you like to work with wood, donate time to a high school shop class, or if you're concerned about the environment, look into the Council on International Education Exchange (212-661-1414), which can link you to agencies that sponsor volunteer environmental programs.

In selecting an appropriate activity, keep in mind your interests. Remember George Kauffman, the former computer salesman who delivers hot meals to shut-ins? He loves his "work" because he enjoys people. "This is the perfect job for me," states George. "I like to make new friends, and I like to help them solve their problems."

Now you might be tempted to think: "I don't have any special talents. I've worked at home all my life." Even so, you may have more valuable experience than a typical executive — at least in certain tasks. When a high school principal needed someone to plan the school's all-night graduation party, he turned to Maggie Lindaman, age fifty-four. The reason? She has six children (including three teen-agers), incredible enthusiasm, and a ton of ideas.

According to the graduating seniors, the

party was a huge success. They loved the hypnotist. The jugglers kept them awake. The prizes were outstanding. And the dance music was in tune with their taste.

Where did all of these ideas come from? Maggie contributed her fair share, but many came from other housewives. No member of Maggie's committee had a master's degree in planning. But they held Ph.D. degrees in life — making them infinitely suited to planning an all-night party for 370 teen-agers!

If you are tempted to think that you have little to offer — think again. If you have been in sales, you probably are a natural at planning programs. If you were a manager, you have talents in designing, marketing, and evaluating projects. If you have been a secretary, you know how to meet the public and how to organize an office. Believe me, there are churches, schools, and agencies in your community that need your skills. To repeat: the key to successful voluntary service is to link your talents with an organization that needs your talents.

Finding such organizations and then evaluating them is crucial. The starting point is to visit with friends and acquaintances who serve as volunteers. That's what I did several years ago, when I was looking for volunteer work.

A neighbor mentioned that our community's park and recreation board needed a member.

I was so impressed with his enthusiasm and the need for volunteers that I called the mayor, submitted a résumé, and attended my first board meeting. And I must say, volunteering to serve on the park board is one of the best things I have ever done. Not only were we able to build bike paths throughout the city, but we planted hundreds of trees after a tornado ripped through our city and constructed a playground for handicapped children.

On those days when I feel a bit blue, I head for Central Park and walk on a trail that *we* constructed. Then I watch handicapped children playing on equipment *we* purchased. And even though my role in all of these projects was modest, I always leave with my mood brightened and my outlook cheered.

The final step in locating the perfect volunteer opportunity is to make contact with an *established* service organization. Established agencies have outstanding training programs and know how to utilize volunteers. Some truly wonderful organizations are making our world a better place in which to live. They include:

ACTION (American Council to Improve Our Neighborhoods) sponsors three programs. *The Foster Grandparents* program pairs older adults with children who have disabilities and need special attention. *Senior Companions* matches volunteers with homebound elderly who need friendship and assistance with shopping and transportation. *Volunteers in the Retired Senior Volunteer Program* (RSVP) serve as Meals-on-Wheels drivers, museum tour guides, classroom or health care aides, carpenters, electrical or plumbing contractors, credit counselors, or tax preparers. "Basically, whatever you want to do is probably something that RSVP needs people to do in your community," states ACTION spokesperson Patita McEvoy. "If you're not sure what you would like to do, we can help you figure it out."[14] To reach any ACTION program dial 1-800-424-8867.

SCORE (Service Corps of Retired Executives) is composed of more than 12,000 retired executives who offer free counseling to fledgling entrepreneurs. Art Kaenian, sixty-seven, formerly the director of industrial relations and safety for Ethan Allen Furniture, is one of SCORE's volunteers. He recently helped a young homemaker start a cake-decorating store. The woman had a good product, but unfortunately she didn't know how to market it or how much to charge.

Art completed a market survey and provided creative ideas for getting started. Today the business is a success. States Art: "Those of us with business experience have been where they are going. Why let them get into trouble and have to bounce back? After all, small businesses have always been the nucleus of the American economy."[15] To locate SCORE offices, use your local telephone directory.

One organization that is helping people learn to read is the *Coalition for Literacy* (800-228-8813). There is a tragic statistic that one out of five Americans is functionally illiterate. Consequently, the need for volunteers to tutor adults is huge, and growing. The Coalition provides free training and all the assistance you need in order to help others master the written word.

If you have a special interest in children, you might consider the following agencies: *T-L-C* (Teaching-Learning-Communities) recruits older adults to serve as mentors to junior high school students who are in danger of quitting school (313-994-4715). The *National School Volunteer Program,* sponsored by the National Association of Partners in Education, coordinates volunteers with community schools (800-992-6787). *Family Friends* matches volunteers fifty-five and over with disabled youngsters twelve and under and their families in eight cities: Washington,

D.C., Los Angeles, Hartford, Miami, Omaha, Cleveland, San Antonio, and Salt Lake City (202-479-1200).

One of your best bets in finding a good place to volunteer might come through your former employer. The Chevron Corporation has a senior mentor program that matches three hundred creative high school students with an equal number of retired engineers, geologists, oceanographers, astronomers, artists, and other professionals, each of whom assists a student on a ten-week project. These pairings have produced a miniature hydroelectric plant built by a retired engineer and a student, as well as a book on laws dealing with outer space written by a retired attorney and a student.

Scott Paper of Philadelphia sponsors SERVE (Scott Employee Retiree Volunteer Effort), which uses a computer program to match retired volunteers with local agencies. Levi Strauss, Dow Chemical, and Honeywell have similar programs.

The charitable programs of some corporations are truly amazing. During the 1984 summer Olympics, Los Angeles wanted to diminish pollution by planting a million trees that would filter over 400,000 pounds of pollution out of the atmosphere each day. General Telephone Company paid for the cost of 250,000 trees, recruited six hundred volunteers, and sent them to three hundred local schools in search of seventy thousand children to help plant the trees! The last tree was planted five days before the Olympic games started.[16]

Then, too, there are opportunities to use your talents in foreign lands. Over five hundred of the 5,200 volunteers in the Peace Corps are fifty years of age or older. Peace Corps spokesman James Flanigan confirms that the Corp is in an active drive to look for older volunteers.[17]

Peace Corps volunteers serve for two years, but sometimes twenty-four months isn't long enough to complete the job. Odilon Long joined the Peace Corps in 1967, three days after he retired from his work at a telephone company. Nineteen years later he was still in the Peace Corps, having worked in a half dozen poor countries.[18]

Finally, one of the best resources in locating a volunteer organization is the talent bank of the American Association of Retired Persons. The talent bank matches your skills and interests with AARP's needs and legislative interests. The talent bank also helps organizations such as the American Red Cross, the National Park Service, and the March of Dimes to locate qualified volunteers. To register, write to AARP Volunteer Talent Bank,

Dept. M, 1909 K St. NW, Washington, DC 20049.[19]

In this chapter we've seen that there is a great need for volunteers. But I want to emphasize one point that should govern all your decisions about volunteering: help thyself by helping others. Those who benefit the most from volunteer services are not the recipients, although they appreciate work done on their behalf, but rather the volunteers themselves. It is they who reap the greatest rewards, including

* A chance to make friends
* An opportunity to develop new skills
* A chance to do the things that one does best
* An opportunity to work with a respected community organization
* A chance to see the results of one's work[20]

But perhaps most important, *volunteer work helps you focus on that which is truly important in your own life and in society.*

Leonard Davison, a Boston attorney, heads each week to Children's Hospital, where he checks in at the volunteer office, puts on an orange smock, and gathers up an armful of children's books and games. Then he heads to the rooms of chronically ill children. When the children see him coming, they beam, knowing that the next few hours will be a respite from their problems.

One patient who made an indelible impression on Leonard was a twelve-year-old fighting leukemia. "One day I had a very tough day at the firm," stated Davison, "and I almost didn't come to the hospital because I was so tired. When I saw him, I said, 'Boy, did I have a hard day.' And he looked at me and said, 'Yeah, I had a pretty tough day, too.' Suddenly I realized I hadn't had a tough day at all." The boy has since died. "I still have his picture," Davison says. It's there reminding him of what is important in life — even after a tough day at the office.[21]

PART V
RELATIONSHIPS

Men, Women, and Change

The moment has come to take a *creative* look at how retirement influences the marital relationship, doubtless one of the most important relationships in our lives. Why is it that retirement has a positive effect on some marriages, while, for others, estrangement sets in? And why is it that some couples use retirement to discover new patterns of sexual intimacy, while others let the bed grow cold?

Chapter 13, "Intimacy in Retirement: Falling in Love Over and Over Again," examines *practical strategies for pepping up a marriage.* Marital relationships fall into one of four categories: we are either enemies, strangers, friends, or lovers. Want to become a lover? A special section in this chapter is devoted to new ways of recapturing sexual excitement, regardless of age.

For those who are remarried and for the

many who would like to be one day, we will take the time in Chapter 14, "Starting Over: Making a Second Marriage Work," to find out why *you are never too old for romance*. And we will learn how to avoid the pitfalls that cause 60 percent of all remarriages to end in divorce.

Chapter 15, "Living Alone — and Liking It," is dedicated to those who are not married and who live alone. If you have chosen a single life or if you grieve over the loss of a husband or wife, this chapter will help alleviate loneliness. In addition, practical suggestions will be offered for discovering new friendships.

CHAPTER THIRTEEN

Intimacy in Retirement: Falling in Love Over and Over Again

He's Protestant, I'm Catholic. He's Anglo, I'm Hispanic. He's a Republican, but I'm a Democrat. He tells me I'm gorgeous. I'm not. But sex gets better all the time because we are nuts about each other.
San Antonio woman, in a letter to columnist
Ann Landers

Make no mistake — retirement can be one of the best times of life.[1] What makes it fulfilling? As we have seen, it is then that you finally have time to do things you enjoy. You have the chance to form new friendships, develop hobbies, take exotic trips, and help improve the world. Best of all, retirement is a golden opportunity to renew your wedding vows and to fall further in love with your spouse, to a level deeper than anything you have ever known.

Frankly, not all the news is good. Retirement can be hard on marriages, frighteningly so. States Harry Baxter, sixty-nine, "We fight more often now. We get on one another's nerves. And we can't agree on how to spend our time."

Fortunately, others report that retirement has had a positive influence on their marital life. "I feel very close to my wife," muses Robert Vante, sixty-eight. With a shy glance he adds: "Our sex life has never been better. Our kids would be embarrassed if they knew what we do for fun."

What are the secrets for staying in love in retirement? How do you keep the fire of passion burning, even if you have been married for three, four, or five decades? And if disputes threaten your relationship, how do you solve them in an amicable way? Let's see.

Enemies, Strangers, Friends, or Lovers: What Is the State of Your Marriage?

Some couples spend their retirement years engaged in marital warfare. They are *enemies*. States Emma Dickenson, sixty-two:

We argued most of our married life. But when he retired, our relationship became worse. First he belittled me. Then he abused me. Now he is threatening divorce.

496

What am I going to do? I have no money, and my children can't help. Every day is hell. I fear he could kill me.

"Throw the bum out," you might suggest. Perhaps so. But that misses the point, since many men and women have difficulty getting out of bad marriages. Some remain married because they are economically dependent. ("How would I support myself?") Others worry about appearances. ("What would the kids think if we split?") Still others hope that retirement will bring relief from tension.

Unfortunately, retirement does *not* salvage a troubled marriage. Says Katherine Wilson, "It solved nothing. Now we fight twenty-four hours a day."

In general, partners who were in love with one another before retirement will continue to be lovers. But in retirement fragile marriages can turn nasty. The reason for this is that boredom sets in. Spouses get on one another's nerves. And since there are no children around, accusations fly without inhibition.

If solutions to problems can't be found, patterns of abuse sometimes follow. It's not always physical; some of the most damaging forms of abuse are psychological, in which partners belittle one another.

Regrettably, many victims of abuse see no hope. Says Norma Eddington, fifty-four, "I feel trapped, but I can't leave after twenty-eight years of marriage. I don't know of any alternative."

Psychologists call this phenomenon co-dependency, a sad state in which two adults mutually hurt one another yet are unable to extract themselves from the relationship. As the distinguished psychoanalyst Anna Freud said: "For many, I'm afraid, pain and suffering are desired."[2] She's right. If you've existed for years in a destructive relationship, you may think that marital conflict is a *normal* state of affairs, which it isn't. But unless your attitudes are changed and solutions found, retirement will be a never-ending series of hostilities.

Fortunately, if both partners value the marriage, relationships do change and creative solutions can be found. But sometimes outside help is needed. Today many older couples enter counseling because they don't want their retirement destroyed by unresolved marital conflicts. Others seek help simply because they want to deepen and strengthen their relationship.

Victor Frankl, the noted philosopher, states that to be human is to be free. We are *free* to choose our attitude. We are *free* to find solutions to our most difficult problems. And we are *free* to chart a new direction for our marriage.

You might think that it is impossible to start over, especially if you are about to retire. Perhaps so. Nevertheless, if your marriage is fraught with problems, you need to find solutions. For some this might mean a late-life divorce, particularly if you are abused and/or you have sought professional counseling and it has not been helpful.

Nevertheless, I would encourage you not to lose hope. If you and your spouse are estranged, spend time with people who will affirm and love you. And if you can't find ways to minimize hostilities, talk to a member of the clergy or seek out the services of a professional counselor.

Never forget one important point: there are few, if any, perfect relationships. Most have troubles, and, in truth, most are severely tested at one time or another.

Nevertheless, one of the most important factors in building a strong relationship is the willingness to find creative solutions to nagging problems. It isn't easy. But once wounds are healed, your love for your spouse will be renewed and your retirement years will assume a richer, deeper meaning.

Strangers. Have you ever felt that you were living with a stranger — someone whom you really did not know? George M. Crampton, sixty-six, of Tampa, Florida, did:

After the first few months of retirement it was clear that I didn't understand my wife. No matter the topic, we always seemed to have different points of view.

Last week she was very busy with her volunteer work. I asked her what she does with her time, and she seemed surprised and irritated at my question. She replied tartly: "It would take too long to explain."

Her response made me feel like we were strangers. Right then I decided that we had to spend time with one another or we would be married in name only.

Are you and your spouse friends? Or strangers? If you feel that your marriage isn't as strong as it once was or that you've drifted apart, take time to evaluate the problem. Here are the ten symptoms of a troubled marriage. Read each statement carefully, then ask yourself whether the statement is true of your marriage and yourself.

* Our sex life is boring.
* We have few *mutual* friends.
* My spouse does not compliment me.

* It's been at least a month since I did anything special for my spouse. I don't feel motivated to do anything special.
* We argue quite a bit but aren't able to resolve our problems.
* My spouse does not seem interested in me, nor does he (she) inquire as to what matters in my life.
* I find myself thinking about what it would be like to be married to another person.
* I find myself forgetting important dates, such as our wedding anniversary and my spouse's birthday.
* My spouse nags me, asking me to do things that I don't want to do.
* I often think that other couples have better marriages than ours.

If you can answer "yes" more easily than "no," take it as a warning signal that your marriage may be in trouble. But don't panic. Marriages move in cycles. At times we feel close to our mate. But in other instances, we feel estranged and sometimes terribly alone. Cycles, by and large, are normal.

Mick and Beck Johnston successfully raised

four children. While their relationship had the normal stresses and strains, they always maintained respect for one another. But shortly after retirement Mick noticed that his wife's mood had changed.

She seemed more quiet than normal. She did not seem interested in what I was doing. And we hadn't made love in several weeks.

I asked her what was wrong and she said, "Nothing." Then I mustered my courage and asked the truly tough question: "Do you feel as close to me as you once did?" She replied in a very soft but firm voice, "No, I don't." I asked her why that was and she said that lately we had had few common interests.

I said nothing, but I was hurt by her response. I knew, however, that she was right. We had grown apart. It didn't happen intentionally, it just happened.

That night I told her that I loved her. She smiled and gave me a hug. And she said, "I hope the old feelings we had toward one another will return."

I asked her if we needed to see a counselor. She laughed and said: "Not on your life. What we *do* need however, is to be able to do things together. If you take a look at your schedule, there is little time for us."

She was right. I was busier now than when I was working. Right then I decided that I better make our marriage a top priority.

Marriage partners *do* drift apart. It's natural, and some would say inevitable as we pursue busy careers, raise families, and attend to our personal agendas. But the real issue is: *Do you care enough about the relationship to rekindle the love that has been lost?*

Frankly, this is an issue of the head, not the heart. True, there should be a romantic spark in your relationship, but the critical issue is whether you want to make a *commitment* to rediscovering your love and a *commitment* to resolving festering problems.

If you and your spouse choose to resolve your conflicts, there is hope for the relationship. But to do so you must spend time with one another, and you must find courage to look squarely at the issues that have driven you apart. Here is how one couple tackled their problems:

We made a commitment to discuss those problems which were driving a wedge between us. Our talks were tense. At times tears were shed. We discussed problems that had been festering for years. And we came to understand one another a lot better.

The breakthrough? One day my wife looked at me and with a reassuring smile said: "Can't we put all of these problems to rest and start over?" I gave her a big, big hug. The next day we spent the afternoon planning a second honeymoon.

I would like to say that we have all our problems solved and that we lived happily ever after. That's not the way it works in the real world. We still have plenty of conflicts. But we are learning — after all of these years — that we can solve most of them.

You need not remain strangers in retirement. But to move to the next level — friendship — you must address that which keeps you apart. Don't get into the trap of thinking you must resolve all the problems at once, but if you can diminish the hostility, you're on the road to reestablishing your friendship. More important, you are on the way to reestablishing *trust* — the glue that holds all marriages together.

Friends. When I asked husbands and wives to identify their best friend, they would often smile and point to the one they love. Their spouse. What does it mean to be married to your best friend?

We know how to fight with one another. More important, we know how to make up!

He overlooks my imperfections. I'm no raging beauty, but he loves me for who I am.

She puts up with my idiosyncrasies. She never makes me feel guilty because I spend so much time on the golf course.

He challenges me. He asks what I am reading and what I am thinking about. He never lets me get intellectually lazy.

She makes me feel like a stud. That's some feat when you get to be seventy years of age.

He never forces sex. If I don't feel like it, he says, "That's fine. I'm not sure I am up to it either."

She always looks on the bright side of things. Her optimism keeps me going.

He's handsome — more handsome than the day I married him.

All I can say is that we would rather be with each other than with anybody else in the whole world.

What are the hallmarks of a good friendship? Listen to what George Burns said of his friend Jack Benny: "Jack and I had a wonderful friendship for nearly fifty-five years. Jack never walked out on me when I sang a song, and I never walked out on him when he played the violin. I suppose that for many of those years we talked every day."[3]

Good friends — married or not — talk almost every day. They laugh together, play together, work together. But most of all, even if things get rough, they never walk out on each other.

To deepen your friendship with the person you married, it's important to define the issues that keep you apart. Equally important is the ability to find workable solutions to perplexing problems.

The number one factor in creating strong friendships is, however, simple sensitivity to one another's needs. If there is one thing that turns strangers into friends, it is a concerned attitude and a caring presence. Remember: it is not the big things we do for one another that build friendships, but rather the small acts of kindness done daily that create trust.

What can you do *today* to deepen your friendship with the one you love? Try saying:

Do you have time for a walk? I want to

spend some time with you.

Here is a little something I bought for you. I hope you enjoy it.

I'll clean the house tonight (or cut the grass or clean the car). You've done enough for one day.

Put on your best dress (or suit). I'm taking you out for a surprise evening.

You've had a busy day. I'm fixing you a special dinner.

I'm taking your car in for new tires. I want you to be safe.

I'm going to run an errand — is there anything I can get for you while I'm out?

I bought two tickets to ____. Let's have a special evening on the town.

You've said that you always want to go to ____. Guess what I've planned for your birthday?

How about a hug? I just want you to know how much I love you.[4]

If you can't say them, try thinking how nice it would be to hear them. Then try again.

Lovers. The fourth category of marriages is perhaps the best and the rarest. Permit me to be candid: There is a world of difference between being "best friends" and being "true lovers." True — you can have a satisfying retirement knowing that your spouse is a good friend. But it doesn't compare to having a friend who is also a terrific lover.

What does it mean to be a lover? Well, for one thing it means you can have as good a sex life at age sixty as you could at age twenty-five. In fact, it might be better simply because you know what turns each other on.

In one study, more than 40 percent of the respondents indicated that *sex had improved as they grew older*. In another study, almost 10 percent of the sixty-five-plus group made love fifteen or more times a month, and 60 percent looked forward to continuing a satisfying love life.

"We enjoy each other more in all ways as we grow older," said one respondent, "and now we have more time to be intimate." Another replied: "My answers sound like we're sex maniacs but we are only loving, caring people." Their age? She's eighty, he's eighty-eight.[5]

You *can* have good sex as you grow old. But if you believe sex is for the young, you are defeated before you start. Listen to the wisdom and wit of author Dave Barry:

The biggest myth . . . is that as you grow older, you gradually lose your interest in sex. This myth probably got started because younger people seem to want to have sex with each other at every available opportunity, including at traffic lights, whereas older people are more likely to reserve their sexual activities for special occasions, such as the installation of a new pope.

But there's no reason for us to feel that getting older should stop us from having sex. Our role model in this area should be . . . Job, who, if I remember my Sunday School lessons correctly, remained sexually active for several hundred years.

With that in mind, there's no reason why we can't continue to lead sexually fulfilling lives well into our Golden Years, as millions of older people have done before us, including, for all we know, your own parents.[6]

To be lovers you need to become more passionate, more involved in your marriage. Here's how to do it.

Friends and Lovers: Strategies for Reestablishing Intimacy

Strategy one: Learn to communicate with one another. Upon hearing this suggestion some might protest: "What, I've lived with him (her) for thirty years. I know how to communicate!" Don't be so sure.

In my experience the number one complaint spouses have of one another is "She (he) doesn't listen." The second greatest complaint, usually mentioned by women: "He (she) doesn't share his (her) feelings."

Margaret Hension, fifty-eight, married a "strong-silent" type of man, thirty-two years ago. She learned to adapt, even though there were times in her marriage when she felt lonely.

> My husband is a rational person who hides his emotions. Consequently, there is part of him that I do not know.
>
> I have tried to accept him as he is. But there are issues we can't discuss. For example, he won't discuss our financial affairs. He has never been able to show affection to our children. He has difficulty complimenting me or anyone else. There are times where I have no idea what is going on in his head. When I ask him if everything is OK, he responds with a polite "yes." But when he retreats to his den, I know things are bad. Unfortunately, I can't break the silence.
>
> What I want to know is this: Can the silence be broken? Is there some way for us to talk about issues that will shape our future?

The answer is a qualified "yes." It isn't easy to resume talking, especially if you never learned well in the first place how to touch one another's deepest concerns and greatest hopes. How do you go about establishing new ways of communicating? How do you connect in new and creative ways?

First, be honest with your spouse. Explain that you feel "shut out" and you want to enter into his or her life in a deeper, more meaningful way. Then, when your spouse responds, look into his or her eyes and for those few precious moments block out everything that might interfere. Pay attention to every word, gesture, and facial expression. Listen for the messages hidden between the lines. Nothing is more difficult. But nothing builds trust so well.

Then, gently probe. Begin by asking *informational questions:* "What do you think about when you're alone in your den?" "Are you worried about something?" "Is there anything that I can do to make our retirement better?"

Then ask *feelings questions:* "You seem discouraged. Anything the matter?" "Do you miss seeing the kids?" "Do you wish that we lived closer to them?" "If you could change one thing in retirement, what might it be?"

If these questions shock your partner, don't be surprised if the response is short and

511

muted. But continue! In fact, don't let a day go by without raising questions. Never nag, but keep probing. The path to another person's soul is traveled only by raising questions in a gentle, considerate manner.

When your spouse finally articulates a meaningful response, seek to understand rather than evaluate. Unfortunately, our first reaction is to judge what is being said. As Carl Rogers notes in *On Becoming a Person*, "When someone expresses some feeling or attitude or belief, our tendency is almost immediately to feel 'That's right'; 'That's stupid'; 'That's abnormal'; 'That's reasonable'; 'That's incorrect'; or 'That's not nice.' Very rarely do we permit ourselves to understand precisely what the meaning of his statement is to him. I believe this is because understanding is risky. If I let myself really understand another person, I might be changed by that understanding. And we all fear change. So as I say, it is not an easy thing to permit oneself to understand an individual, to enter thoroughly and completely and emphatically into his frame of reference. It is also a rare thing."[7]

Seek to understand. But if you note hostility, do not respond with anger. If you do, both of you will suffer and the lines of communication will again grow cold.

Raising questions shows you care. But it also

breaks the cycle of estrangement. Regrettably, many older people feel alienated from their loved ones and friends. Studies suggest that 45 percent of those over sixty-five years of age are lonely. Who are these people, and why do they feel alone?

Some live alone in apartment buildings where the doorbell seldom rings. But many of the loneliest people in the world are those who live in single-family homes with a spouse.

Why should these people be lonely? After all, there arc neighbors nearby. They have acquaintances galore. And perhaps they have been blessed with children and grandchildren.

They are lonely because no one takes the time to ask the questions that touch the nerve endings of their soul. Close physical proximity is no guarantcc of psychological intimacy. As one of my students told me: "You can be in the middle of a rock concert with twenty thousand people and feel like the loneliest person on earth." Loneliness is negated only when someone asks questions that transcend the superficial babble that so often surrounds our lives.

What if you and your loved one are raising questions but not making headway in revitalizing your relationship? A modest suggestion: *change your physical location.* Sometimes conversation flows most easily *away* from home.

Paula and Greg Simpson, from St. Paul, Minnesota, travel 146 miles north to Lost Land Lake Lodge located in Hayward, Wisconsin, whenever irritations threaten to get out of control. Says Paula, "The drive through Wisconsin farmland is beautiful. It gives us a chance to cool down and to talk about what's bothering us. By the time we get up north, we usually have everything worked out."

Another couple simply takes a walk in a community park whenever tensions build. And Eric and Sally Reston head for a Bed and Breakfast Inn located in a rural setting ninety minutes away from home: "A few hours sitting on the porch talking about what is happening is all that we need to get back on track," says Eric.

Remember: to have a close relationship with the person you love, express those concerns that nibble away at tranquility. Raise questions. Listen with your heart as well as with your head. In so doing, your relationship may be transformed. Elton Mayo once noted: "One friend, one person who is truly understanding, who takes the trouble to listen to us as we consider our problem, can change our whole outlook on the world."[8]

Strategy two: Make a candid assessment about

the state of your marriage. Pull no punches. If you're estranged, admit it. If your sex life is unfulfilling, discuss it. And if you have little in common, confront your aloneness. In short, what you want to do is to see if the flame of passion has burned out in your marriage.

To help you and your spouse address critical issues, take the following test.[9] If your answer is "No," give yourself one point. If your answer is "Sometimes," give yourself three points. And if your response is "Yes," give yourself five points.

Marriage Burnout Signals

Have you
____found yourself looking for excuses to leave or stay away from the house?
____quit caring about your appearance when your spouse is due home?
____no interests or hobbies in common?
____quit laughing with your spouse?
____stopped meeting your spouse with a smile when he/she gets home?
____changed your sleeping habits?
____lost interest in having the house be neat and clean, inside and out?

___changed your eating habits?

___lost interest in the planning and preparation of meals?

___made more visits to your doctor this past year than in previous years?

Do you

___and your spouse have fewer and fewer couple friends?

___and your spouse have little interest in each other's work, hobbies, and avocations?

___no longer compliment your spouse?

___resent your spouse's family and friends?

___often feel angry?

___think members of the singles' Sunday School group have more fun than you do?

___spend time planning activities for yourself that don't include your spouse?

___sleep in separate bedrooms when neither of you even snores?

___feel less sexually attractive?

___and your spouse communicate only on a factual level?

Now total your score and check it against

the following scale to determine whether your marriage is strong and stable or needs revitalization.

Marital Burnout Scale

Stage One: 0 to 25. Plenty of fire in your marriage! Continue, however, to stoke the flame.

Stage Two: 30 to 50. Not enough oxygen; your marital flame is smothering. Turn up the gas!

Stage Three: 55 to 75. Embers; heading for a blackout. You and your mate have your work cut out for you if you are to have a satisfactory retirement marriage.

Stage Four: 80 to 100. Ashes! Professional help needed fast.

Now for a moment, let's assume that you want to better your score. What do you do? This takes us to a third strategy for rekindling the marital flame.

RECALL WHY IT IS THAT YOU MARRIED ONE ANOTHER AND GET IT BACK

With your spouse present, each working independently, write down six reasons you fell in love with one another. I can't predict what might be on your list, but here are some typical comments:

She was incredibly good looking!

He was an incurable romantic.

Her smile was warm and soft.

He was gentle and kind.

She made me feel special.

He would make a wonderful parent.

We had *great* chemistry!

Now read to each other what was on your list. Then share the *most important reason* you married the person you love. Completing this exercise will not solve marital problems, but I promise you one thing: you will not go to bed with anger in your heart.

It's easy to forget the reasons we made life-long commitments to one another. We become preoccupied raising a family, building a career, and making a mortgage payment. Soon our chief concerns are the marital *tasks* rather than marital *relationships*. Rather than focusing on what we can do to feel closer to one another, we focus attention on who is going to pay the bills, buy the groceries, or run Junior to his baseball game. In addition, we forget to do those things that make a marriage meaningful, whether it be surprising a spouse with chocolates, going out for a special evening, or simply buying a tender greeting card. Without these perks the marriage soon becomes a mechanized affair as we go about our separate tasks and the days turn into years.

Recalling why you married one another is a helpful step in getting a marriage back on track. But it is also important to recall significant experiences. That's what my wife and I did yesterday as our son, Brent, left for his first year of college. It was a bittersweet moment as his 1977 Buick LeSabre, loaded with all his earthly possessions, left our driveway. As we waved good-bye we had lumps in our throats and tears in our eyes.

That evening my wife had prepared, unknown to me, a special candlelight dinner. But I had a surprise up my sleeve as well.

Two days after our son's birth, I'd sneaked some special wine into my wife's hospital room. We decided on his name. Then we offered a toast to his future. Finally, we said a little prayer of thanks for the new life that had been entrusted to us.

Last night — almost nineteen years later — I again brought out a chilled bottle of the same special wine. This time we toasted all the joys which our son had provided us through the years.

After dinner we retreated to the backyard and reminisced, not only about our son but about twenty-one years of married life. We laughed as we recalled our first vacation, spent in a broken-down resort in northern Minnesota. We talked about how our roles had changed over the years, since I am now the cook and Karen is the gardener. We recalled tough economic times and illnesses in which the outcome was in doubt.

In short, we discussed our *shared history* — a history that no other people in the world could share or fully understand.

I can't emphasize this point enough: *It is important to relive your history,* and not only when something major happens, such as sending your child off to college. At least weekly you should review your accomplishments and share your little disappointments. You need to recall often those moments when you felt most in love. And you need to affirm the internal strength which you *collectively* possess to meet whatever challenges loom ahead.

True, marriage comes with few guarantees. But the key is not to demand perfection in one another. For as one astute philosopher noted: "God help the man who won't marry until he finds a perfect woman, and God help him still more if he finds her."[10]

If you demand perfection in a partner, you are bound to be disappointed. For most people have at least a few characteristics that others find irritating.

Nevertheless, if you look past the irritants and concentrate on those qualities that attract you to your spouse, understanding evolves. And a deepened love abounds. As Rebecca Nestrom said of her husband of thirty-three years: "Yes, he forgets to pick up his newspapers, and yes, he leaves his shoes all over the house. But I love him for who he is." She paused and with a twinkle in her eye added: "Furthermore, I never give up hope that I might reform him — even if it is in the thirty-fourth year of our marriage!"

How to Make Sex Sizzle!

You want to revitalize your sex life. You are not alone. Studies confirm that once the kids leave the house and the pressures of the job are off, many couples want to enliven their lovemaking. Marriage therapist Shirley Aussman calls this a period of *liberation*. "Couples turn to each other to fill the gap left by the children and feel a renewed sense of romance and support from each other. There is a new interest in enriching their sexual life."[11]

To enrich your sex life and make things sizzle, first *clear your mind of negative attitudes*. One of the worst is the belief that you are sexually over the hill. "There are *so* many stereotypes," laments Maggie Kuhn, of the Gray Panthers. "The worst part of it is that older people believe these lies about age, and younger people are taught to expect them! Old people drool. They take laxatives all the time. Their sex organs are dried up. They are stuck in the past. Senility is judged an inevitable part of age. But old age is not chronology. It's self-image and mind."[12]

Kuhn is correct: whether or not you have a good sex life is largely dependent upon your attitude. If you believe that sex is a gift to the young, then you will have only fleeting memories of passionate moments. But if you and your spouse believe that it is possible to have a better sex life at sixty-five years of age than at twenty-five — then you are a candidate for a stunning and mutually fulfilling sex life.

True, you may not have sex as often as you once did, for biological reasons. But frequency is not the critical factor in developing a great sex life. Quality is far more important.

But to have a high-quality sex life *you must be honest with your spouse about what attracts you and what you hope to get out of your love-*

making. According to Michael E. Metz, of the University of Minnesota's Program in Human Sexuality, "Nothing helps enhance the vibrancy of the relationship as much as talking about one's sexual interests, feelings, desires, and ideas. Research consistently suggests that the ability to discuss these things and to creatively decide how to sexually please each other are indispensable to sexual satisfaction."[13]

Unfortunately, we often don't take the time to understand one another. In the movie *Annie Hall*, two therapists on a split screen ask a pair of lovers, Woody Allen and Diane Keaton, the number of times they have sex. "He wants sex all the time," she groans. "At least four times a week." Woody replies sadly, "Practically never. Four times a week at most."[14]

Why is honesty such a critical factor in a healthy sexual relationship? In a thoughtful article appearing in the newsletter *Sex Over Forty*, the author states: "When one partner lies or pretends with the other, it inevitably leads to suppressed anger, resentment, and discontent. If these emotions are held long enough, they will explode and cause far more problems than if the person has been honest to begin with. When erotic situations arise, let your partner know how you feel and proceed from there."[15]

Now you might be thinking: "Well, I have lived with my spouse for thirty years. I ought to know what gets her (him) excited. And she (he) *should* know what turns me on." Don't be so sure. The reason? As we age, sexual priorities change. Or as the American writer and dramatist Lillian Hellman notes: "People change and forget to tell each other."[16]

Perhaps in our child-rearing years all that we could have hoped for were a few moments of uninterrupted lovemaking. But in retirement, things change. The house is quiet. You have time to love. Perhaps best of all, you no longer have to worry about the kids crashing into your bedroom at the most inopportune time!

Now is the time to focus your energy on rekindling your passion. The only thing standing in your way of developing a more fulfilling sexual life is the attitudes you and your spouse bring to the bedroom.

Be liberated! What is it that your spouse would *really* enjoy?

If you are a *man* remember this: the single most important key to a woman's satisfaction with a sexual relationship lies in her partner's attitudes *after* lovemaking. In one study only 19 percent of women surveyed considered orgasm the most important part of sex. More important to the others was the husband's willingness to lie close after intercourse, caressing, talking, letting the spouse know that she is loved and valued.[17]

If you want your sex life to improve — think about your spouse and why you love her. Put aside those little irritations that keep you from expressing positive thoughts. And remember: a robust hug given in the middle of the day may be more meaningful than anything said at night.

In addition, it is important to realize that it may take your wife longer to get sexually excited as she grows older. This is a normal, physiological response to aging and should not be taken as a sign of a troubled marriage or that she is less attracted to you.

The key, however, is never to rush your wife into having an orgasm. Or worse, inquiring why it is "taking so long." Because if you do, it will be taken as a sign that you are more interested in fulfilling your needs than meeting hers. Far better to take your sweet ol' romantic time. Remember: foreplay can be as exciting to you as it is to her.

If you are a *woman*, it's important to understand that your husband's sexual needs also change as he grows older. He may find it more difficult to obtain a spontaneous erection. The force of his ejaculation may diminish and it will take him longer to get a second erection.

More important is that many men silently wonder whether their wives find them sexually attractive. If a man is unable to come to a climax, he may wonder whether the passage of time has eroded his manhood. Assure him it has not.

Now more than ever, your husband will be dependent upon you for great sex. In his youth, he quickly climaxed. But now it takes longer. Therefore you must become assertive; he needs your eroticism to stir his sexual energy. He also needs to know he hasn't missed a beat in his romantic skills.

Never forget — the quality of sex does not deteriorate with age. In fact, it often improves. In the first nationwide survey of healthy men and women over sixty-five, respondents were asked, "Does sex change after retirement?" "No," replied 58 percent of the men and 60 percent of the women; "Yes — it *gets better*," said 23 percent of the men and 24 percent of the women.[18]

Of course one of the best ways to make sex sizzle is to vary your sexual routines. The French author Balzac once said, "Marriage must constantly conquer the monster that devours; its name is habit."[19] Nowhere is that more true than in the bedroom. After thirty or more years of marriage, we have developed predictable ways to make love. Now is the time to change them, particularly if your love-making has lost its spark.

Start by making sex a priority, rather than something fitted in at the end of the day. Why put off that which can be enjoyed earlier? Stanford psychiatrist Dr. Herant Katchadourian asks: "When . . . the couple is alone in the home, why must sex be postponed until the eleventh hour at night? Why not early mornings? Why not weekends or afternoons?"[20]

If you can't decide on a time, try taking turns defining the time, setting, and plan for your "date." Use your imagination. Have sex *before* a romantic dinner. Undress each other. Give each other a massage. Spend a night in a luxurious hotel. Go out for breakfast — then come home to make love. Or make love in a car, just like you did when you were a kid! Yes, older people still enjoy the backseat of a car. In one study of 83,000 married women, a startling 18 percent reported making love in a car, and 21 percent enjoyed it outdoors.[21]

The key is to let your imagination run free, and that might mean using some romantic props. One of the best is to make love by candlelight. Nor Hall, a Jungian analyst, found that "the Romans had a lot of ways of talking about fire, associating it with passion. It cast a rosy glow that is associated with the state

527

of being enraptured. The external object expresses an internal state."[22]

Or — get this — enter the bedroom through a window! After all, Cupid was known to fly in and out a window. "You should always admit your lover through a window; that makes it a little more difficult," says Hall, echoing the Roman poet Ovid, who suggested that lovers should prefer windows over available doors, which may explain the reputations of Don Juan, Errol Flynn, and Douglas Fairbanks as second-story men.[23]

Now your style might not be jumping in and out of windows, and the back seat of your Toyota might not be too appealing. However, the point is to never let your sex life become boring. "A rebellious sex life within the bonds of a couple," notes psychoanalyst Otto Kernberg, "can be the cement that preserves a marriage."[24]

Obviously, both partners should make an effort to enrich their lovemaking. But don't be surprised, men, if your wife takes the lead. In the famous Kinsey studies done some forty years ago, the rate of lovemaking in the marriage was totally dependent on the male. That's not true anymore. In one recent study, 14 percent of the women surveyed sometimes call in late for work simply because they felt in a loving mood before the work day began.[25]

In another study the sexiest wives enriched their lovemaking by altering bedroom routines. They wore sexy nightgowns, played romantic music, and wore different perfumes.[26] The result? Said one man: "When we make love, I feel as if my wife wants to do it to infinity. It's maddeningly good."[27]

To repeat: *make intimacy a priority*. But don't believe that you have to make love every day to be happy. According to a Masters and Johnson study, most individuals over the age of sixty are satisfied with one or two climaxes per week.[28] In another study of fifteen hundred households of all ages, the typical American had sex an average of fifty-seven times a year — or about once a week.[29] If you and your spouse feel comfortable with both the quality and frequency of sex, relax and celebrate your love when those romantic moments occur.

Now permit me to change the focus of our discussion. We have already noted that it's possible to have the best sex ever in mid to late life. But suppose you have had a heart attack? Or perhaps you are going through menopause? Can you *really* continue to enjoy sex as you once did?

In most cases, the answer is a strong, affirming *"yes."* True, if you have had a *heart attack,* your physician may ask you to limit all physical exertion for a period of time. This gives your damaged heart muscle time to heal. But your doctor will also want you to gradually increase your activities — and that includes vigorous activities in bed! If you're worried about having another heart attack in the middle of a moment of ecstasy, relax. Subsequent heart attacks due to sexual intercourse virtually never occur. If they do, it is almost always due to the *psychic* stress of having sex with a new partner, often a younger partner, and in an unfamiliar surrounding or circumstance.[30]

If you have recently gone through *menopause,* you may experience some discomfort when having sex due to the fact that there is a decrease in your body's ability to produce estrogen. This, in turn, leads to a decrease in lubricating fluids and can diminish the elasticity of the vagina. Fortunately, in most instances this discomfort is mild and temporary. Thomas H. Walz and Nancee S. Blum, two authorities on sexual health in later life, noted that you must "be patient. The vagina may stretch back to normal with use, or it may be assisted by oral or vaginal estrogen preparations (combined with progesterone). In the meantime, water-soluble lubrications such as K-Y Jelly can alleviate some of the discomfort."[31]

If you have recently undergone a *hysterec-*

tomy, you may wonder what effect it will have on your sexual life. A hysterectomy is a traumatic event that can lead to depression, which may then result in a decline in sexual desire.

But a hysterectomy does not diminish libido. In fact, some women report *increased* sexual pleasure after a hysterectomy because they'd previously been experiencing pain from enlarged uterine or ovarian tumors. The key to resuming an active sex life is to know that you are as sexually healthy after a hysterectomy as you were before. And there is no reason not to believe you can engage in an active and passionate love life. But if problems with hot flashes and vaginal dryness persist, see your physician for advice on practical remedies.

What if you don't look as good at age sixty as you did at age twenty? Take heart; few of us do. We may have put on weight, added wrinkles, lost some weight.

Fortunately, the most important factor in a good sexual relationship is *psychological* rather than physical health and attitude. This is not to suggest that physical characteristics are unimportant. In fact, the more you can keep yourself in good shape, the more attractive you will be to your mate. But ultimately, good sex is not dependent upon preserving a youthful figure. If it did, many of us would be in deep, deep trouble! The critical factor in a good sex life is open and honest communication and a deep, abiding respect for one another.

To repeat: *the way to good sex is through the mind.* Or, to put it another way — good sex begins with good conversation.

Sadly, even in retirement we may not take the time to find out what is *really* happening to our spouse. Most of us in fact spend only *twenty-eight minutes* a week expressing how we feel about one another and ourselves.[32] It's not difficult to understand, then, why sex can easily become a mechanical and superficial affair.

Talk tenderly to one another before going to bed. Cuddle and caress. And then, after your love has been shared, remind each other of how fortunate you are to have one another. If you do, the passion will never die. And the commitments made at the altar years ago will burn bright into the future.

We have seen that there is one thing about marriage that is always true: it gets better or worse. It becomes richer or poorer. Deeper or shallower. It never, ever, remains the same.

If you are married and want to have a successful retirement, become romantic. Spend time with one another. Share your hopes as well as your fears, and your aspirations as well as your failures.

Never take one another for granted, and, by all means, keep courting until the day you die. Plan dates. Hug spontaneously. Alter sex routines. Through these simple things you will discover that you and your spouse are friends. And, in all likelihood, terrific lovers.

CHAPTER FOURTEEN

Starting Over: Making a Second Marriage Work

The lessons you learn from your first marriage don't necessarily help you to survive the second.
Norman M. Lobsenz

If you have been divorced or your spouse has died, you may believe that your retirement will be spent alone. That's not necessarily true, since over 1,500,000 million people remarry *annually*, a 63 percent increase since 1970. Unfortunately, *60 percent* of all remarriages end in divorce, and an untold number can best be described as "fragile unions" — marital relationships in which the passion is gone and romance has been forgotten.

Why do some second marriages succeed and others fail? Why are some couples able to solve their differences, while others call an attorney? And why is it that some individuals refuse to take a second chance on marriage, even when an affectionate and willing partner appears?

I decided to explore. What I found is that a second marriage — particularly one in mid-life to late life — can be magnificent. But developing such a relationship doesn't happen by chance. It takes patience, hard work, and a commitment to ride out the marital storms that inevitably arise.

If you are thinking about remarrying, this chapter is for you. And if you recently walked that path, read these paragraphs carefully, for it is possible to learn from the mistakes of others. More important, by focusing on second marriages that are strong and durable, we can uncover the secrets of staying in love throughout your retirement years.

Stay Ready – You Are Never Too Old for Romance

"There may be snow on the roof," the old saying goes, "but there's still a fire in the furnace."

Doubt that fact? Turn to the classified advertisements in retirement magazines. Here are a few choice examples from a recent issue of *Active Senior Lifestyles:*

WWF, 62, attractive, classy, would like to meet a suave gentleman, 6′ plus, educated, 62-70, with a zest for life.

WWM, young 65 year old, would like to meet a classy young lady, late 50s to early 60s . . . No smoke, lite drinker, travel to warm places, let's talk.[1]

There is no doubt: even if years have passed since you last were on a date, the fires of romance and passion can still exist. And well they should. As W. H. Auden, an Anglo-American poet, critic, and very wise man once wrote, "We must either fall in love with Someone or Something or else fall ill."[2]

An exaggeration? Not really. Health experts have observed that married people are healthier than unmarried people and that death rates are *consistently* higher among single and socially isolated people.

In one study of 4,775 adults in Alameda County, California, those who had the weakest social ties — as measured by marital status, nature of family relationships, number of friends, and membership in churches and community organizations — had *significantly higher death rates* than those with the strongest social ties, even after adjustments were made for age, sex, and health status.[3]

James S. House, of the University of Michigan, states that mortality rates are approximately 100 percent to 300 percent higher for socially isolated men and 50 percent to 150 percent higher for socially isolated women compared to those who have strong social networks. "That's roughly in the same ballpark as the effects on mortality that have been estimated for smoking," states House.[4]

This is not a recommendation that you rush to the altar in order to live longer! What I am suggesting, though, is that it is important to develop close, loving ties to other people. How to begin?

Start by joining organizations where you can meet people with similar interests, values, and aspirations. As Abigail Van Buren ("Dear Abby") says, "Decent people are found where decent people gather. If you want to hook a mountain trout, don't go fishing in a herring barrel."[5] In addition, let it be known that you are back in circulation, since there will likely be at least one matchmaker who will enthusiastically step forward and introduce you to others.

Don't assume you won't have enough nerve to ask someone to arrange a date. After all, why stay at home, lonely, when there are other people like yourself who would enjoy your company?

Frank McKinney's wife died after a beautiful thirty-four-year marriage. "The pain of losing Maria was almost unbearable. I was very lonely, but I didn't feel comfortable in groups, especially when other couples were present. I watched a lot of television."

Fortunately, Frank's best friend noted his depression and his retreat from life. "You need female companionship," he said. "And I know the perfect person for you."

"No way," replied Frank. "I'm not ready for that."

"When do you think you will be ready?" asked his friend.

"Probably never," was the response.

But Frank's loneliness grew, as did his desire to find a special confidante. He called his friend, who, in turn, lined up the date. "I was as nervous as a teen-ager on his first date," said Frank. "But it was love at first sight. We talked into the early hours of the morning. And the next night she fixed me a terrific dinner in her apartment. I never thought I could fall in love again, but it happened. And if it happened to me, it can happen to anyone."

Yes — it can happen to you, too, no matter how old, wrinkled, out of shape, fat, thin, or whatever you think you are. No matter your physical condition, you can make yourself attractive and appealing.

First, in order to feel better about yourself, get into top physical condition. Reread chapter 9, and start a vigorous exercise program. If you have a weight problem, a small investment in a weight-loss clinic can do wonders for your morale as well as your figure.

Then take a close look at your wardrobe. If it's dated, purchase a new suit or dress and invest in some contemporary, upscale casual clothes. If your budget permits, add a little jewelry or other bit of flair.

Then assess your attitude. Remind yourself that you are a loving, capable person. And that you have much to offer others.

As you meet people, don't demand perfection, for everyone has unique qualities. In addition, be honest about your feelings. As author William Novak says: "In love, as in any other investment, the reward is directly proportional to the risk. Do not let the fear of rejection hold you back."[6]

But do have fun together. Go to events that you enjoy — exhibits, concerts, plays, athletic events, or whatever. But don't neglect quiet walks and candlelight dinners. Indulge all sides of your personality.

Your goal? To learn all you can about your new friend, for the interest you express in that person will be returned to you a hundredfold.

What if you find someone who becomes more than a friend? How will you know if it is infatuation or true love? Judith Viorst has the perfect answer: "Infatuation is when you think that he's as sexy as Robert Redford, as smart as Henry Kissinger, as noble as Ralph Nader, as funny as Woody Allen and as athletic as Jimmy Connors. Love is when you realize that he's as sexy as Woody Allen, as smart as Jimmy Connors, as funny as Ralph Nader, as athletic as Henry Kissinger and nothing like Robert Redford in any category — but you'll take him anyway."[7]

Stay Calm: Never Make a Commitment before You Are Ready!

Most people who one day find themselves alone waste no time establishing new relationships. In fact, most remarry within three years of their marital breakup, and more than one out of every six will remarry almost as soon as their divorce is finalized.

Why do we make lifelong commitments so quickly? Sylvia Weishaus, a therapist who counsels remarried couples, observes: "It's natural to need to feel loved when you've just been rejected. But remarrying on the rebound is self-defeating. Unless one takes the time to learn something from the collapse of the first marriage that will make the second stronger, he or she is likely to repeat the destructive behavior or pick another unsuitable partner."[8]

If you're unsure whether you're marrying for the right reasons, consider these three good reasons *not* to marry.

Do not marry for money. This may seem like strange counsel, especially if you have a zero balance in your checking account and are living on the edge of poverty. But marital counselors agree: money does not buy lasting happiness. True, you might get a kick out of dining in the most exclusive restaurant in town. But unless you are sharing an evening with someone you enjoy, the fancy silverware, the expensive wine, and the lush ambience will soon seem hollow.

Don't marry for convenience. Suppose you were divorced a number of years ago and still haven't met a suitable partner. If someone suddenly appears who seems okay, doesn't offend you, promises security, and seems reasonably well adjusted, you might jump at the chance to form a more serious relationship.

But don't. If there isn't a romantic spark between you before marriage, it's unlikely to appear after. If his or her personality doesn't light your fire now, it probably won't five months from now.

Never succumb to pressure. No matter how much you're in love, take your time before making a permanent commitment. The last thing you need is to be swept off your feet, only to discover that the person you dated is different from the person you married.

Sociologist Irving Goffman made an astute observation when he noted that all of us have a "public self" and a "private self." The public self is that part of us we let others see. It represents our best attributes — those strengths of which we are proud.

But everyone, says Goffman, also has a "private self." Located deep in the private self are all the negative attitudes we harbor, including our fears, shortcomings, and limitations. We rarely reveal the private self to others, at least not intentionally. The reason is simple: we fear that if others see our faults, they may reject us.

Rejection doesn't always occur, of course. In fact, love is often born during those moments in which we share our weakness. And trust often develops when we learn that our limitations are understood, even accepted by that all-important other person.

What happens if you don't like the private self of the person you are dating? What if the mask unintentionally slips, and his or her anxieties unnerve you? What if your prospective lover is put off by the shortcomings you reveal?

I cannot tell you what to do, but I do know this: There comes a time to take a risk and accept one another — shortcomings and all. In so doing, you accept each other's limitations as well as strengths, shortcomings as well as attributes. Remember, if you can identify with the best characteristics in others, you are less tempted to look for the worst.

Nevertheless, marriage remains a calculated gamble. Can you really get along with one another, not for an evening or two, but for the rest of life? Can you talk openly about issues you find troubling? If problems arise, can they be dealt with in a nondefensive manner? And perhaps most important, do you share similar values — values that can sustain you when disputes threaten your relationship?

If you can say yes to these questions, I would encourage you to state your wedding vows. For as Soren Kierkegaard, the Danish theologian, has correctly noted: "To cheat oneself out of love is the most terrible deception; it is an eternal loss for which there is no reparation, either in time or in eternity."[9]

Jacklyn Remington, fifty-seven, had some deep fears that almost cost her a new love. Outwardly she is self-assured and articulate; inwardly she mourns the passing of a husband who treated her like a queen. Now, long after his death, she still believes that no man anywhere could measure up to her lover of twenty-seven years.

There is a deeper reason, however, for her reluctance to form new relationships. Last year she was diagnosed as having breast cancer. Her figure has been altered through a mastectomy, and her future is uncertain.

Now we are at the core of human existence, for the key to forming new relationships is not the new wardrobe, the glittery jewelry, or whether you dine at fancy restaurants. The key is whether you can find someone who will love you for who you are, as you are.

The poet Rainer Maria Rilke once said, "Love consists in this, that two solitudes protect and touch and greet each other."[10] What does it mean to protect, touch and greet one another?

Jacklyn Remington can tell you. On a beautiful summer evening she took Paul Sherman to be her husband. Why did she marry now, when at one time she thought no one would ever satisfy her hopes, let alone her standards?

Her new spouse from the start clearly accepted her for who she was. He didn't ask her to change her values, nor was he threatened by the strength of her first marriage. And if perchance the cancer reappeared, they would meet it head on and love one another *joyfully* until the end of their days.

In preparing to write this book, I encountered many marriages that at some point had severe testing. There was one couple that I will never forget because their story is unique.

John and Elizabeth Johnson were in their mid-70s. They approached me holding one another's hand. Their appearance was frail. Their wardrobes were tattered. They were, in his words, "dirt poor."

They informed me that Elizabeth had at most three months to live. It was stated perfunctorily, with no indication of fear. "How do you cope when the prognosis is so bleak?" I asked.

John smiled, and I realized that he had an understanding of life that I needed to learn. "We live one day at a time and we make the most of it," he said. "No matter the pain, no matter the discomfort, we try to have fun. Then just before we go to sleep, we kneel by our bed and pray. I always put my arm around her. And I thank God that he has given us one more day to be together."

Ultimately, that's the goal of any marriage — to be able to protect, touch, and greet one another tenderly, always. So don't rush into marriage. Ask questions, and if you find yourself sharing the intimacies of your heart, which is the foundation for a lasting, beautiful marriage — move ahead.

Be Realistic: Identify Problems that Threaten Your Relationship

When five hundred divorced men and women were asked to identify the major reasons for the breakup of their marriage, they cited infidelity, loss of love, alcoholism, and lack of communication most often. But according to a study in the *Journal of Marriage and the Family*, second marriages tend to end because of conflicts related to money, stepchildren, and the "unfinished emotional business" from the first marriage, including feelings of anger, guilt and remorse.[11]

To avoid these problems in your second marriage, let's take a close look at money issues, not surprisingly the number one problem affecting second marriages.

MONEY

It's a fact: Money problems will probably threaten your second marriage often and more severely than any other issue. Why? Because when you enter a second marriage you establish a *business relationship* as well as a *marital relationship*.

Think back to your first marriage. How much money did you bring to the relationship? Probably very little.

Now think about your current assets. You

may not be a millionaire, but you probably have saved some money. And your spouse's financial holdings may be equally impressive.

Now consider the following decisions that must be made in a new marriage:

* Who will manage the money in your new relationship?
* Which spouse is the "saver" and who is the "spender"? Can your differences be reconciled?
* Who will pay the bills?
* Who will be responsible for the mortgage payments?
* Who will be responsible for investments?
* How much risk should be taken in investments?
* Which assets will be merged and which will be independently owned?
* Should money be loaned to children? If so, how much and how often?
* Should there be separate savings and checking accounts?
* Should there be a household budget? Who is responsible for managing it?

These issues should be addressed forthrightly, since their resolution will affect you, your spouse, and your extended family for years to come. One forty-year-old woman, an only child whose sixty-five-year-old mother remarried three years ago, recalls: "One reason I was so upset when my mother remarried after Daddy died is that I felt like her new husband was just after her for Daddy's money. Her new husband gave his house to his oldest son and then moved into my mother's house. Daddy always used to say he didn't mind dying because he knew that long after he was dead, his great-great-great-grandchildren would be running up and down the hallways, just like I used to do. But of course he left the house to my mother in his will, and now I'm afraid if she dies first, her new husband will get everything and my children and grandchildren will have lost everything Daddy expected them to have."[12]

There are ways to avoid such dilemmas. Here is one suggestion: Before you remarry write a *prenuptial agreement,* which is a legally binding document. The agreement will stipulate who controls financial assets, how they might be distributed in your marriage, and how they will be dispersed if you die or if the marriage ends in divorce.

To prepare a prenuptial agreement, you must locate an attorney who can advise on what should be included. The difference between a will and a prenuptial agreement is that a will, by definition, is signed and changed by one party, while a prenuptial agreement needs both parties for any modification.[13]

Frankly, some people are dismayed at the notion that they should consult an attorney before they marry. As financial columnist Jane Bryant Quinn notes: "When lawyers walk in, some think, love flies out the door."[14]

But a prenuptial pact is designed to *strengthen* a marriage, not weaken it. If you doubt that fact, think about the following problems that could have been prevented with a little financial planning.

Margaret marries a prosperous dentist. She brings to her marriage a $125,000 inheritance. She does not have a prenuptial agreement. Her new husband's lifestyle requires a lot of money for his five children and his expensive cars. He takes control of Margaret's money and invests it in a tax shelter for one of his sons — a guitar factory that later goes bankrupt. The marriage is dissolved and Margaret is forced to spend $25,000 in an unsuccessful attempt to reclaim her money. A prenuptial agreement would have protected Margaret's inheritance from being blended with community property.

Ted and Sally have been married only four months. One evening Sally announces nonchalantly, "Oh, by the way, we have to repay Mother the eight thousand dollars I owe her." Ted is horrified: "What else might she be hiding?" A prenuptial agreement would have placed all the financial information on the table *before* they were married.

Linda has been married for only a year when her husband develops cancer. Before the marriage he had placed all his insurance and money market funds in a joint account with his parents. He had also given them a lien on his house to protect it from his ex-wife. Merle dies six weeks after his illness is diagnosed. He leaves almost nothing for his wife, their child, or his three children by his previous marriage. His parents believe the money belongs to them. A prenuptial agreement and a change of beneficiaries would have prevented this tragedy.[15]

If you think you could benefit from a prenuptial agreement, have a frank discussion with your fiancé(e) about money and the role it will have in your relationship. Think about these factors:

* How much money you earn and how you will support yourself in retirement.
* Whether you intend to work in retirement, and, if so, for how long.
* Assets you own, including savings accounts, stocks, bonds, money market funds, annuities, and money owed to you. What portion will be blended, and what will remain separate property?
* Whether you are in debt. Is your own cash flow sufficient to support your indebtedness?
* Whether anyone is dependent upon you for financial support. Who is and for how much and how long?
* Whether your ex-spouse has rights to your pension; if so, how much and for how long?
* Whether any large bills are forthcoming, such as college tuition expenses.
* Whether you wish to retain control of the assets you bring to the marriage.
* How much life insurance you have.

Who are your beneficiaries? Do you plan on changing your primary beneficiary?

* Where your money will go after you die. Remember — anything given to the surviving spouse may eventually go to his or her children.
* Whether you will have joint checking and savings accounts. How will you handle credit-card payments?
* What percentage of your income, if any, should you save? Who will be responsible for investing it?
* Whether you should purchase a new home; if so, who is responsible for the mortgage?
* Whether you have a will. Does it need revision?

If these questions are difficult to resolve or cause disagreement between you, consider seeing a lawyer. One issue to target specifically is whether financial assets should be blended. For many, this is not an issue. Glorya Olds of Santa Fe, New Mexico, says: "I felt if I loved him enough to marry him, I loved him enough to merge [our assets] — and it has worked wonderfully."[16]

Blending assets, however, is not always wise. Listen to the following story.

A couple in their fifties came to an attorney's office to draw up a prenuptial agreement. The woman had considerable money. Her partner, recently divorced, had no financial assets and many obligations to his former wife and their children.

They wanted their prenuptial agreement to say that *everything* would be shared equally. The husband-to-be, however, wanted to take over the management of his wife's money because, despite her investment success, he was convinced that he could do better.

"I was scared to death for her," the attorney recalls. "But what could I say? I couldn't insult him."

Six months after the wedding, the husband had reinvested most of the wife's portfolio. Six months after that, the attorney discovered that the investments were doing poorly and that a considerable amount of money had been lost. "They're still very much in love," notes the attorney. "She seems to be taking it well. But it just shouldn't have happened."[17]

Some might think that that's the risk she took. True. But in your case it is important to decide prior to the marriage whether that risk should be taken. If you're at peace with the decision, don't fret over what others might think. But if you prefer another arrangement, make your wishes known *before* your wedding vows are spoken. A marriage can be quickly tarnished by financial misunderstandings, and if your spouse goes so far as to misappropriate financial resources without your knowledge, grounds for a divorce are firmly established.

A most creative version of the prenuptial agreement, and one that has particular appeal to retirees, is for each spouse to retain control of the assets each brought individually to the marriage. But everything acquired or earned *after* the marriage is considered "community property." For example, if one partner owned $75,000 worth of stock on the date of the marriage, that would continue to stay in his or her name. But if the stock appreciated to $100,000 afterward, the $25,000 capital gain would belong to the two of them.[18]

There are, of course, many other ways to structure a financial relationship. An attorney can guide you through the possibilities, but listen carefully to counsel. Legal advice given now can save you a bundle in financial and emotional costs later.

One financial issue deserves special attention, and that is whether you should loan money to your children, stepchildren, and even more distant relatives. Be careful. A fifty-year-old Chicago woman recalls: "I made every mistake possible when my daughter asked me for a twenty-five-thousand-dollar loan for a down payment on the home she wanted to buy. My financial situation was simple. I had a forty-thousand-dollar-a-year job, a heavily mortgaged house, and a thirty-thousand-dollar certificate of deposit. Without telling her of my financial position I said yes — and cashed in my CD."

The outcome? The daughter added hot tubs, a greenhouse, and a stereo system to her home — but never repaid the loan. The mother told her daughter she resented the way the money had been used. The daughter became defensive. The relationship turned bitter.[19]

As I mentioned earlier, if you are retired or close to retirement, you may have accumulated considerable wealth. That fact is not lost on close relatives nor is it lost on stepchildren. In fact, they may begin to see you as a personal banker who can be tapped for emergency funds. Should you become their financial friend? Here are four good reasons *not* to give a loan.[20]

Never give money you can't afford to lose. You might have a nice pension and some investments, but who knows what financial emergencies might occur down the road? As we know, inflation can take a big bite out of savings. And since there are very few items that are decreasing in cost, don't take chances with your retirement nest egg, especially when you're living on a fixed income.

Don't make a loan if the borrower is irresponsible. Judy Barber, a licensed family therapist who specializes in the psychology of money, advises: "It's important to consider the individual adult child. You need to know what the money is for and what's the likelihood that your child will follow through, not only in using it for the proposed purpose but in paying it back."[21]

Withhold the loan if you don't think it's a good deal for you. Suppose, for example, that a stepchild requests $15,000 for a new car. Why does the stepchild need a *new* car if a used car would be just as adequate? If you have $15,000 to loan, think about whether you'd prefer to see it spent on something that will *appreciate* in value.

Don't give a loan when you sense you're being manipulated. A grandchild, for example, might suggest that you "prove" your affection by loaning money. Don't fall for the bait. If the strength of your relationship is contingent upon a loan, it isn't much of a relationship. "Frequently," says financial planner Paul Westbrook, "grandparents who are tapped by their grandchildren fear that if they don't pony up for the car Jennifer wants, the child's love will evaporate. Yet it rarely happens. . . . The funny thing is that when grandparents say no, the grandchild's nonplussed reply is usually, 'Well, I asked.' "[22]

Is giving money to a relative *always* a bad risk? No. If you have adequate funds for retirement and there is a genuine need, you might take delight in helping a relative.

But draw up the loan in a businesslike fashion. State the terms, including the rate of interest and when the loan is to be repaid. Make clear what will happen if the loan is not repaid and what options there may be if you had an unexpected need for the money. Above everything else, make clear that this is a *loan,* not a gift.

STEPCHILDREN

There is a second problem endemic to many second marriages: conflict between stepparents and stepchildren, and how to manage it.

Today nearly 40 percent of all remarriages include stepchildren and, regrettably, conflict between stepparents and stepchildren can be a formidable threat to the marriage. In one survey of two thousand remarried people, *17 percent* of the couples with stepchildren divorced during the three years of the study. But divorce occurred in only *ten percent* of marriages without stepchildren.

Some harsh facts: few stepparents can truly love a stepchild in the same way that one loves one's own child. And rarely does a stepchild feel more affection for the stepparent than for the biological parent.

If you have difficulty developing a lasting relationship with stepchildren, take encouragement from Dr. Benjamin Spock, probably the best known child-care expert of the past three decades. Ten years ago, Spock became a stepfather. His thoughts? "I had no idea of how painful it would be to feel rejected by someone within my own family or how hard it would be to react rationally."

His stepdaughter spent the first several years largely ignoring him. But then she treated him rudely. Especially uningratiating was that she would leave plates of rotten food under her bed, along with wet towels.

Mary Morgan, her mother, coped by shutting her daughter's bedroom door. "Although I found comfort in closing her door and shutting off the pain," she noted, "this kind of denial was not Ben's style. He would go into my daughter's room each morning after she left for school to hang up her wet towels, gather up the garbage, and expect that somehow this would teach her to do it herself. Not at all. It only taught her that if she left wet towels on the floor and food under the bed, Ben would clear them all away in the morning. She had him beautifully house-trained and she knew it. He knew better but he couldn't seem to stop."[23]

In time, Dr. Spock gained a clearer understanding of the dynamics between stepparent and child: "In retrospect it's clear to me that no matter how much I was suffering, my stepdaughter was suffering even more. But at the time I was so resentful of her attitude toward me that I didn't have room in my heart, as the expression goes, to feel much sympathy for her."[24]

What can you do to keep your relationship with stepchildren on track? Here is some advice from Dr. Spock, who in time developed a trusting relationship with his stepdaughter.

Remember that to the child, a remarriage of a parent is the final severing of the original, intact family. Even a thirty-five-year-old whose parent has been dead for ten years might resent your appearance because it truly symbolizes the end of his or her original family.

Stepchildren tend to see stepparents as intruders within their family. Consequently they may become rude and antagonistic. Don't respond in kind, and never assume that you are a failure as a stepparent.

Remember, sometimes the child's reluctance to show affection or even polite acceptance is based on her loyalty to the absent parent. The child may believe that if affection is shown to a stepparent, there is no longer love for the deceased parent. Or worse — she has now let the parent's place be taken by a stranger.[25]

There are other things you can do to nurture your relationship with adult stepchildren. If possible, spend time together. Take an interest in their careers, hobbies, and avocations. Stay away from disputes between child and parent. And be reticent about playing the role of peacemaker, even when you're asked; far better to avoid family fights that you did not create and probably cannot solve. This doesn't suggest that you are uncaring, unfeeling, or unconcerned. It *does* suggest that you have confidence in your loved ones' ability to work out differences without your interference.

I have one more suggestion for improving relationships between stepparents and stepchildren, and it's best illustrated in a beautiful letter written to, of course,

Dear Abby:

My heart went out to "Upset in Minnesota," who had saved his money to splurge on a nice Father's Day brunch, only to have his father show up with his new wife. No doubt "Upset" was looking forward to the father-and-son brunch.

I notice that so many letters in your column contain problems created by the second wife, who always wants to be "in the picture," so to speak. In most cases, the second marriage is a traumatic experience for the children, who deserve more consideration than they really get.

As a second wife, during the early years of our marriage, I encouraged my husband to attend his family's graduations, weddings, family reunions, and special occasions without me. Though etiquette decrees that the spouse should be invited, there is nothing that says the spouse cannot decline, and I found it was very much appreciated when I did. I might add that the rewards I have received for insisting that my husband attend without me have far outweighed the small sacrifices I made.

Now, in my old age, I have the love and friendship of these children — and their children. They are a part of my family.

A Well-rewarded Second Wife

Abby replied as follows:

Dear Second Wife: Most second wives have two strikes against them when they marry a man with a ready-made family. And second husbands usually have to try harder when they're No. 2. I admire your sensitivity and insight. It paid off handsomely. Other "seconds" could learn from you.[26]

UNFINISHED BUSINESS

Dealing with the emotional fallout from the first marriage can seriously impinge on the second. There are two types of fallout. One is evident when a spouse dies, thus ending a successful marriage. The other appears when a first marriage ends in divorce.

What happens to the surviving spouse of a good marriage? Often they *deify* the deceased. As Donna Hodgkins Berado, a sociologist at the University of Florida, says: "The widowed have a tendency to sanctify their former mates, remembering all their positive qualities and forgetting the negative."[27]

Sometimes surviving spouses state flatly that they will never remarry. Why? No one could possibly measure up to their former spouse.

But in time wounds heal and special friendships are formed. Vows never to remarry are cancelled. And wedding plans move ahead.

If the new marriage is based on mutual trust and respect, comparisons to a former spouse are made realistically and with gentle humor. "Yes, he knew how to make money," said Alma Beckinridge. "But did he remember my birthday? No, he was a tad forgetful."

But if the new marriage is fraught with tension, the new spouse draws comparisons between the new and the old. "Richard, my first husband, was more sensitive." "Mary, my former wife, was more cheerful." "Doug was more considerate." "Sandy was more loving." "Peter was brighter." "Judy was more dependable."

Such comparisons might never be verbalized, but they are insidious; once the image is gilded, the old spouse becomes an idol and the stature of the new spouse dwindles rapidly.

In one sense, comparisons between old and new spouses are normal, even inevitable. But if you find yourself tempted to turn your old spouse into a saint, take a moment to recall his or her shortcomings. Better yet, focus attention on the *positive qualities* of your new spouse. If you can highlight characteristics you find endearing and attractive, the tendency to compare abates. Indeed, comparisons will seem a waste of time.

If you're on the receiving end of unfair comparisons, speak up, for comparisons are hurtful. In time, they will undermine your self-confidence and diminish your love for one another. Don't engage in marital warfare, however. As one commentator noted aptly: "People who fight fire with fire usually end up with ashes."[28]

Another serious type of emotional spillover occurs when a previous marriage has ended in a contentious divorce. Some couples learn to remain friends after a divorce, but these are the exception, not the rule.

Most feel victimized by their former spouse, and the anger runs deep. "I'll never get over what he did to me," said one individual. Replied another: "My anger is always present, just hidden from view."

Anger often gives way to another destructive emotion — guilt. "What I regret most," says one father, "is how the divorce hurt our children." Says another husband, "If I had spent more time with my wife, her affair would never have happened."

Anger and guilt are not diffused simply because one establishes a new marital relationship. Indeed, destructive feelings can lie just beneath the surface, threatening to erupt at any moment.

How do you come to peace with your feelings? How do you let go of regrets that gnaw at peace of mind? There is no magical formula.

But the key is to be able to admit mistakes and move on. "True, I did some dumb things," says Juan Cortez. "But how long should I punish myself? How long do I do penance?"

If your former marriage is finalized on paper, let it be finalized in your heart. Where you may have made mistakes, admit them. If children are involved, nurture them. But also focus loving attention on your new spouse, now. If you don't, yesterday's problems can put a stranglehold on tomorrow's joys.

If you are mentally stuck in a previous relationship or can't get beyond your anger or your hurt, see a counselor. If the emotional spillover threatens your new marriage, join a support group. But don't burden your new spouse with your anger or your guilt, because few things damage a new relationship faster than a constant replaying of old tales. Remember: it is far better to build a new life than sift through the ashes of the old, looking for something that isn't there.

Be Resilient: Second Marriages Demand Patience, Nurturing, and a Whole Lot of Love

Now we come to the final suggestion for

making a second marriage work: Be flexible, for rigidity is a deadly enemy to a successful relationship.

As we age, we often become opinionated and more judgmental. We make statements such as, "That dress doesn't look good on you." "Why do you let your children take advantage of you?" "You should have more meat in the spaghetti sauce." "You spend too much time with your children."

Such comments may have been expressed in an earlier marriage. But in general, twenty-year-olds tend to be less secure in their opinions because they don't have a bank of information on which to base their advice. But after a half-century of experience, we have pretty firm ideas as to how the food should be seasoned, the house should be organized, and what to do in our spare time. Consequently there tends to be conflict in second marriages simply because we have definite perspectives on how to live our lives.

Of course, a certain amount of gentle chiding in most marriages is normal, providing it goes both ways. Yesterday my wife tried out a new recipe. She took a beautiful piece of fresh fish, put it directly on the barbecue grill, and turned the gas jets on high! Then she practically drowned the poor creature in a sea of pepper.

"What are you doing?" I asked, with a hint of disbelief. "The heat will bake the fish dry," I noted. "And the pepper will make it inedible."

My wife looked at me and gave me that now-Robert-I-know-what-I-am-doing look, which, incidentally, I have come to expect at moments like this. I bit my tongue but was convinced that the fish was ruined.

My wife watched as I took the first bite. "Do you like the fish?" she asked with a mischievous grin. I muttered a one-word apology: "Sorry." It was the most delicious fish dinner I've ever eaten.

All marriages have such moments. But personal quirks can, indeed, be annoying:

> My husband expects me to fold his laundry. But why should I? It's his underwear!
> My wife has to eat at 6:00 P.M. It can't be 5:45 or 6:15. It just drives me crazy!
> He always has to have red meat and a baked potato. Where has he been nutritionally for the last ten years?
> She is always listening to the radio. It drives me nuts! I would like to have just one evening of peace and quiet.

Fortunately, most spouses make accommodations to one another's idiosyncrasies. However, if you sense that the romantic flame is dimming due to your personal habits, ask one simple question: *"What is it like to be married to me?"* Answered honestly, this question cuts to the heart of marital dilemmas because suddenly you see yourself through your partner's eyes.

Stan and Sue Gordon walked into the office of Harry P. Dunne, Jr., a family therapist in Norwalk, Connecticut, believing that their twenty-year marriage was over. They wanted help in getting through a divorce. "We love each other, but we can't live together," they explained.[29]

Rather than help terminate a marriage in which love was still evident, the therapist asked each to answer the question: "What is it like to be married to me?"

Accusations flowed. Sue was absolutely certain that everything would be all right if Stan did not wear his feelings on his sleeve. And it would help things if he didn't run off in a huff and leave her alone after an argument.

Stan, on the other hand, insisted that he would stay home more if Sue were not so messy and sharp-tongued.

Several days later Sue saw a calendar that had been carelessly tossed on the dining room table. She blew up. How could Stan criticize her for keeping a messy house when he was the one always cluttering it up with useless things? "Why did you bring that calendar home?" she yelled.

Before Stan responded, Sue realized that she, not her husband, had probably left the calendar there. Her first impulse was to defend her error by saying, "Even if you didn't bring it home this time, it's just like you." But instead she asked: *"What would it be like to hear what I have just said?"*

She was saddened by her comment and told Stan: "That was a nasty thing for me to say, and I'm sorry."

Stan couldn't believe his ears. As Samuel A. Schreiner, Jr., who chronicled their story, observed: "It was as though she had taken an unexpected step backward in a familiar dance, and he had to step forward to match her. He was totally disarmed. What once would have become a battle never got started."[30]

This marked the beginning of a transformation in their relationship. They no longer think of their marriage as terminal. After some painful lessons they are taking the time to understand each other again.

If you're willing to learn how your partner sees you (which can be fun as well as illuminating), and *if you are committed to changing your-*

self rather than your partner, the chances of your remarriage succeeding dramatically improve.

What kinds of changes might you make? Ask a second question: *"What can I do to make life better for you?"*

If there is tension, the question asked aloud might evoke a flood of pejorative statements: "You could get home on time each night." "You could spend less money." "You could quit being so messy."

Quick, angry retorts are predictable in friction-filled marriages and may be more evident in second marriages. But the types of comments that heal misunderstandings are these:

The One Thing You Can Do Is . . .

Tell me that you love me.

Listen without judging me.

Criticize me only when I am strong.

Compliment me when I feel weak.

Hold me when I am afraid.

The next task is to move to a deeper, far more significant level of communication, a level in which each shares his or her vulnerability and his or her pain.

The real problems in a marriage are not reflected in whether the toothpaste clutters the counter or whether dirty dishes line the sink. These are only reflections of habits. The real issue is whether we can lovingly nurture one another in new and creative ways. What does it mean to *nurture* one another? On one level it means being reluctant to criticize, since harsh criticism rarely changes behavior. It only undermines confidence.

But nurturing also means to build up and to make strong. How do you "make strong" a marital union? How do you learn from the mistakes of a former marriage and apply the lessons learned to a new one? And how do you strengthen the union, when the normal stresses of life threaten to tear it down?

It is important to communicate those things about your partner that you *admire,* since in a world where so many are quick to criticize, we seldom receive the affirmation we need. Bosses tend not to give it. Neighbors may not know us well enough to give it. And friends assume that we already know why our company is valued, so they don't give it. Spouses should give it — but don't, often enough.

If you want your marriage to last, never assume that your wife knows why you love her. And never assume that your husband knows why you value his affection. Far better to articulate those things that bring you together than rehash issues that drive you apart.

Chris and Todd Johnson of San Francisco, California, married shortly after they retired. "The first year," she noted, "was difficult. We got on one another's nerves. I had to put up with his independence and he had to put up with my children. To make matters worse, we didn't know one another nearly as well as we thought."

"We almost split," he added. "But one day we went for a walk. I held her hand, something I hadn't done in a long, long time. And I told her all the reasons why I married her."

"It was just what I needed to hear," she said.

The result? "Our differences diminished. Our arguments stopped. We became aware that we married one another for sound rational reasons. And a host of romantic ones."

Today the Johnsons still have to deal with what Chris calls "his peculiarities" and what Todd affectionately refers to as "her uniqueness." But they walk hand in hand every evening. And never do they let the sun set on their anger.

Such is the composition of a truly successful second marriage.

Playwright Robert Anderson observed: "In every marriage more than a week old, there are grounds for divorce. The trick is to find, and continue to find, grounds for marriage."[31]

How do you find the "grounds for marriage"? How do you avoid the mistakes of a previous relationship, and how can you make your second marriage strong and durable?

There is no neat formula for keeping a second marriage on track. But this much we know: All loving couples share certain commonalities, things which perhaps second-time spouses have to work a little harder at remembering. Among the most important ones to incorporate into a second marriage are the following:

* They *anticipate problems,* mindful that each brings a different set of values, experiences, and expectations to the second marriage.
* They *contain the emotional spillover* from a previous marriage.
* When conflict emerges, they *use their collective wisdom* to find creative solutions.
* They seek to *change themselves* before seeking to change their partner.
* They *speak often of their love,* ever mindful of the need to affirm each other.

CHAPTER FIFTEEN

Living Alone – and Liking It!

What a lovely surprise to finally discover how unlonely being alone can be.
Ellen Burstyn
American actress

For many reasons, you may live alone. What if you don't wish to marry, or can't? Can retirement lived alone be as good as one shared with a special person?

The answer is an emphatic "Yes!" Many single people are having the time of their life in retirement, freed from hostilities and old hurts that sometimes choke marital relationships. They don't need to worry about offending a spouse when planning their personal calendar. And they are able to form beautiful friendships that sustain them in every season of life.

Regrettably, there is a downside to this portrait of single living. Many older people suffer from loneliness, which, if unchecked, can lead to sadness, despair, even suicide. It is an unfortunate fact: Americans over sixty-five are nearly *twice* as likely to take their own lives as the rest of the population. Many feel alone and utterly disconnected from other people, making this horrifying statistic almost understandable.

If you are struggling with loneliness, I hope you will take encouragement from this chapter. It is true — loneliness is a wrenching emotion that casts a dark cloud on all aspects of life. But it is a darkness that can diminish, especially when strong and vital relationships are formed.

How do you connect in meaningful ways to other people? How do you establish joyous relationships, especially when your efforts at finding them have failed? And what should you do in those terrifying moments when you feel abandoned by those whom you love? The starting point in resolving these difficult issues is to understand why we are lonely, and how loneliness makes its unwanted presence felt in our lives.

Why Do I Feel So Alone?

Some of the most intense feelings of loneliness occur after the *death of a spouse*. This is true in loving, supportive marriages but, interestingly, it is also true in fragile marriages in which survivors not only mourn the death of a loved one but grieve for the successful marriage they were not able to achieve.

Ronald Carpenter, sixty-six, was married for thirty-four years. Like many marriages his had its ups and downs, but upon his retirement he and his wife vowed to put their differences aside and try to truly enjoy their years of leisure.

It wasn't to be. Shortly after his retirement his wife complained of shortness of breath. He rushed her to a hospital, where she died of a massive coronary infarction. When I asked Ron to describe the hardest part of his tragedy, he replied: "I miss my wife's companionship, but what I find so hard to reconcile is that we believed the best days of our marriage were ahead of us." He paused and with considerable emotion added: "We waited too long to resolve our differences."

Most couples have an idealized notion of what their marriage will be like in retirement. They hope that differences will be resolved and accommodations made so that retirement will indeed be the best time of their life.

But if death comes prematurely, these hopes can be quickly and cruelly dashed. The surviving spouse is confronted with two tragedies: the loss of a companion *and* the close marriage that never materialized.

Compounding the problem is that friendships made as a couple often fade when one becomes single. One widow comments: "I miss my husband terribly, but I also miss our friends. Why is it that people are so kind at the funeral but forget about you six months later?"

I don't know the answer, but this much can be said: The months following the death of a spouse are disquieting. Familiar routines are shattered. There is no one to talk to or even argue with. Worse yet, there is no one to help plan for the future. Says Henry Reardon, sixty-eight:

My friends telephoned me every night for two weeks after my wife's funeral. But the calls gradually stopped, as did the sympathy cards.

Then I realized for the first time what it meant to be alone — not for an hour or two, but probably for the rest of my life. I panicked, thinking about my future, wondering what purpose there was in going on.

I went through every room, looking at pictures and reminders of the special times we enjoyed together.

But then I realized I was alone — *totally*

alone. At that moment, there was no one anywhere who could comfort.

Surviving the death of a loved spouse is one of the most difficult challenges he'll ever face. But a second problem is equally ominous: some of the most intense feelings of estrangement occur when there are *strained relationships between parent and child.*

Shortly after Fred Lindstrum, sixty-six, retired, he moved to White Plains, New York, in order to be near his grandchildren. More important, he hoped that the move would bring a reconciliation between his oldest son and himself. His hopes were dashed, for his son expressed little interest in spending time with his father. Nor did he show the slightest concern for his father's well-being. "I might as well be living a thousand miles away," complained Mr. Lindstrum. "I hardly ever see my grandchildren."

What the elder Lindstrum didn't realize was the depth of his son's resentment. In a terrifying moment of honesty, thirty years of pent-up hostility erupted: "You were never there when it counted," said the son. "I remember playing Little League baseball and looking up in the stands hoping my father would show up. You never did." The young man paused and added poignantly: "Now that you are retired and have time on your hands, you want me to become your best friend. Doesn't that seem ironic, when you were never able to give me any time?"

Mr. Lindstrum, stung by the criticism, looked at the floor, and his eyes welled with tears. No other words were spoken, not even a good-bye. The next weeks were hell for both father and son. The younger Lindstrum had pangs of guilt over his outburst, and the elder couldn't sleep, knowing he had failed as a parent.

Fortunately, turbulence in relationships often has a curious reward: if you wait long enough, wounds heal. It doesn't happen instantaneously, but it does happen eventually, sometimes in almost undetectable ways.

In the months that followed, Mr. Lindstrum and his son reached out to one another in small yet meaningful ways. Telephone calls increased, and there was even an evening of lighthearted fun, when they went together to a New York Mets game.

The turning point came on Mr. Lindstrum's seventieth birthday. He walked hesitantly to the mailbox, fearing that no one had remembered his special day. But there in the middle of the junk mail was a humorous birthday card. Inscribed were the following words from his son: "Want to start over? Dinner is on me."

Mr. Lindstrum sprinted to his pickup truck and hurried to his son's home. At first, no words were spoken. But then a soft and reassuring hug was given that forever buried the enmity.

If you are estranged from an adult child, be patient. This does not imply that a curtain of silence should fall between you. But it does suggest that you can't force a relationship when it's not wanted.

All friendships have ebbs and flows. There are times when we feel close to one other and there are moments in which we feel estranged and wholly separate from those we love.

If the tide has gone out on a relationship you value, accept it. But when those precious moments of reconciliation come, don't question the motive. Let go of *all* resentments. As Katherine Anne Porter stated: "Love must be learned and learned again and again; there is no end of it. Hate needs no instruction, but wants only to be provoked."[1]

Misunderstandings are a major source of alienation. But another burden, equally difficult, can be the *absence of meaningful friendships* — those friendships that have the power to encourage, sustain, and validate our lives.

Susan Langford, sixty-one, of Dallas, Texas, took pride in her many friends. But the glue that kept these friendships together was their common bond of work. Unfortunately, most of the friendships faded once she left the office.

On my last day at work my colleagues said: "We will call you." "We will get together." But the telephone has been silent.

One day I asked my former colleagues to lunch. They spent most of the time discussing business deals.

I listened but I felt like an outsider. Not once did anyone ask me about my retirement. Not once did they say they missed me.

When I asked Susan what advice she would give to people approaching retirement, she replied:

Tell them that the friends they had at work may not be their friends after they leave. You have to start over in establishing new friendships. It took me almost a year to understand that.

Of course, friendships come in all shapes and descriptions. There are old friends whom we seldom see but whose memory we value. There are acquaintances whose presence we enjoy. And there are probably a host of people we could telephone if help were needed. Nevertheless, what we long for is to have one or two special friends with whom we can share our struggles as well as our joys. These relationships are based on trust and respect. Equally important, they are based on a common desire to deepen the friendship.

Close physical proximity is no guarantee of finding such soul mates, unfortunately. Gloria Carpenter, sixty-six, lives in a retirement community in Sarasota, Florida, with 150 residents. She knows most by name, yet they remain strangers.

> Every evening all residents eat in the congregate dining hall. You would think that over dinner we would share what is happening in our lives, but it seldom happens.
>
> Some eat in silence. Others talk in platitudes. Most show little interest in getting beyond themselves.
>
> Last night I was seated with three other people who seemed preoccupied with their thoughts. They didn't talk much and not once did they ask me how I was doing. When the meal was over, everyone scattered.
>
> I sat alone for the longest time. "Why

is there so little sharing of things that are important?" I asked myself. "How is it that you can feel so terribly alone, when you are surrounded by dozens of people your own age?"

If your goal is to establish new friendships and deepen old ones, here is what to do.

Developing Lasting Friendships

The typical advice given to those who wish to escape loneliness is to stay active and involved in their community. For if you are confined to your home, you will not meet new people. And if you exclude yourself from social gatherings, friendships will not take root.

This advice is well taken, but the real starting point in overcoming loneliness is to *become your own best friend.*

What does it mean to befriend yourself? It means being able to go to a concert or an athletic event, knowing that you can enjoy it without company. It means treating yourself to a special meal, buying a good bottle of wine, and toasting a good memory or a special plan for the future. It means being able to go for a walk and not lament that there is no one by your side.

Regrettably, many people have never

learned to enjoy their own company. There is a story of a man who came to see the famous psychoanalyst Carl Jung for help with his depression. Jung suggested that he cut back his fourteen-hour workday to eight hours, go directly home after work, and spend the evenings in his study, quiet and alone.

So the man tried. He went to his study, shut the door, read some of the works of Hesse and Mann, played a few Chopin etudes and Mozart rondos.

Several weeks passed and he returned to Jung, complaining that his mood had not improved. On learning how the man had spent his time, Jung said, "But you don't understand. I didn't want you to spend time with Hesse or Mozart or Mann or Chopin. I wanted you to be all alone with yourself."

The man looked terrified and said: "I can't think of any worse company."

Jung replied, "Yet this is the self you inflict on other people fourteen hours a day." He could have added that it was the self he inflicted on himself all the time.[2]

If you feel terribly alone, may I make a suggestion? Don't run off to the nearest singles' club. Don't plan a big party or surround yourself with people all the time.

Instead, think about a special place in the world which you love and which comforts your soul. It might be the ocean, or the mountains. It could be the plains, or a picturesque lake. Visit that place and drink deeply of its serenity. That's what Charles Wilkenson, sixty-four, did after his wife's death, and it marked the beginning of his recovery.

Everyone told me to make new friends. "Get back in circulation," said a neighbor. "Join a retirement club," advised a friend.

But what they didn't understand is that I needed to be alone. So I decided to take a vacation in the Boundary Waters that separate Canada and Minnesota.

I went to a sporting goods store and bought some new camping equipment. I also purchased a lightweight canoe.

As I returned from the store, I felt a sense of peace as well as considerable excitement about the trip I was about to take.

I spent two weeks alone in the wilderness. At first, I longed for company. But each succeeding day I felt better. I liked the idea of being alone and hearing the loons and the wildlife. I felt a sense of self-sufficiency as I portaged the canoe, set up camp, and made my meals.

Once I returned home, my neighbors

came by to hear about the trip. Everyone seemed friendlier and was curious to know how I did. "Isn't it interesting," I said to myself, "that these people are changing?"

Then I realized that it was I who had changed. I was more at peace with myself. I was having fun. And people wanted to be around me.

It's a fact: people are attracted to individuals who are involved in life. When someone is full of energy, it energizes others. And when someone has a good tale to spin, the room lights up with life.

This brings me to an important suggestion for diminishing loneliness: *Never go to bed without a plan for the next day.* Norman Mailer aptly noted, "Growth in some curious way, I suspect, depends on being always in motion just a little bit, one way or another."[3]

Carole Levetti's self-confidence was shattered when her husband left her for a younger woman.

My husband didn't say a word after our divorce papers were signed. There was no thank-you for the children I bore or for the times we shared. He simply put on his coat and walked out of the room.

The following months were difficult. At the urging of a friend I went to see a psychologist. "The best antidote for your depression," he noted, "is to stay busy." He told me to exercise religiously and to write three goals that I would strive to accomplish each day.

At first I resisted his suggestions. The last thing I wanted to do was exercise. But I began to take short ten-minute walks twice a day. One night I managed to write down three things I wanted to accomplish the following day.

To my surprise, the more I focused my goals, the better I felt. I felt new energy and a desire to be with others. Best of all, my depression started to lift.

How do you summon the courage to form new relationships when you're depressed? How do you initiate action when your energy reserves are on empty?

Start by making firm resolutions, such as going for a daily walk, reading a book, or telephoning a friend. Then increase the complexities of the task: What hobbies lie dormant, waiting to be developed? What new avocations could you pursue? Finally, convey to a trusted friend *exactly* how you feel. If you're lonely, share the pain. If depressed, convey your discouragement. And don't be reluctant to simply say: "Can we spend some time together? I'm having a tough day."

Why are we reluctant to share that which we feel? Why are we hesitant to expose our weakness?

I believe we're reluctant to share what we feel because we fear that we might be rejected if we show our vulnerability. Or at the very least, we think, we'll not be held in high esteem if others see the dark corners in our lives.

Nevertheless, you pay a big price for not showing your vulnerability. Painful memories are buried, not resolved, when you hole up. And others ignore you, not realizing your need for a trusted friend.

But when you dare trust another person, the trust is almost always reciprocated and the foundation for a solid friendship is firmly established.

Several years ago, a colleague stopped by my office at the University of Minnesota and asked whether we could go to the student union for a cup of coffee. He seemed agitated, and I knew that this was not going to be an ordinary conversation. As we walked to Coffman Memorial Union, he confided that his fifteen-year-old daughter had run away from home after a bitter family quarrel. "I have no idea where she is," he said anxiously, "and

I fear for her safety."

In a quiet corner of the student union we communicated at a level that few colleagues ever experience. I tried to convey a note of optimism, but, frankly, there were few positive words that I could summon. Mainly I listened as he shed copious tears.

Several days later he stopped by the office again. His outlook visibly brightened, he indicated that his daughter had been located and her anger was subsiding. And he noted that his resentment had softened to the point where he was able to admit to her that he had made some mistakes. Then, as he was about ready to leave the office, he grasped my hand firmly and thanked me for my time.

Out of that conversation has grown a wonderful friendship. We now make it a point to meet periodically in the same location in the student union. We often discuss work-related projects, but most of the time we talk about what is happening in our lives including our hopes and fears, our disappointments as well as our joys.

I don't know why, but most friendships are nourished in human struggle. They're not formed when we brag about our accomplishments, nor are they cemented when we articulate our achievements. It seems that the most precious of all relationships are fostered when we expose our vulnerability and our pain. As Kahlil Gibran observed once, "We tend to forget those with whom we have laughed — but we never forget those with whom we have cried."[4]

I have one final suggestion for forming new friendships: *Summon the courage to tell people you love them.* For if affection is left unverbalized, the friendship will slowly perish.

Gale Sayers and Brian Piccolo were outstanding running backs for the Chicago Bears when they decided to room with one another in 1967. It was a new experience, for Sayers had never had a close relationship with a white person, and Piccolo had never really known a black person. But by sharing a room, they developed a great friendship, characterized by humor.

Before an exhibition game in Washington, D.C., a studious young reporter quizzed them about the nature of their relationship:

"How do you two get along?" the writer queried.

"We're okay as long as he doesn't use the bathroom," said Piccolo.

"What do you fellows talk about?" asked the reporter, ignoring the wisecracks.

"Mostly race relations," Gale replied.

"Nothing but the normal racist stuff," Piccolo added.

"If you had your choice," the writer went on, "who would you want as your roommate?"

Sayers replied that if he had to pick a big white Italian fullback from Wake Forest, he'd select Piccolo. But submerged under the levity was a deep respect and loyalty to one another — a friendship that is considered one of the best in the history of professional sports.

Then, unexpectedly, tragedy hit. Piccolo was diagnosed as having cancer. He wanted desperately to play football but found himself in hospitals more than on the playing field. Gale Sayers flew to his bedside to be with him as often as possible.

Sayers and Piccolo had planned to sit together at the Professional Football Writers annual dinner in New York, where Sayers was to receive the George S. Halas Award as the most courageous player in professional football. Sayers stood up to receive the award and tears flooded his eyes. As he took the trophy, he said: "You flatter me by giving me this award, but I tell you here and now that I accept it for Brian Piccolo. Brian Piccolo is the man of courage who should receive the George S. Halas Award. I love Brian Piccolo, and I'd like you to love him. Tonight, when you hit your knees, please ask God to love him too."[5]

"I love Brian Piccolo." How often do you

hear such words being spoken? Unfortunately, not very often.

It's amazing, however, what happens when tender feelings are expressed. Walls that separate, crumble. Misunderstandings evaporate. Loneliness diminishes. And, best of all, friendships that can weather life's storms are set firmly in place.

What are the secrets for being alone but not lonely? Take an interest in others. Never go to bed without a plan for the next day. Share your vulnerability and never be afraid to let others know of your love, for, as G. K. Chesterton correctly noted, the meanest fear of all is the fear of sentimentality.[6]

But when loneliness occurs, take a moment to reflect on these insightful words: "Loneliness leaves its traces in man, but these are marks of pathos, of weathering, which enhance dignity and maturity and beauty, and which open new possibilities for tenderness and love. . . . Loneliness is as much a reality of life as night and rain and thunder, and it can be lived creatively. So I say, let there be loneliness, for where there is loneliness, there is also sensitivity, there is awareness and recognition of promise."[7]

PART VI
SPIRITUALITY

Through the Years

The primary goal of this book has been to help you prepare for the best years of life. But many cast a wary eye toward their future. The reason? They are dealing with major problems that cast a dark shadow over their lives.

I think, for example, of John Knutson, sixty, who was stricken with cancer shortly after retiring. Or I think of Marla Dickenson, fifty-nine, whose own retirement plans have been delayed as she cares for aged and frail parents. Then there are Nancy and Rick Carlson, who are worried about a daughter whose life has been tragically altered by an automobile accident.

When you are in the peak of health and surrounded by friends, it's easy to glow with optimism. But staying optimistic if health deteriorates or there is a sudden change in your financial outlook is trying indeed. How do you do it?

This is reaching to the heart of what constitutes a successful retirement. Ultimately, a successful retirement is not contingent on how many stocks one owns or whether it is possible to travel to exotic locations but rather on *living with inner peace* regardless of external situations that threaten our lives.

How do you maintain hope when everything seems hopeless? How do you maintain faith when you feel abandoned by your Creator?

To answer these questions, I consulted with someone who knows far more about faith than I. He lived many years ago and was known as a man of great wealth and eminent virtue, yet in the span of a few terrifying years he lost everything he owned.

Here are his offerings — tested in fire — for staying hopeful when life takes an unexpected turn against itself.

CHAPTER SIXTEEN

A Message from Job

The Lord blessed the latter part of Job's life more than the first. And so he died, old and full of years.

Job 42: 12, 17

Dear Brother Job:

In a few months, I will be retiring. Frankly, I am not too optimistic about the future. I have little wealth. I have few friends. Worse yet, I have some health problems that threaten the quality of my life.

As I recall, you, too, faced many hardships. Your children died unexpectedly. Your health failed and you lost all of your wealth. In your despair, you were tempted to curse God and die. Instead you decided to live by faith and were rewarded with a bountiful life.

What I want to know, Brother Job, is,

is it possible to stay cheerful as you grow old? Is it possible to stay optimistic when health declines? And is there hope for me, someone who has little faith?

Any ideas that could help me as I approach retirement would be greatly valued. I eagerly await your reply.

Sincerely,
An old soul

Dear old soul:

Thank you for your letter. I was somewhat amused when you said you were going to retire. As you know, retirement is a relatively new concept. In my day we worked until we died. There was no Social Security system, no pension funds, and little time for leisure. In fact, if you reached fifty years of age, it was considered a remarkable achievement.

Nevertheless, I understand your concerns as you plan for your retirement. Especially since you are confronting problems that could diminish your happiness.

I must state at the outset that my knowledge is somewhat limited. I know little about economics, so I have nothing to say about your financial difficulties. I am not a psychologist, so I cannot advise you about forming new friendships. And since I am not a physician,

I will not make recommendations about how to regain your strength.

However, I did experience my share of disappointments. I lost wealth and was thrown into poverty. I received a terrifying medical diagnosis and almost died of a tragic disease. And on the heels of all these terrible things, I lost my children and nearly my sanity.

What did I learn from these experiences? What advice would I give to someone who is experiencing hardship? Here, in retrospect, is what I learned.

First, it is important to obtain competent advice. This is true whether your problems are financial, psychological, or spiritual.

I speak with conviction about this point, for I did not receive competent counsel. My three advisers, Bildad, Eliphaz, and Zophar, never took time to understand me. Consequently, I felt betrayed by their insensitivity to my problems.

I would encourage you to carefully evaluate all advice. Be especially cautious of those who can profit at your expense. And be suspicious of those who promote ideas that seem too good to be true.

Frankly, some of the unhappiest people I have met are those who blindly followed a stranger's counsel. I almost fell into that trap myself when listening to the recommendations from my advisers. But in a marvelous moment of insight, I asked myself: "Why do I rely so much on the wisdom of strangers? Why do I have so little confidence in my own experience?"

From that day forward I learned to trust my intuition as well as my ability to make sound decisions. This is not to say that I turn a deaf ear to others. But if forced to decide between the recommendations from a stranger or follow the inclinations in my heart, I always sided with the stirrings in my soul.

This leads me to an important suggestion: *you must not be timid in your search for solutions to problems.* Frankly, I sensed a bit of helplessness in your letter, which I understand given your difficulties.

However, when confronting major problems, it is important to approach them from many points of view. Therefore ask questions of those who understand your problems. Ask your friends how they would manage your predicament. Better yet, imagine yourself as a counselor who is asked for advice on the misfortunes you are experiencing. What might you tell your audience?

The central challenge in life, I discovered, is not to feel powerless when threats appear. Therefore I would encourage you to go to the library and learn everything you can about that which plagues your life. Talk to those who have similar difficulties — especially those who are living triumphantly in spite of their problems. And always look for multiple solutions, for in my experience there are *many* possibilities for solving the riddles that touch our lives.

Once you have gained new understandings, *find a quiet place to assimilate what you have learned*. This is particularly true when making major decisions.

My habit when confronting important issues was to walk to the foothills in the land of Uz. There I sifted through what I heard, evaluated what was said, and affirmed a new direction for life.

Those moments spent in solitude were very precious. For in the quietness of nature I was able to gain a clearer perspective on my problems and a sharper focus on how to live my life.

May I make a suggestion? I think you need to flee the noise that surrounds your life. Go to a place where serenity abounds. Then ask questions that touch the nerve endings of your soul: What can be learned from my disappointments and mistakes? How do I transform negative experiences into positive ones? And how can I develop a deeper faith so that when other disappointments come, I can transcend them?

I must caution you, however: the answers will not readily appear. But if you approach life as an empty cup without any preconceived notions about how your problems should be solved, you will resolve your most troubling issues.

Now I come to one of my most important discoveries: If you are going through difficult times, *don't fall victim to fear.*

How do you keep apprehensions under control? How do you keep fear at bay?

The key is to live in the *present,* for if you are consumed with regrets over your past, or if you fall victim to worry over the future, you can never be content.

Frankly, I never fully understood the importance of living in the present. The reason? I worried incessantly about the future. Would my health improve? Could I regain my wealth? Would my associates forsake me? And perhaps most troubling, would God abandon me?

Soon I was a nervous wreck. Everything looked bleak. Nothing in my life brought joy or serenity.

So it is for most of us. We become so preoccupied with tomorrow's battles that we fail to enjoy today's tranquility. If I had my life to live over, here is what I would do differently: I would live for today and quit worrying about what might happen tomorrow.

I must now pause, old soul, and talk very directly to you. I know that you are worried about your medical problems. In fact, you spend endless hours contemplating what will happen if your health declines.

I make one request: Quit imagining the awful things that might befall you. Instead, concentrate on the tiny joys that are graciously placed on your path every day. Take note of your neighbor who greets you affectionately each morning. Express gratitude for the medical care you are receiving — the best that any generation has ever received. And if someone expresses kindness to you, respond in like manner and celebrate the moment. For if you do these things your joys will grow and your problems will diminish.

Now I come to one of the most difficult things for me to learn, and that was the *importance of forgiving those who did not measure up to my expectations.*

I must confess that my problems left me somewhat cynical. Contrary to public opinion, I was not a patient man. I became angry with those who challenged my integrity. I even became combative with God as I contemplated all the injustices in the world.

I realized, however, that all my self-righteous pronouncements were not enhancing the quality of my life. I realized, too, that if I was to experience inner peace, I needed to build bridges to my adversaries and forgive those who harmed me.

To speak candidly, I think you, too, need to let go of your anger. I note the friction between you and your children. And I hear the unsolicited advice you give to your wife. Even when silent, you make judgments on the lives of people you love.

Please, old soul — be silent. They do not need your counsel. Give them the freedom to make mistakes and overlook their insensitivities. For if you express love *and ask nothing in return,* their gratitude will follow you all the days of your life.

Now I come to the most important lesson I learned through my travails. In spite of all that I went through, *I believe that at the heart of this universe there is a benevolent God* — a God who was with me through the most trying moments of my pilgrimage.

To be certain, there were many days when I would not utter such an affirmation. But I will say this: The only thing that saved me from my harrowing experiences was a firm belief that there was a God who loved me and would protect me from the random insults of life.

How did I arrive at this conclusion? To begin with, I earnestly wanted to discover answers to questions that plagued me. I wanted to learn how to maintain faith when darkness abounded. And I wanted to discover how to stay confident when disappointments marred my outlook.

I therefore raised questions that helped me transcend my limited view of the world. For when I dared question that which was sacred, I found that I was free to discover new realities and a deeper understanding of life.

Of course, there were those terrifying moments when no solutions to my problems appeared. But rather than becoming angry, I learned it was best to become quiet, affirming that in another time and perhaps another place, answers would flow. To my surprise, when I stopped demanding answers, they often appeared.

Asking questions about the meaning of life was the first step in developing a deeper faith. But my biggest challenge was to decide whether the world was a friendly place — or whether I was a stranger in a hostile land.

In my lowest moments, I was tempted to conclude that the world was hostile. But at the point of my greatest despair, I made an unlikely decision: I reaffirmed that the world was indeed friendly, in spite of all the evidence to the contrary.

From that moment forward, my perspective

was radically changed. No longer was I threatened by those who verbally assaulted me, for I knew that there were those who would love me. My grief over the deaths of my children diminished, as I was comforted by their memories and the realization that I had known them. My anxiety over material goods lessened, for I realized that the important aspects in life carry no monetary value. And although my health status remained uncertain, I knew that I could live at peace regardless of how many days I was given to live.

I would like to tell you that these discoveries came easily — but, alas, they did not. I struggled with my faith, and there were times in which I was tempted to become an aging, cynical old man.

But I resolved not to let that happen. By affirming that life was good and that every day was a gift, I experienced a personal renaissance — a marvelous freeing feeling that no matter what I might experience, I would be able to survive the sudden detours. Equally important, I would be able to celebrate those unexpected joys that came my way.

So, old soul, here in brief is what I would say as you plan for your retirement years: Trust your intuition and your ability to make credible decisions for tomorrow. Forgive those who have been thorns in your side and love those who make each step on your journey worthwhile. Live for today and let go of regrets of yesterday. For if you do these things, you will come to understand that life is a precious gift that should be joyfully lived, no matter your age.

Sincerely,
Job

APPENDIX

Survey on Retirement, Health, and Happiness

Your help is needed! Please take a few moments to answer the following questions on a separate piece of paper. You do not need to include your name.

The purpose of this brief questionnaire is to learn how older adults are meeting their health care needs. *Your experiences could be of great help to others confronting similar situations.*

The aggregate results of this questionnaire will eventually be published. Direct quotes may be taken from the answers; however, no individual will be identified by name. The answers to all questions are voluntary. If you do not want to answer a question, feel free to skip it and go to the next one.

1. Describe your overall health and what steps, if any, you are taking (exercise, diet, etc.) to improve your well-being.

2. Do you have a physician whom you can call if medical help is needed? If so, are you satisfied with the medical care you receive? Why or why not?
3. Have you ever had difficulty locating competent medical assistance? If so, describe the situation and its resolution.
4. Have you ever had a problem with your mental health? If so, describe the problem you experienced and whether you were able to obtain satisfactory professional help.
5. Have you been admitted to a hospital during the past two years? If so, were you satisfied with the care you received? Why or why not?
6. Does your physician explain to you the nature of the medications you are taking and what might be their side effects? Have medications ever caused a problem?
7. Have you found your pharmacist helpful in responding to your questions? Why or why not?
8. Do you ever worry about how

you would pay for a serious illness? Why or why not?

9. Does your religious faith contribute to your happiness? If so, in what ways?
10. If you had one suggestion to give to someone planning retirement, what would it be?
11. Was this book helpful to you? If so, what was most useful?

Please mail your response to:

Survey on Retirement, Health, and Happiness
Robert Veninga, Ph.D.
P.O. Box 8186
St. Paul, Minnesota 55108-0816

Thank you for your assistance. Responses will be collected through June 31, 1993.

Notes

Introduction: A Personal Note from the Author

1. Jo Coudert, "Risky Business," *Woman's Day*, March 24, 1987, page 32.
2. Neil Steinberg, "No Place like Home," *Mature Outlook*, May/June 1987, pages 81-83.
3. Eric Erickson, *Childhood and Society* (New York: W. W. Norton, 1963), pages 247-274.

Chapter 1. The Secrets of a Successful Retirement

Epigraph. George F. Will, "At Baseball School with Pete Rose," *Minneapolis Star Tribune*, April 3, 1989, page 8.
1. Unless footnoted, the case studies are realistic depictions of the lives of 135 individuals. In some instances composites have been drawn for illustrative purposes. Names are pseudonyms and locations are fictional.

2. Albert Myers and Christopher Anderson, *Success Over 60* (New York: Summit Books, 1984), page 29.

3. *Ibid.*

4. Norman M. Lobsenz, "Why Do We Keep Working?" *Parade* magazine, September 14, 1986, page 16.

5. Jeffrey Sonnenfeld, "Heroes in Collision: Chief Executive Retirement and the Parade of Future Leaders," *Human Resource Management,* Summer 1986, Vol. 25, No. 2, page 317.

6. Norman M. Lobsenz, page 16.

7. *Ibid.*

8. Ruthan Brodsky, "As Much to Gain as Give," *Modern Maturity,* April/May 1987, page 50.

9. Christy Wise, "Americans Find that Older Is Better Overseas," *Minneapolis Star Tribune,* February 24, 1988, page 1E.

10. Albert Meyers and Christopher Anderson, page 72.

11. Michael J. Bandler, "Something Important beyond Me," *Dynamic Years,* November/December 1985, page 33.

12. *Ibid.*

13. Ellen Brandt, "Secrets of Success After 60," *Parade* magazine, December 13, 1987, page 4.

14. Adapted from Mark Reiter, "The Smartest Thing I Did in My 60's," *50-Plus,* February 1987, page 84.

15. David Hobman, *The Social Challenge of Aging* (New York: St. Martin's Press, 1987), page 47.

16. Gene Prigge, "Zest for Life Keeps Woman Young at Heart," *St. Paul Pioneer Press Dispatch,* August 7, 1983, page 4C.

17. Adapted from Caroline Bird, "Profile of Tomorrow," *Modern Maturity,* April/May 1983, page 37.

18. Paul Dienhart, "Changes in Attitude, Changes in Latitude," *Update,* Vol. 13, No. 6, July 1986.

19. Caroline Bird, page 37.

20. *Ibid.*

21. *Ibid.*

Chapter 2. Early Retirement: Is It for You?

1. Greg Anrig, Jr., "How to Retire Early," *Money,* November 1988.

2. Troy Segal, "Early Retirement: It Pays to Plan Early," *Business Week,* February 27, 1989, page 134.

3. *Ibid.,* page 24.

4. Greg Anrig, Jr., page 60.

5. *Ibid.*

6. Nancy Goode, "Silver Linings: Retirement Better than Most Expect," *Mature Outlook*, October 1985, pages 92-93.

7. Jay Stuller, "When Emeritus Isn't Enough," *Dramatic Years*, May/June 1983, page 37.

8. Troy Segal, page 134.

9. *Ibid.*

10. Greg Anrig, Jr., page 59.

11. Dana Shilling, "Retirement: Early, Normal, Late, or Never," *Sylvia Porter's Personal Finance*, April 1989, pages 66, 68.

12. Joseph Campbell, *The Power of Myth* (New York: Doubleday, 1988), page 3.

13. The story of Colonel Sanders has been adapted from "The Courage to Keep a Dream Alive," *Financial Freedom Report*, April 1989, pages 39-40.

14. Robert Brody, "Getting Off Your Workaday Treadmill," *50-Plus*, September 1988, page 28.

15. Daniel Jaspen, J. P. Palmquist, "What I Wish Someone Had Told Me About Retirement," *Retirement Living*, February 1978, page 28.

Part One. Money Sense: Handling Your Finances

1. Denise M. Topolnicki, "The Pre-Retiree: A Supersaver, a Positive Thinker, a Terrible Planner," *Money*, April 1989, pages 195-196.

Chapter 3. *A Short Course in Financial Planning*

Epigraph. Denise M. Topolnicki, "The Pre-Retiree: A Supersaver, a Positive Thinker, a Terrible Planner," *Money,* April 1989, pages 195-196.

1. The following materials may be helpful to you in analyzing your retirement finances: *Think of Your Future* (Scott, Foresman, 19800 East Lake Avenue, Glenville, IL 60016); *Retirement: Currents and Trends for 1989 and Beyond* (PaineWebber, Service Center, P.O. Box 22746, Rochester, NY 14692); *Wake-Up Call* (Lutheran Brotherhood, 625 Fourth Avenue S., Minneapolis, MN 55414).

2. "Figuring What You'll Need," *Family Wealth,* Spring 1989, page 29.

3. "Tackling the Health-Care Crisis," *Modern Maturity,* June/July 1989.

4. Lisa M. Keefe, "Dwindling Dollars," *St. Paul Pioneer Press Dispatch,* September 13, 1988, page 3C.

5. Diane M. O'Brien, "How to Pick an HMO," *Active Senior Life Styles,* March 1988, page 10.

6. "When You Leave a Group Plan," *Consumer Reports,* August 1990, page 545.

7. Lani Luciano, "HMO, Yes or No?," *Money,* July 1988, pages 114-115.

8. Adapted from *How to Use Private Health Insurance with Medicare* (Washington, D.C.: Health Insurance Associates of America, January 1987), pages 12-13.

9. Adapted from Ellen Schultz, "Five Sins to Avoid When Investing for Retirement," *Fortune,* March 27, 1989, pages 24, 28.

10. *Ibid.*

11. Jane Berryman and Nancy Way, "Their Retirement Plans Dashed by the Crash, a Couple Must Rebuild Their Finances," *Money,* May 1988, page 181.

12. Ellen Schultz, *Fortune,* March 27, 1989, page 28.

13. Walter L. Updegrave, "Six Smart Ways to Plan for Retirement Income," *Family Wealth,* Spring 1989, page 61.

14. *Ibid.,* page 63.

15. Fred W. Fraley, "Stocks That Pay and Pay and Pay," *Changing Times,* October 1990, pages 44-45.

16. Laura Saunders, "Retirement Tax Strategy," *Forbes,* June 27, 1988, page 240.

17. *Ibid.*

18. Daniel P. Wiener, "Do-It-Yourself Investing," *U.S. News and World Report,* June 6, 1988, page 76.

19. Jan M. Rosen, "Finding a Planner Can Be a Task," *The New York Times*, June 18, 1989, page 18Y. Note: Among the financial advisers the term "financial adviser" applies to a broad spectrum of disciplines, including accountants, stockbrokers, life insurance agents, bankers, lawyers, and financial planners.

20. *Ibid.*

21. David J. Morrow, "The Financial Planning Jungle," *Fortune*, 1989 Investor's Guide, page 198.

22. Adapted from Harry J. Lew, "How to Find a Quality Financial Planner," *Money Maker*, December/January 1988.

23. "How to Check Out a Financial Planner," *Money*, August 1988, page 28.

24. Marie Hodge and Jeff Blyskal, "Where to Get Financial Advice," *New Choices*, March 1989, page 44.

25. Junius Ellis, editor, *Money 1988* (Birmingham, Ala.: Oxmoor House, 1988).

26. Denise M. Topolnicki, "How to Leave a Lasting Legacy," *Family Wealth*, Spring 1988, page 101.

27. *Ibid.*

Chapter 4. New Rules: Protecting Your Retirement

1. Jane Bryant Quinn, "Debt: What's Too Much?" *Newsweek,* May 23, 1988.

2. *Sylvia Porter's Active Retirement Newsletter,* Vol. 2, No. 5, May 1989, page 7.

3. William Doyle, "Paying Off Debt Is Almost Always the Wise Thing to Do," *St. Paul Pioneer Press Dispatch,* June 8, 1988, page 11D.

4. "Money Talks," *Savvy,* May 1988, page 36.

5. "Pension Management," *Personal Investor,* September 1989, page 54.

6. Harry J. Lew, "How to Retire Early," *Money Maker,* October/November 1989, page 52.

7. Adapted from Eric Schurenberg, "The Art of Tending to Your Savings Plans," *Family Wealth,* Spring 1988, pages 41-42.

8. *Ibid.,* p. 42

9. Manuel Schiffres, "Social Security: Should You Count on It?," *Changing Times,* October 1988, page 71.

10. *Ibid.*

11. Linda Demkovich, "Social Security at 50," *Modern Maturity,* August/September 1985, page 30.

12. Merton C. Bernstein, Joan Brodshaug Bernstein, "The Case for Social Security," *Fortune*, May 9, 1988, page 150.

13. Adapted from Marie Hodge, "Social Security," *New Choices*, June 1989, pages 49-55.

14. "Your Questions Answered," *Changing Times*, November 1990, page 110.

15. *Your Social Security Benefits* (New York: 50-Plus Publishers, 1989), page 43.

16. *Ibid.*, page 40.

17. Adapted from *Your Social Security Benefits* (New York: 50-Plus Publishers, 1988).

18. Eric Schurenberg, "How to Handle a Plump Pay-out," *Family Wealth*, Spring 1989, page 45.

19. Adapted from *Your Pension* (Washington, D.C.: Pension Benefit Guaranty Corporation, 1989).

20. Adapted from Peter A. Dickinson, editor, *The Retirement Letter*, Mid-February 1989, No. 246.

21. Adapted from *United Retirement Bulletin*, August 1989, Vol. 15, No. 8, No. 172, page 1.

22. *Ibid.*, page 9.

23. Manuel Schiffres, "Low Risk Investments to Make Now," *Changing Times*, May 1988, page 26.

24. *Ibid.*

25. Denise M. Topolnicki, "Suddenly Bonds Are Both Sexy and Safe," *Money Guide to Taxes, Money* magazine, 1987, page 86.

26. Manuel Schiffres, "20 Ways to Cash in on High Yields," *Changing Times,* April 1989, page 34.

27. *Ibid.*

28. Walter L. Updegrave, "Six Smart Ways to Plan for Retirement Income," *Family Wealth,* Spring 1989, page 62.

29. Jane Bryant Quinn, "Stocks Still Wise Choice for Long Term Investors," *St. Paul Pioneer Press Dispatch,* October 17, 1989, page 7C.

30. Adapted from "Building For Retirement: How to Select Mutual Funds," Merrill Lynch Asset Management, Inc., 1988, pages 2-3.

Chapter 5. Retiring on a Modest Income

1. Sarah Oates, "Saving Pennies Stacks Up Dollars," *St. Paul Pioneer Press Dispatch,* May 31, 1988, page 1B.

2. *Ibid.*

3. A national survey of prescription drug prices and pharmacy services demonstrated that you can save considerable money on prescriptions by undertaking comparative shopping. For example, in one study the cost of Tagamet, which is used to treat stomach ulcers, ranged from $8 to $35. Procardia, which is used to relieve chest pains, sold for $26 at one pharmacy and $58.60 at another. For further information see Bill Crawford, "Drug Price See-saw," *AARP News Bulletin,* Vol. 30, No. 8, September 1989, page 1.

4. It is important not to *overinsure* your home. Consider a $100,000 single-family house with a $90,000 mortgage. A real estate evaluation might indicate it is worth $100,000, but that includes the land on which the house sits as well as its foundation, neither of which would disappear in a fire. The actual cost of rebuilding the house could be considerably less — $80,000, for example. Therefore some experts suggest that home owners could be paying for insurance that they do not need. If the $100,000 home were to be destroyed, most insurance companies would only reimburse the owner for the replacement cost, regardless of how much it was insured for. To save dollars on your insurance costs, get an accurate appraisal of how much it would cost to have the home rebuilt in the event of a disaster.

Insure it for that amount, but never pay for insurance you do not need.

5. John F. Dolan, "Half of the Elderly Eligible for SSI Don't Get Benefits," *AARP News Bulletin*, Vol. 3, No. 3, March 1989, page 15.

6. Clint Willis, "How to Retire on the House," *Family Wealth*, Spring 1988, page 53.

7. Jane Bryant Quinn, "Trading Down Helps Older Home Owners," *St. Paul Pioneer Press Dispatch*, September 15, 1989, page 14E.

8. *Ibid.*

9. I am indebted to Clint Willis, "How to Retire on the House," *Family Wealth*, Spring 1988, pages 52-55, for some of the suggestions in this section.

10. *Ibid.*, page 53.

11. *Ibid.*

12. Hugh Vickery, "A Mortgage Turned Upside Down," *Insight*, July 13, 1987, page 43.

13. *Ibid.*

14. Andrea Rock, "The Truth about Post-Job Jobs," *Money Guide*, Fall 1989, page 74.

15. "Work in the Future," *AARP News Bulletin*, July/August 1987, page 13.

16. Gail Rosenblum, "A New Job — a New Life," *New Choices*, January 1989, pages 27-28.

17. Kate McEnore, "Older Workers a Sought-after Resource," *St. Paul Pioneer Press Dispatch,* October 22, 1989, page 1.

18. Eric and Cynthia Shuman, "The Post-50 Job Hunt," *Dynamic Years,*" January/February 1983, pages 20-21.

19. *Ibid.,* pages 23-25.

20. Caroline Bird, "The Freedom Road," *Modern Maturity,* June/July 1988, page 43.

21. Peter Weaver, "Going Back To Work — Part-time," *Mature Outlook,* January/February 1989, page 20.

22. Alice M. Pytak, "Is Unretirement in Your Future?," *Dynamic Years,* July/August 1985, page 26.

23. Jay Stuller, "When Emeritus Isn't Enough," *Dynamic Years,* May/June 1983, page 36.

Chapter 6. Don't Make a Move — Yet

Epigraph. Michael Sumichrast, Ronald G. Shafer, and Marika Sumichrast, *Planning Your Retirement Housing* (Washington, D.C.: American Association of Retired Persons, 1984), page 2.

1. Doris Little, "Home Is Where the Heart Is," *Active Senior Lifestyles,* February 1987, page 15.

2. Allen Evans, "The Empty Nester's Home-Buying Guide," *Sylvia Porter's Personal Finance,* June 1989, page 56.

3. You can get names and addresses of papers through *Ayer's Directory of Publications* or *Editor and Publisher,* available at your local library.

4. Allen Evans, page 58.

5. *Ibid.*

6. Jaclyn Fierman, "What It Takes to Be Rich in America," *Fortune,* April 13, 1987, page 25 (1987 real estate values).

7. Bob Lane, "How to Pick the Best Real Estate Agent," *Dramatic Years,* May/June 1983, page 22.

8. *Ibid.,* page 23.

9. *Ibid.*

10. Leonard Wiener, "IRS Traps for the Unwary Home Seller," *U.S. News and World Report,* May 22, 1989, page 43.

11. *Ibid.* At age 55 you are able to keep tax-free up to $125,000 of the profit from the sale of your principal residence. To qualify, you must have lived in the home for *three* of the past five years. What if you are a nursing home resident? Thanks to recent legislation, you have to have lived at your home for only *one* of the previous five years in order to escape the tax on the sale of your house.

12. Michael Sumichrast, page 121.

13. *Ibid.*, page 122.

14. Linda Hubbard, editor, *Housing Options for Older Americans* (Washington, D.C.: American Association of Retired Persons, 1984), page 2.

15. *Ibid.*

16. Michael Sumichrast, page 207.

17. "Communities for the Elderly," *Consumer Reports*, February 1990, page 123.

18. *Ibid.*, page 208.

19. David W. Myers, "Seniors on the Move," *Personal Investor*, January 1990, page 69.

20. *Ibid.*, page 208.

21. *Ibid.*, page 207.

22. *Ibid.*, page 70.

23. *Ibid.*, page 212.

24. *Ibid.*

25. *Ibid.*, page 213.

26. *Ibid.*, page 125.

27. *Ibid.*, page 69.

28. *Ibid.*, page 72.

29. *Ibid.*

30 *Ibid.*

31. Eric Shuman, "Retirement Moves," *Dramatic Years*, July/August 1983, page 33.

32. Tam Westover, "Where The Living Is Easy," *Active Senior Lifestyles*, August 1987, pages 30-31.

33. *Ibid.*, page 32.

34. *Ibid.,* page 33.

35. Michael Sumichrast, page 105.

36. *Ibid.,* page 107.

37. *Ibid.,* page 218.

38. "Hit the Road!" *Active Senior Lifestyles,* May 1989, page 34.

39. *Ibid.*

40. *Ibid.,* page 35.

41. Barbara Braun Hansen, "Supportive Housing," *Minnesota Guide to Senior Housing,* October 14, 1987, page 21.

Chapter 7. Twelve Great Retirement Locations

1. Eric Shuman, "Retirement Moves," *Dynamic Years,* July/August 1983, page 36.

2. Adapted from Eric Shuman, pages 32-37.

3. *Ibid.,* page 37.

4. *Ibid.*

5. Richard D. Lyons, "Stimulation of College Towns Lures Growing Number of Retirees," *Minneapolis Star Tribune,* December 19, 1987 page 1S.

6. 1990 real estate values. Source: "Putting a Price Tag on the American Dream: From Starter Homes to Mansions, Coast to Coast," *USA Today,* January 25, 1980, page 5B.

7. Eric Shuman, page 37.

8. Roy Hemming, "Finding the Right Place for Your Retirement," 50-Plus Publishers, 850 Third Avenue, New York, NY 10022, 1987. (To order call 1-800-247-8080.)

9. I would like to acknowledge the following resources, which were helpful in writing this section: Peter A. Dickinson, *Retirement Edens Outside the Sunbelt* (New York: E. P. Dutton, 1981); John Howells, *Retirement Choices,* (San Francisco: Gateway Books, 1987); Richard Eisenberg and Debra W. Englander, "Great Places To Retire," *Family Wealth,* 1989; Peter A. Dickinson, *The Retirement Letter,* No. 250, Mid-May, 1989.

10. Peter A. Dickinson, *Retirement Edens Outside the Sunbelt,* (New York: E. P. Dutton, 1981), page 34.

11. Richard Eisenberg and Debra W. Englander, page 81.

12. *Ibid.,* page 79.

13. *Ibid.*

14. *Ibid.,* pages 79-80.

15. Peter A. Dickinson, "Retirement Winners," *Bottom Line,* August 15, 1985, page 13.

16. *Ibid.*

17. Peter A. Dickinson, *Retirement Edens Outside the Sunbelt,* page 242.

18. John Howells, *Retirement Choices* (San Francisco: Gateway Books, 1987), page 87.

19. *Ibid.,* page 88.

20. *Ibid.*, page 80.

21. *Ibid.*, page 81.

22. *Ibid.*

23. *Ibid.*, page 69.

24. *Ibid.*

25. *Ibid.*, page 117.

26. *Ibid.*

27. "Bisbee: Old World Charm," Greater Bisbee Chamber of Commerce, P.O. Box BA, Bisbee, AZ 85603.

28. Richard Eisenberg and Debra W. Englander, page 79.

29. John Howells, page 248.

30. Richard Eisenberg and Debra W. Englander, page 80.

31. *Ibid.*

32. *Ibid.*

33. Peter A. Dickinson, *The Retirement Letter*, No. 250, Mid-May, 1989, page 2.

34. Peter A. Dickinson, *Sunbelt Retirement* (Washington, D.C.: American Association of Retired Persons, 1986), page 152.

35. Adapted from Stephen Baker, "Mexico Still Makes the Most of Your Pension Dollars," *Business Week*, August 13, 1990, page 123.

36. Lawrence J. Kaplan, *Retiring Right* (Wayne, New Jersey: Avery Publishing Group, 1987), page 205.

37. James T. Yenckel, "Cheap Living Abroad Leaves More Money for Retirement Travel," *Minneapolis Star Tribune,* March 20, 1988, page 1E.

38. *Ibid.*

39. Among the organizations that specialize in preview tours of various retirement locations are: National Retirement Concepts, 1454 North Wieland Court, Chicago, IL 60610 (800-888-2312) and Lifestyle Explorations, P.O. Box 57-6487, Modesto, CA 95355 (209-577-5081).

Chapter 8. Retirement Blues: Stop Worrying and Start Living

1. Albert Myers and Christopher Anderson, *Success Over Sixty: How to Plant It, How to Harvest It, How to Live by It* (New York: Summit Books, 1984), page 202.

2. Jim Vetsch, "Retirement Planning," *Active Senior Lifestyles,* November 1989, page 26.

3. Albert Myers and Christopher Anderson, page 38.

4. "I'd Like to Thank My Nanny, My . . . ," *Modern Maturity,* February/March 1983, page 66.

5. "Retirement Can Be a Blessing to a Couple's Sex Life," *Dynamic Years,* January/February 1983, page 66.

6. Albert Myers and Christopher Anderson, page 38.

7. *Ibid.,* page 39.

8. *Ibid.,* page 229.

9. *Ibid.*

10. Eric W. Johnson, *Older and Wiser* (New York: Walker, 1986), page 77.

11. James Lincoln Collier, "Most of Worry Doesn't Do Any Good," *Reader's Digest,* April 1988, page 184.

12. *Ibid.*

13. *Ibid.*

14. Ann Knowles, "Think Your Way out of Depression," *Dynamic Years,* January/February 1983, page 63.

15. Adapted from Ann Knowles, page 62.

16. Kim Ode, "Growing Old Gracefully Is a Very Personal Experience," *Minneapolis Star Tribune,* June 4, 1989, page 1E.

17. James Lincoln Collier, pages 184-185.

18. Laurie Jones, "Imagery May Help You Cope with Stress," *Minneapolis Star Tribune,* March 28, 1989, page 3E.

19. Albert Myers and Christopher Anderson, page 37.

20. *Ibid.,* page 37.

21. *Active Aging,* Vol. 9, No. 8, July 1988, page 8.

22. *A Woman's Notebook,* page 22.

23. Dennis Prager, "The Secret of True Happiness," *Redbook*, February 1989, page 88.

24. *A Woman's Notebook*, page 15.

25. Caroline Bird, "Profile of Tomorrow," *Modern Maturity*, April 1983, page 37.

26. Nadine Stair, "If I Had My Life to Live Over," *Association for Humanistic Psychology Newsletter*, July 1975, page 2.

27. Cathy Perlumutter, "Comic Relief," *Prevention*, March 1988, page 16.

28. Jane Brody, "Evidence Keeps Mounting that Humor Can Be Hazardous to Most Illness," *Minneapolis Star Tribune*, May 15, 1988, page 2E.

29. *Ibid.*

30. "You Know What They Say," *Reader's Digest*, July 1988.

Chapter 9. Ten Tips for a Healthy Retirement

Epigraph. Elliot Carlson, "Join the Wellness Revolution," *Modern Maturity*, June/July 1986, page 39.

1. David Ragan, "Health Styles of the Rich and Famous," *50-Plus*, March 1987, pages 93-94.

2. Philip Goldberg, *Executive Health* (New York: McGraw Hill, 1978), page 130.

3. "Start Exercising — and Stick with It," *Parade* magazine, December 4, 1988, page 8.

4. Gordon Slovut, "Older Swimmers not like Fish out of Water When It Comes to Sex," *Minneapolis Star Tribune*, November 8, 1987, page 18C.

5. *Ibid.*, page 22.

6. Robin Marantz Henig, "A Healthy Dose of Exercise," *AARP News Bulletin*, Vol. 21, No. 10, October 1980, page 9.

7. "Novices Advised to Take It One Step at a Time," *USA Today*, February 15, 1990, page 12C.

8. *Ibid.*

9. Robin Marantz Henig, page 8.

10. *Ibid.*, page 57.

11. *Ibid.*

12. Paul Recer, "Healthy Diets Ignored in U.S., Researchers Say," *Minneapolis Star Tribune*, March 21, 1988, page 3E.

13. Adapted from *Diet Nutrition and Cancer Prevention: A Guide to Food Choices*, U.S. Department of Health and Human Services, NIH Publication No. 85-2711 (Washington, D.C.: 1985), pages 25-31.

14. Joanne Silberner, "A Call to Get the Fat Out," *U.S. News and World Report*, August 8, 1988, page 61.

15. Adapted from Michael Murphy, "Osteoporosis: Its Onset Is Optional," in *Women in Their Dynamic Years,* a special AARP publication (Washington, D.C.: 1989), pages 23-24.

16. Tim Friend, "Cancer Patients Still Unaware of New Treatments," *USA Today,* May 3, 1989, page 1D.

17. Robert L. Veninga, *A Gift of Hope* (Boston: Little, Brown, 1985), page 200.

18. It is particularly important to obtain a second opinion concerning coronary bypass surgery, since as many as half of the 100,000 elective heart bypass surgeries done each year may not be needed. (Source: "Editorial Questions Heart Bypass Operations," *St. Paul Pioneer Press Dispatch,* September 25, 1987, page 3A.)

19. Peggy Eastman, "Unlike 'Birds of a Feather,' Some Drugs Don't Go Together," *AARP News Bulletin,* Vol. 30, No. 3, March 1989, page 1.

20. Jane Brody, "Elderly Sensitive to Adverse Drug Reactions," *Minneapolis Star Tribune,* February 19, 1990, page 15C.

21. "Pharmacists Assail Medication Errors," *St. Paul Pioneer Press Dispatch,* January 16, 1982, page 5.

22. Joe Graedon, "Doc's Handwriting Can Be Lethal," *St. Paul Pioneer Press Dispatch*, May 28, 1983, page 8.

23. *Ibid.*

24. "Pharmacists Assail Medication Errors," page 5.

25. Ann Meyer, "Drug Deals: To Save on Prescriptions, It Pays to Shop Around," *Mature Outlook Newsletter*, June 1988, page 9.

26. "Ask Your Pharmacist," *Time*, June 27, 1988, page 12.

27. "30 Percent Cut in Breast Cancer Deaths Seen if More Doctors Call for Mammograms," *St. Paul Pioneer Press Dispatch*, March 16, 1990, page 12A.

28. Adapted from Robin Marantz Henig, "Take Care!," *AARP News Bulletin*, Vol. 31, No. 1, January 1990, pages 16-17.

29. Shelley Levitt, "It's Never Too Late to Stop Smoking," *New Choices*, February 1990, page 69.

30. *Ibid.*, page 70.

31. *Ibid.*

32. Linda Hubbard, "In Search of 40 Winks," *Modern Maturity,*, April/May 1982, page 73.

33. Charles T. Kuntzleman, *Maximum Personal Energy* (Emmaus, Pa.: Rodale Press, 1981), page 89.

34. *Ibid.*, page 103.

35. Harry E. Yates, *Managing Stress* (New York: AMACOM, 1979), page 123.

36. Adapted from Charles T. Kuntzleman, page 91.

37. Ann Landers, " 'Miracle' Diet Pill Is Product of a Charlatan," *Minneapolis Star Tribune,* February 23, 1988, page 7E.

38. Peter Michelmore, "Beware the Health Hucksters," *Reader's Digest,* January 1989, page 115.

39. William Fassbender, *You and Your Health* (New York: John Wiley and Sons, 1977), page 375.

40. Paul Insel and Walton Roth, *Core Concepts in Health* (Palo Alto, Calif.: Mayfield Publishing Company, 1985), page 333.

41. "Tips for Combating Food Quackery," *AARP News Bulletin,* Vol. 29, No. 10, November 1988.

42. Peter Michelmore, page 117.

43. Adapted from Marvin Levy, Mark Digman, and Janet H. Shirreffs, *Life and Health* (New York: Random House, 1984), page 458.

Chapter 10. Health Costs: Protecting Yourself from Financial Ruin

Epigraph. "Now that Catastrophic Coverage Will Be Repealed, Purchasing a Medigap Policy Is More Important than Ever," *Money,* January 1990, page 77.

1. "Nursing Home Costs Force Many into Poverty, Study Says," *Minneapolis Star Tribune*, November 9, 1987, page 7B.

2. Junius Ellis, *Money Guide to a Secure Retirement* (Birmingham, Ala.: Oxmoor House, 1989), page 171.

3. *Ibid.*

4. *Medicare* (Baltimore: Social Security Administration, April 1990).

5. Robert A. Gilmour, "How to Cover the Gaps in Medicare," (Great Barrington, Mass.: American Institute for Economic Research, 1986), page 24.

6. *Medigap Insurance Cost Comparison Study* (St. Paul, Minn.: Department of Commerce, 1990), pages 8-9.

7. "Medigap Annual Premiums," *St. Paul Pioneer Press Dispatch*, February 2, 1990, page 1A.

8. Robert A. Gilmour, page 26.

9. Marie Hodge and Jeff Blyskal, "Coping with Medicare," *New Choices*, January 1990, page 61.

10. Lani Luciano, "HMO, Yes or No?," *Money*, July 1988, page 115.

11. *Ibid.*, page 120.

12. *Ibid.*, page 115.

13. *Long Term Care Insurance: Is It Right for You?* (St. Paul, Minn.: Metropolitan Senior Federation, 1989).

14. "Don't Be a Victim of Future Shock," *Savvy Woman,* January 1990, page 24.

15. *Long Term Care Insurance: Is It Right for You?* page 6.

16. "Don't Be a Victim of Future Shock," page 24.

17. *The Complete Guide to Long Term Care for 1990* (Potomac, Md.: Phillips Publishing), page 14.

18. *Ibid.,* page 120.

19. "Don't Be a Victim of Future Shock," page 24.

20. *Long Term Care Insurance: Is It Right for You?* page 11.

Chapter 11. The World Awaits: The Lure of Retirement

Epigraph. "Malcolm Forbes," *Minneapolis Star Tribune,* March 9, 1990, page 2B.

1. Charles N. Barnard, "Thanks for the Memory . . . ," *Modern Maturity,* April/May 1988.

2. Peg Beemer-Moore, "Long Cruises: More Fun, More Romance, More Adventure," *Active Senior Lifestyles,* October 1989.

3. I would like to acknowledge the following resources used in this section: George S. Bush, "Cruising Into Summer," *Mature Outlook,* March/April 1990, pages 45-49; Shirley Slater and Harry Basch, "The Best Cruise Buys of 1990," *New Choices,* February 1990, pages 38-42; George S. Bush, "Creative Cruises," *Mature Outlook,* September/October 1989, pages 35-41.

4. George S. Bush, "Cruising Into Summer," page 90.

5. Shirley Slater and Harry Basch, page 42.

6. *Ibid.*

7. Adapted from Dan Moreau, "Castles for Rent," *Changing Times,* February 1988, page 56.

8. *Ibid.*

9. *Ibid.*

10. *Ibid.,* page 57.

11. Mary Granfield, "A Sampler of Villa Rental Agencies," *Money,* October 1990, page 153.

12. Adapted from Julie Sinclair Eakin, "Trading Places," *New Choices,* December 1989, page 29.

13. *Ibid.,* page 30.

14. *Ibid.*

15. Pamela Lanier, "Morning Glories," *Mature Outlook,* July/August 1988, page 34.

16. *Ibid.*

17. Adapted from Edwin Kiester, Jr., "B&B — America's Way," *Modern Maturity,* October/November 1984, page 27.

18. *Ibid.*

19. *Ibid.*

20. "Traveling in a Group," *United Retirement Bulletin,* October 1989, page 6.

21. Warren Cohen, "Elderhostel Has Wide Appeal," *United Retirement Bulletin,* March 1990, page 8.

22. Warren Cohen, page 8.

23. *Ibid.*

24. Beverly Shaver, page 77.

25. "Budget Travel: How to Vacation at Universities," *Parade* magazine, June 25, 1989, page 16.

26. "Out-of-the-Ordinary Vacations," *Mature Outlook Newsletter,* July 1989, page 7.

Chapter 12. Charitable Giving: On Becoming a Volunteer

Epigraph. Barbara Kantrowitz, "The New Volunteers," *Newsweek,* July 10, 1989, page 36.

1. The story of Jack and Sally Costello has been adapted from Kathryn Strechert Black, "The Good We Do," *New Choices,* December 1989, page 62.

2. "Volunteering in the 1990's," *United Retirement Bulletin,* October 1989, page 9.

3. "Cities Can't Keep Up with Aid for Needy," *St. Paul Pioneer Press Dispatch,* December 20, 1989, page 13A.

4. "The New Volunteers," *Newsweek,* July 10, 1989, page 38.

5. Christine Rosheim, "Homelessness and Health Care in the United States" (unpublished paper, 1990), page 8.

6. According to a 1988 Gallup survey, 47 percent of those between the ages of 65 and 74 are engaged in some type of volunteer service activity.

7. "Healing an Old Wound," *Newsweek,* July 10, 1989, page 49.

8. "Self-Help for Hispanics," *Newsweek,* July 10, 1989, page 47.

9. *Ibid.*

10. Wade Nelson, "The Millionaire Who Clothes the Homeless," *Mature Outlook,* November/December 1987, page 15.

11. Russ Hodge, "The Charitable Chairman," *50-Plus,* July 1986, page 62.

12. Ilene Springer, "Helping 'em Get It Right," *AARP News Bulletin,* Vol. 29, No. 4, April 1985, page 16.

13. *Ibid.*

14. Margaret Opsata, "Get Up, Get Out, Volunteer!" *50-Plus,* July 1986, page 59.

15. *Ibid.,* page 61.

16. Adapted from Margaret Opsata, pages 58-65.

17. Christy Wise, "Americans Find that Older Is Better Overseas," *Minneapolis Star Tribune,* February 24, 1988, page 2E.

18. *Ibid.*

19. Louise Crooks, "Volunteer Workers: Our Greatest Asset," *Modern Maturity,* April/May 1989, pages 10-11.

20. Charlotte J. Lunsford, "Volunteering in 2001," *Vital Speeches of the Day,* Vol. 54, No. 23, page 731.

21. Annetta Miller, "The New Volunteerism," *Newsweek,* February 8, 1988, pages 42-43.

Chapter 13. Intimacy in Retirement: Falling in Love Over and Over Again

Epigraph. Ann Landers, *Minneapolis Star Tribune,* January 23, 1989, page 3C.

1. According to the Roper Organization, a New York-based research firm, nearly one-third of those older than sixty indicated that retirement marks the best period in their lives. (Source: "Mind over Mirror: You're as Old as You Feel," *Mature Outlook,* March/April 1987, page 94.)

2. Robert Coles, "People Who Lean Too Much," *New Choices,* May 1990, page 93.

3. Quoted in Alan McGinnis, *The Friendship Factor,* (Minneapolis, Minn.: Augsburg Press, 1979), page 35.

4. Adapted from Nanci Hellmich, "Equalizing the Relationship Between Sex and Love," *USA Today,* March 21, 1990.

5. Marilyn Mercer, "Men, Women and Sexuality Today: A Report," *New Choices,* June 1990, pages 30-33.

6. Dave Barry, "Are We There Yet?" *St. Paul Pioneer Press Dispatch,* June 10, 1990, page 6E.

7. Carl Rogers, *On Becoming a Person: A Therapist's View of Psychotherapy* (Boston: Houghton Mifflin, 1961), page 16.

8. Quoted in E. Borman, W. Howell, R. Nicols, and G. Shapiro, "Interpersonal Communication in the Modern Organization," (Englewood Cliffs, N.J.: Prentice Hall, 1969), page 178.

9. Adapted from Nancy Badgwell, "To Rekindle the Marital Fire," *Women in Their Dynamic Years,* special AARP publication (Washington, D.C.: 1989).

10. Erma Bombeck, "What Does Marriage Mean Today?" *Los Angeles Times,* Thursday, October 19, 1980, page E17.

11. Nancy Badgwell, page 18.

12. Albert Myers and Christopher P. Anderson, *Success Over Sixty* (New York: Summit Books, 1984), page 29.

13. Nancy Badgwell, page 18.

14. Anthony Pietropinto and Jacqueline Simenauer, *Husbands and Wives: A Nationwide Survey of Marriage* (New York: Times Books, 1979), page 78.

15. "You Want More Sex, Your Partner Doesn't: What to Do When Desire Differs," *Sex Over Forty*, Vol. 8, No. 2, April 1990, page 3. Subscriber information can be obtained by calling 919-929-2148.

16. *Passages Journal* (Philadelphia: Running Press, 1986), page 8.

17. Jim Sanderson, "Pillow Notes to Husbands," *Women in Their Dynamic Years*, a special AARP publication (Washington, D.C.: 1989).

18. "A pension — and thou beside me," *Dynamic Years*, January/February 1983, page 66.

19. Bob Logan, "The Meaning of Love," *Golden Years*, February 1989, page 27.

20. Edwin Kiester, Jr., "Good Sex Makes Good Marriages," *50-Plus*, July 1988, page 29.

21. "Sex Revolution Puts Pep in Marriages," *USA Today*, March 15, 1983, page 9A.

22. Quoted in Carole Nelson, "What Is the Elusive Thing Called Romance?," *St. Paul Pioneer Press Dispatch*, February 14, 1982, page 1, "Accent."

23. *Ibid.*

24. Daniel Goleman, "Psychologists Take Clinical View of Love," *Minneapolis Star Tribune*, December 23, 1984, page 8F.

25. "Sex Revolution Puts Pep in Marriages," page 9A.

26. *Ibid.*

27. Alexandra Penney, "Six Mistakes Most Wives Make," *Ladies' Home Journal*, March 1988, page 45.

28. "Sex Changes in Men Over Forty," *Sex Over Forty*, premier issue, June 1982, page 3.

29. "U.S. Sex Isn't What You Think, Study Says," *Minneapolis Star Tribune*, February 19, 1990, page 7A.

30. Thomas H. Walz and Nancee S. Blum, "Sex in Midlife," *New Choices*, July 1989, page 62.

31. *Ibid.*

32. Edward Wakin, "Happily Ever After?" *50-Plus*, June 1985, page 20.

Chapter 14. Starting Over: Making a Second Marriage Work

Epigraph. Norman M. Lobsenz, "How to Make a Second Marriage Work," *Parade* magazine, September 1, 1985, page 12.

1. Bill Hanvik, "Moonlight and Roses: It's Never Too Late for Romance," *Active Senior Lifestyles*, June 1988, page 17.

2. *Ibid.*

3. "Living Alone Can Be Hazardous to Your Health," *Business Week,* March 5, 1990, page 20.

4. *Ibid.*

5. Abigail Van Buren, "How Do You Meet Someone? Here Are Tips," *St. Paul Pioneer Press Dispatch,* June 25, 1990, page 2C.

6. Brad Lindeman, "How to Overcome Loneliness," *Active Senior Lifestyles,* February 1987, page 40.

7. Judith Viorst, "What Is This Thing Called Love?" *Redbook,* February 1975, page 12.

8. Norman M. Lobsenz, page 12.

9. Leo Buscaglia, *Love* (New York: Fawcett Crest, 1972), page 8.

10. Alan Loy McGinnis, *The Friendship Factor* (Minneapolis, Minn.: Augsburg Publishing House, 1979), page 27.

11. *Ibid.,* page 12.

12. Susan Hazen-Hammond, "Twice in a Lifetime," *Mature Outlook,* July/August 1988, page 54.

13. Neal A. Kuyper, "The Business of Remarriage," in *Women in Their Dynamic Years,* a special AARP publication (Washington, D.C.: 1989), page 47.

14. Jane Bryant Quinn, "Post-Marital Pacts Are Increasing," *St. Paul Pioneer Press Dispatch,* April 20, 1989, page 8C.

15. Neal A. Kuyper, page 46.

16. Susan Hazen-Hammond, page 56.

17. Mary Rowland, "Yours, Mine and Ours," *New Choices,* April 1990, page 75.

18. *Ibid.*

19. Patricia Schiff Estess, "When to Say 'Yes' and How to Say 'No,' " *Parade* magazine, July 24, 1988, page 4.

20. Adapted from Leslie Laurence, "A Debt in the Family," *New Choices,* July 1990, page 78.

21. *Ibid.*

22. Patricia Schiff Estess, page 4.

23. Pat Gardner, "Becoming a Stepfather Proved to Be Chaotic for Child Expert Spock," *Minneapolis Star Tribune,* June 27, 1990, page 1E.

24. *Ibid.*

25. *Ibid.*

26. Abigail Van Buren, "Second Wife's Easy Pace Wins Her Loving Place," *St. Paul Pioneer Press Dispatch,* September 6, 1989, page 11D.

27. Susan Hazen-Hammond, July/August 1988, page 56.

28. *A Woman's Notebook* (Philadelphia: Running Press, 1983), page 46.

29. Adapted from Samuel A. Schriner, Jr., "One Question that Can Save Your Marriage," *Woman's Day,* October 1989, page 35.

30. *Ibid.*

31. Brad Lindeman, "Keeping Love Alive," *50-Plus,* September 1986, page 60.

Chapter 15. Living Alone — and Liking It

Epigraph. *A Woman's Notebook* (Philadelphia: Running Press, 1983).

1. Robert L. Veninga, *A Gift of Hope: How We Survive Our Tragedies* (Boston: Little, Brown, 1985), page 168.

2. Adapted from Morton Kelsey, *Encounter With God* (Minneapolis, Minn.: Bethany House, 1972), page 83.

3. *Passages Journal* (Philadelphia: Running Press, 1986), page 32.

4. Robert L. Veninga, page 60.

5. Adapted from Alan Loy McGinnis, *The Friendship Factor* (Minneapolis, Minn.: Augsburg Publishing House, 1979), pages 40-41.

6. *Ibid.,* page 42.

7. Clark Moustakas, *Loneliness and Love* (Englewood Cliffs, N.J.: Prentice Hall, 1972), page 103.